JUNIUS, LORD CHATHAM:

A Biography,

SETTING FORTH THE CONDITION OF ENGLISH POLITICS

PRECEDING AND COTEMPORARY WITH

THE REVOLUTIONARY JUNIAN PERIOD,

AND SHOWING THAT THE GREATEST

ORATOR AND STATESMAN

WAS ALSO THE GREATEST

Epistolary Writer of his Age.

BY

WILLIAM DOWE.

Search then the ruling passion; there alone
The wild are constant and the cunning known;
That clew once found unravels all the rest;
The prospect clears and Wharton stands confest.
POPE.

That terrible Cornet of Horse.
WALPOLE.

A trumpet of sedition.
GEORGE III.

NEW YORK:

MILLER, ORTON & CO., 25 PARK ROW.

LONDON: TRÜBNER & CO., 12 PATERNOSTER ROW.

1857.

Miller & Holman,
Printers and Stereotypers, N. Y.

THIS ESSAY,

TOUCHING

THE MOST POPULAR ENGLISH WRITER OF A FORMER PERIOD,

Is Dedicated to

THE MOST POPULAR ENGLISH WRITER OF THE PRESENT,

CHARLES DICKENS,

By one repeatedly thankful to him for the pleasantest reading hours of his life—since the morning of Ivanhoe, and the Bride of Lammermoor—and a sincere admirer of the resolved and genial democrat, who, being the most famous and flattered author of his time, has always chosen to stand by the side of the people, laboring for and with them, and sympathizing with their wants, feelings and interests; and who now seems willing to advance a new claim to a more general applause, by the opinion that all his countrymen should learn the use of arms, and thus be enabled to stand erect, on a level with the people of other nations in the Old and New World.*

THE AUTHOR.

* See "Household Words," No. 319, p. 363.

PREFACE.

THE historic reader is struck—or should be—with the facts that Lord Chatham is represented as in some degree out of his senses—full of a certain perversity, secret, evasive, scowling, and implacable—during a portion of his career; and that the period of his strange, unexplained lunacy was the very period of the Junian epistles. In the earlier part of the *lustrum*, 1767–1772, the great baffled minister was doing something under a cloud, and behind a curtain; and Junius, at the same time, in all his fortitudes, girding at the king, lords, and commons of England. A remarkable coincidence; but not sufficiently remarked, we suspect, by those who meditate that Epistolary Sphinx of the last age.

The same reader has, probably, felt surprise that the orator, whose genius and audacity could raise the monotonous character of British eloquence to the old Greek level of the Agora—and the statesman, who, since the stronger times of the Wolseys and Burleighs, stands up alone to redeem the common run and fatal mediocrity of British statesmanship, should have such an indistinct and meagre biography, and leave some of the best effects of his energetic life to the keeping of tradition; at a period, too, not beyond the memory of some men now living. This veiling of such a bust in the procession of the celebrities, suggests something, in the dispositions of the great man himself and in those of his compeers and countrymen, which does not show itself in a passing glance.

Along with these, there are two other striking considerations. The first is, the general appearance of dislike with which the great peers of that time—the Butes, Albemarles, Russels, Rockinghams, and others—allude to Lord Chatham, in their memoirs, or any letters having reference to that angry period; while their sons and successors continue to the present day the old impressions of aversion—an aversion which certainly seems too deeply rooted to have had its rise in the mere political feuds of the day. The next is, the curious anxiety of Lord Mahon—Chatham's descendant—and, along with him, Lord Brougham, Mr. Macaulay, and others, to make the world believe, against the most glaring contrary evidence, that the vehement orator and statesman was a poor hand at a letter, a feeble sycophant of George III., and, for the rest, a man of crotchets and oddities, which no one could rightly understand then, and which no one need try to understand any more.

Such considerations—calculated, perhaps, to excite certain doubts, and rouse curiosity—were those which first led, in this case, to the method of Lord Chatham's madness, and the conclusions shown in the following pages.

The writer has seen but one attempt to prove that Junius was Lord Chatham: that of Dr. Waterhouse,* of Cam-

* The Doctor's testimony, though garrulous and rambling, is not with-

bridge, Massachusetts, who published his book in 1831, and whose manner of treating the subject did his theory more harm than good. He confines himself to what may be called the classic series, rejecting the Miscellaneous Collection, which confused and puzzled him, and making that desperate which was difficult before. The Doctor, entering the arena, on which he was to cope with the most cunning strategist on record, is confounded by the fact that Poplicola begins by a terrible show of attack on—Lord Chatham! He gives up the Miscellaneous Series as something unaccountable, and rambles on his way to the conclusion with half the evidence. In England, Messrs. Swinden and another produced *rifaccimentos* of the Doctor's argument.

But the Chathamites are not the only inquirers who have stood puzzled before the Poplicolas and Correggios. The Franciscans, too, have flung doubts upon them—on some of them, at least—more disposed to give up the letters than give up their theory. The truth is, those searchers, from the beginning, have had an humble opinion of the Junian legerdemain, and thought they could circumvent that Ulysses of the pen with a few hours' felicitous thinking, and a nice balancing of the evidences discoverable in the letters themselves, and the tenor of the few years embraced by their publication.

The only man who could be Junius is presented in these pages; his life before and after 1767 being the best proof

out a certain merit. He was in his youth a cotemporary of Junius; and, as a medical pupil of Dr. Fothergill, of London, could gather enough from the gossip of the capital to produce the convictions of his after life. He had heard whispers of the truth long before those sectaries, the Franciscans and others, rose to corrupt and darken it with their devices, glosses, and heresies. In this respect, the opinion of Dr. Waterhouse is of higher value than people are disposed to think.

of his identity. That is the main argument. Following it out in the synthetic way, the reader is led inevitably to perceive the means of secrecy, and the nature of the strategy. Lord Chatham is curiously abused by Junius in the very opening of the epistolary war; and this suggests the mode of dealing with the whole cunning system of concealment.

> Suivez le fil de la rivière.
> Un autre répondit : Non, ne le suivez pas ;
> Rebroussez, plutôt, en arrière.

Pursuing this course of contraries, described by Lafontaine, the investigator finds himself in an untrodden way; and the Miscellaneous Series, rejected by other theorists, leads him, against the current of appearances, in the direction of the truth. It shows Junius opposing and denouncing himself; it shows him also arguing in a similar spirit of ambages against Lord Chatham; and presents a succession of epistolary combats and sparrings, in which we can perceive the Mask doing all in his power to confuse and bewilder those who would be most likely to trace him by his political and personal sentiments. In the eighth chapter of this book, that curious and complicated strategy is pointed out, and many letters not included in Woodfall's collection are identified as those of the secret writer. Among these are two, lying eight or nine years away from the recognized Junian period. All this shows the Mask moving over a wider field, and in a stranger way than most people have suspected, and at the same time suggests that there may be as much of his literature yet unreclaimed as we find between the covers of Woodfall's book. There are, doubtless, many lights of this theme still burning in the crypts of the dead London journals; and the inquirer within reach of them may yet use them in forming the complements of a truth given here in its outline and incomplete features.*

WEST HOBOKEN, Sept., 1856.

* In arranging the following pages, the writer has often wished for some of those out-of-the-way books and journals which have cotemporary reference to the Junian literature. But he does not recollect with less gratitude those helps within his reach, in the excellent Athenæum Library, of the city of Boston, remarkable and enjoyable beyond other libraries of this country, for the liberality of its loanings, and an unrestricted access to its valuable shelves—things which the inquirer or student so dearly appreciates, and without which a huge library is little more to him than a huge trouble and disappointment. Along with the free and satisfactory order of the Boston Athenæum, the writer always remembers with pleasure the cheerful genius of the place, the courteous and accomplished Mr. Charles Folsom, prince of librarians.

TABLE OF CONTENTS.

DEDICATION - - - - - - - iii

PREFACE - - - - - - - v

CHAPTER I.

CONSIDERATION OF THE STRATEGY OF JUNIUS, AND THE VARIOUS CLAIMS AND OPINIONS ADVOCATED IN CONNECTION WITH THE AUTHORSHIP OF THE LETTERS - - - - - - - - - - - 1

Influences at work to conceal the Identity of Junius—Pettifogging of the Franciscans—Preliminary glance at the Junian Period—the Strategy that led inquirers to Stowe—Ideas of Sir James Mackintosh, Lord Nugent, and the Duke of Buckingham—List of the Juniuses, Burke, Gibbon, etc.—Heron, the late Quarterly Reviewers, the Duke of Albemarle, Sir Harris Nicholas—Bohn's edition of Junius—Search narrowed to two persons—One of them Junius.

CHAPTER II.

ANTECEDENTS OF JUNIUS — THE POLITICAL CAREER OF WILLIAM PITT, FIRST EARL OF CHATHAM - - - - - - - - 21

William Pitt's opposition career—Early adhesion to the party of the Prince of Wales, and bold attacks on George II. and his policy—The king's antipathy against him — Pitt's alliances and vigorous efforts to force himself into office—George II. resists obstinately—Is defeated—Pitt Paymaster of the Forces—Acts with Newcastle—Plots with Fox—Another vehement seizure of office in 1757—The Secretary stands alone—The Quadrennium—Is forced from office by George III.—The court policy—The king strives to detach Pitt from his family and other alliances—Succeeds in 1767.

CHAPTER III.

LORD CHATHAM'S DESPERATE ATTEMPTS TO CONSTRUCT HIS HELPLESS MOSAIC MINISTRY—HIS STRANGE RETIREMENT, AND THE CONSEQUENT CONFUSIONS - - - - - - - - - 50

Lord Chatham's reckless piece of "joinery"—The truckle-bed—The Duke of Portland and others escape from it—The Duke of Bedford will not go into it—Lord Chatham goes away and shuts himself up—Outcries and calls which he will not hear—Attempts to bring him out—Strange whisperings about him—The Great Seal put in commission, to provoke him—The king tries to bring him back—Exhorts him, prays him, warns him, offers to send his own doctor to see what the matter is—Says he will go himself—All in vain—Curious fact concerning Hayes—Seclusion of Lord Chatham's apartment there.

CHAPTER IV.

LORD CHATHAM'S RESOLUTION TAKEN — THE FEINTS AND PRECAUTIONS MADE USE OF TO BAFFLE THE CURIOUS INQUIRY OF THE WORLD RESPECTING HIS AGGRESSIVE EPISTLES - - - - - 69

Political writing in England — Marchamont Needham, Bolingbroke, Wharton, Smollett, Burke, etc. — First of the Miscellaneous Series of Junius—Curious oblique but significant attack on the character of Lord Chatham and on Lord Camden—Machinery of concealment—The Mask would be thought a Grenvillite—Praises George Grenville—Also tries to look like Burke — Lord Campbell's notion — Lord Chatham anticipates it.

CHAPTER V.

LORD CHATHAM'S UNDENIABLE LITERARY ABILITIES, AND THE REMARKABLE VERSATILITY OF HIS INTELLECTUAL POWERS - - 92

Lord Mahon's efforts to show that Lord Chatham was no letter-writer and could do nothing but make speeches—Pitt's education—Admiration excited by his style of parliamentary eloquence—Its astonishing power and versatility—Pitt's literary tastes—Love of the drama—Was looked on as a dramatic censor and arbiter of elegance in letters—Wrote poetry—Curious verses to Garrick—Translation of Thucydides—Facetious letters in the Chatham Correspondence—This last a meagre collection—Pitt's affected and sarcastic modes of writing and acting—Lord Brougham puzzled by them.

CHAPTER VI.

A CONSIDERATION OF PARALLEL PASSAGES IN WHICH THE POLITICAL SENTIMENTS OF THE MASK AND LORD CHATHAM ARE SHOWN TO BE COINCIDENT - - - - - - - - - - 108

Speeches of 1770, in the House of Lords—The parallels—the instances in which the orator adopted the sentiments of the Junian literature—Mr. Taylor's argument founded on the parallels—Perfect inadequacy of Philip Francis, the amanuensis, secretary, and reporter of the Earl of Chatham—Late admissions of the Franciscans to the effect that the earl had a hand in the letters—That he was the purveyor and assistant of the young War Office clerk—Their argument that the latter was "precocious," and soon lost the early Junian stamina.

CHAPTER VII.

POLITICAL BATTLES OF 1770 AND 1771, IN WHICH JUNIUS AND LORD CHATHAM SHOW THEMSELVES ON THE SAME SIDE, AND MAKE USE OF THE SAME WAR-CRIES - - - - - - - - 131

Hostile relations of Lord Chatham with Lord Bute, the Earl of Mansfield, the Duke of Bedford, the Duke of Grafton, and the king—"Savagery" of George III.—The parliamentary struggle—Suicide of Chancellor Yorke—Lord Chatham's assaults against the King and his Ministry—Junius on the side of the Earl—London and Westminster on the same side—Lord Chatham called a madman by his opponents—He tries to engage in a war against Spain—Vituperates the peace—Junius vituperates the King's personal cowardice—George III. resists, sustaining his Ministers—Opposition fails—Junius abuses the King outrageously—Lord Chatham's political disgust and despondency—His last frown and last blow at Lord Mansfield.

CHAPTER VIII.

A CONSIDERATION OF THE CURIOUS AND COMPLICATED SYSTEM OF ATTACKS AND DEFENSES ADOPTED BY LORD CHATHAM IN THE MANAGEMENT OF HIS MYSTERY - - - - - - - - - - 161

Strategy of the Miscellaneous Series of the letters—Curious and complicated attacks on Lord Hillsborough—Letter of "Nerva," against Lord Chatham and for Mansfield, recognized as Junius's—Mr. Simons, of the British Museum—Letter to a Brigadier-general certainly by Junius—New pamphlet by the same hand—Double discomfiture of Brigadier-general Townsend—Pitt the patron and friend of General Wolfe—Character of that hero—His behavior at dinner with the great War-minister—Lord Mahon's piece of gossip—Pitt's fierce habit of letter-writing.

CHAPTER IX.

COTEMPORARY EVIDENCES; SHOWING THAT THE ACUTEST JUDGES OF THAT PERIOD CONSIDERED JUNIUS TO BE LORD CHATHAM - 189

Motives of men's silence respecting Lord Chatham—Horne Tooke's sentiments respecting Junius—He sees Lord Chatham's policy in the letters—Nearly pushes off the mask—Burke's ideas of Junius—His speeches in the House of Commons concerning Lord Chatham's strange retreat and the audacity of Junius—Burke believed Junius attacked his friends, and even himself, to guard the secret—Wilkes's reverent way of talking to the Shadow—Considers Junius a political Jove—Woodfall's profound respect and obedience—Dr. Johnson's attack on Chatham and Junius together—Alderman Beckford's curious admission of the identity.

CHAPTER X.

LORD CHATHAM'S SPEECHES AND REPORTERS—AFFECTATIONS AND INADEQUACY OF SIR PHILIP FRANCIS, LORD CHATHAM'S AMANUENSIS AND SECRETARY - - - - - - - - - - - - 203

Philip Francis and Mr. Boyd, reporters of the Earl of Chatham—His style the same, however reported—Francis reported for other Lords—Admissions of Lady Francis—Her letter in Campbell's "Lives of the Chancellors"—Her argument that Francis was a precocious genius—The Indian appointment and £10,000 a year—Junius not bribed—Francis's pamphlet on the Regency—Speeches in parliament—Expostulation with Mr. Brougham—His remarkable letters to Edmund Burke—Playing Junius—Burke's way of rebuking him.

CHAPTER XI.

SOME FURTHER CONSIDERATIONS LYING ROUND THE MAIN TRACK OF THE ARGUMENT - - - - - - - - - - - 218

Junius not the sole depositary of his secret—Francis his medium or conveyancer—Lady Chatham—Her accomplishments—She conducted the Earl's open correspondence, and was his amanuensis—Lord Chatham's chirography—Junius and Lord Chatham on the affairs of America—Not at variance, but curiously "at one" on that subject—Lord Chatham's modified sympathy with the Americans—His statue at New York—The War Office—Lord Chatham's familiarity with it—His contempt of Change Alley—Mrs. Ann Pitt, one of her brother's secret political agents both in France and England—Her character—Lord Mahon's representations—Mrs. Pitt's letters—David Garrick—He cowers under the abuse of Junius, and protests he would not for the world pronounce his name.

CHAPTER XII.

RECAPITULATION—PASSING REMARKS ON THE JUNIAN LETTERS PUBLISHED IN THE GRENVILLE PAPERS AND IN THE CHATHAM CORRESPONDENCE—MR. MACAULAY'S LETTER, AND CONCLUSION - - - - - 237

Recapitulation—The Grenville Correspondence—Mr. Smith's theory of Lord Temple's authorship a futile one—The "three letters" mere feints—The *North British Review*—The two letters addressed to Lord Chatham—Cunning demonstrations made for a purpose—Mr. Macaulay's War Office argument—The judge and jury test of this theme—Odium of the letters—It would leave Lord Chatham's character as it was—His biography imperfect without the letters—Junius impossible without the antecedents of Lord Chatham—The fragments of a mutilated character restored in the statue sculptured by Grattan.

JUNIUS, LORD CHATHAM.

CHAPTER I.

CONSIDERATION OF THE STRATEGY OF JUNIUS, AND THE VARIOUS CLAIMS AND OPINIONS ADVOCATED IN CONNECTION WITH THE AUTHORSHIP OF THE LETTERS.

'Tis a spirit; sometime it appears like a lord: sometime like a lawyer; sometime like a philosopher. He's very often like a knight; and, generally in all shapes that a man goes up and down in, between eighty and twenty-three, this spirit walks in.

TIMON OF ATHENS.

We have a number of shadows to fill up the muster-book.

FALSTAFF.

ONE of the classics of the English language,* is an author without a name, who lived and agitated the public mind in the time of Cowper and Burns. He was, as his letters sufficiently show, a man of genius, eloquence and subtlety —the last distinctive the greatest of the three. For, as regards the two first, we may find those who equal or ap-

* In Mayhew's "London Labor and London Poor," we perceive that, among those works which a street seller of books esteems the English classics—such as the Spectator, the Vicar of Wakefield, Tom Jones, and Robinson Crusoe—he numbers the Letters of Junius. This is curious enough; for it is hard to explain why such a political literature should be at all attractive in our day. Perhaps it is the vituperative audacity which girds at all dignities and the great folk, that gives it a name, and generally recommends it in a popular way. On the whole, the letters are a tough kind of reading, and nobody, as yet, we believe, has got them up with the entertaining editions for railway passengers.

1

proach him; but nowhere can we find a cunning to match the artifice which, for over eighty years, has succeeded in confusing and baffling the curious inquiries of the world. Everything proves that he was a wonder of intellectual strength and versatility; but the wonder that he has not been found out is a greater wonder than himself. Not that he has not been recognized. The identity has been known to many, and pointed out by a few, and there is not a discussion of that interesting mystery in which the true name does not necessarily and largely occur; while, in later discussions, it puts itself so prominently forward that one would think few could avoid recognizing it. Still, curiously enough, the general eye wanders over that Junian shape without resting upon it. In spite of a thousand considerations indicating the identity, there seems to have always been a disinclination to challenge it aloud. And this disinclination may naturally be explained as growing by degrees out of a system of precautions and dissuasives, operating, according to the design of Junius, long after he had departed, and also, due to the influences of his family concealing or controlling all sources of correct intelligence on the subject. Indeed, the greater number of those dissertations that have appeared in the Junian controversy—especially those having the greatest air of authority—seem to us far less intended to aid a discovery than to set investigators astray. The advocacy for Sir Philip Francis, aided by his own demeanor respecting it, was wonderfully calculated to divert the public mind from the true merits of the question, and the true way of investigating it. The Franciscans first created the court-room pettyfogging style of evidence. And yet, as we shall perceive in the future pages of this disquisition, the facts which are thought to tell most remarkably in favor of Sir Philip, are those very things which, after all, lead us to the real Junius.

The letters of Junius cover a space of five years, from 1767 to 1773, a time when the press was teeming with letters and pamphlets, on the exciting political subjects of the day. At the former date, George III. was a young man of twenty-seven, and had been about six years on the throne. In the first unpopular decade of his reign he was engaged in a contest with the great circumvallation of the Whigs, whose fathers and grandfathers had made the Revolution of 1688, and established the Guelphic family, and who were, therefore, always invoking the constitution, and patriotically quarreling among themselves for white sticks, garters, regiments, sees, sinecures, pensions, all the emoluments, in fact, of all the offices in the state. Hereditary salvagers, they were always ready to claim salvage. Sir Robert Walpole had done all in his power to keep the armaments quiet and inexpensive, and he and his party had poisoned the whole body politic with the venalities and corruptions of a demoralizing peace. Pitt, by far the greatest, if not the best of the Whigs, forced himself into power in 1756, after a long effort of twenty years, and, with a prodigality which amazed and insulted them, threw away on regiments and line-of-battle ships, on Wolfe, Hawke, Boscawen, Amherst, Saunders, the king of Prussia, and all the fierce vanities of conquest, as much money as would have kept and fattened the whole "country party," during their lives, in the lap of patriotic luxury. But in 1762, by God's blessing, they had succeeded, altogether, in thwarting and pulling him down, and giving away a great portion of what his victories had won for the nation. Since that time, the government was in the condition of a ship with a series of unskilful and mutinous crews. The young king, following the advice of his mother, Princess Dowager of Wales, the Earl of Bute and others of his friends, was resolved to have none but a subservient ministry which would not offend his ears with the Whig jargon or harass his prerogative, and so he kept manœuvring, and shuffling, and changing his servants. The Whigs made use of counter intrigues; their writers assailed the king's friends and the court party, and Wilkes was tried and punished for his irreverent language in the "North Briton." The City of London, always "a fast burgh" of democracy, returned that incendiary to parliament for Middlesex, in 1764, and when the house expelled him, pitchforked him back in triumph—only to see him turned out again.

This grievance was a wonderful lift to the country party. The occasion was vigorously improved, and the outcry great. Meantime, George Grenville passed the Stamp Act, and threw the American colonists into a ferment, preparatory to the War of Independence. In little more than a year, the Rockinghams, coming in turn to the helm, repealed that act, and, at the same time, declared that England had, nevertheless, the right to impose taxes, thus letting "I dare not wait upon I would." The King, who was more of a farmer than a despot, though fated to look very much like the latter in the end, and who found his business only half done, and himself not very well treated by his scolding Bedfords, pennywise Grenvilles, gruff, gawky Temples, and sour Puritanical Rockinghams, now tried to detach William Pitt from his family alliance, and induce him to lead a King's ministry. He succeeded; and Pitt, created Earl of Chatham, became premier, in 1766, with a motley crew of colleagues forced upon him by the stress of circumstances and the astute policy of George III. The result was, that, in a few months, he went away to the country and left them to their fate, in spite of a world of outcries. The ministry of the Duke of Grafton supervened in 1768, that of Lord North —the seventh premier in less than ten years—in 1770, and under these the government sustained a succession of the rudest assaults, urged and directed by the angry and indefatigable Earl of Chatham, who fulminated powerfully in the House of Lords, more terrible, in his flannels, to the peerage of that place, than any Clifford or king-marring Warwick that ever stood there in greaves and corslet.

It is with the confusion of the earl's unfortunate ministry, in 1767, that the warfare of Junius began, and it ended when the defeated Whigs found, in 1772, that they could not overpower the king's friends. During that time, the mask assailed the perverse ministry, deserted by the Earl of Chatham, till it fell into ruins, and took a new shape under the Duke of Grafton, when he fell upon that, too, with increased vehemence, striking at his Grace the Earl of Bute, the Princess Dowager of Wales, and the king himself, with amazing bitterness and fury. He advocated the chief Whig principles, and, like his party, made a vigorous handle of the Middlesex election and London remonstrances, the management of the Colonies, the Court of King's Bench trials of the publishers, the Spanish convention, and all the collateral and minor subjects of popular satire and objurgation. When, in 1770 and 1771, the Whigs, lately divided by the royal influences, made a united attack upon government, under the leadership of the Earl of Chatham, the letters were found seconding the onslaught in the most vehement manner. When Lord North was found too firmly intrenched to be overcome, the jaculation dire of Junius came to an end; he hurled no more missiles, and was silent. This will convey some slight idea of the stage on which he played his part, and the general motives which must have urged the various actors in that stirring political drama.

When the masked writer begins his course of aggression by a curiously indirect, but sufficiently expressive, attack on the two men who most conspicuously and steadily advocated the opinions which we know he entertained on the chief questions of that period; when he begins both his miscellaneous and regular series of letters by such palpable hits at the most popular and venerable Whig in the kingdom, people generally take it as it reads, simply, with an easy, unsuspecting confidence in the candor of the Mask; accept it very much as a man would take an honest friend's declaration, that the Czar Nicholas behaved like a tyrant, in subverting, or helping to subvert, the independent government of Hungary, or some thing of that sort. When Lord Chatham is suggested in this inquiry, it is retorted in a tone of conclusiveness that the masker calls that nobleman a traitor, a lunatic, a worthless idol, and so forth; and this is an argument which has disconcerted thousands upon the threshold. Other considerations, no doubt, have helped to mislead inquiry, but that wonderful gesticulation against the earl, just at starting, is the grand dissuasive. When Junius talked of George Grenville as that wise and honest minister, that pure patriot, the simple enquirers always called out and bid each other take notice that this man was a Grenvillite surely; and this device was found to be as effective as that employed respecting the Earl of Chatham. The querist took the ghost's word for it in both cases. And that impression has long continued. One said Junius was George Grenville himself; others said, no; he was James Grenville; some contended for the other brother, Lord Temple, and the most confident held out for Charles Lloyd, private secretary of George Grenville. A writer, in the *Edinburgh Review*, said to have been Sir James Macintosh, expressed his belief as follows: "A simple test ascertains the political connection of Junius; the only circumstance which could not be concealed without defeating his general purpose. He supported the cause of authority against America with Mr. Grenville, the minister who passed the Stamp Act. He maintained the highest popular principles on the Middlesex election with the same statesman who was the leader of opposition on the question. No other party in the kingdom combined these two opinions. Whoever revives the inquiry, therefore, unless he discover positive and irresistible evidence in support of his claimant, should show him to be politically attached to the Grenville party, which Junius certainly was."* A tradition of something to come out of the library at Stowe has long kept the critics on the *qui*

* *Edinburgh Review*, vol. xliv., July, 1826.

vive. The *London Magazine,* in 1827, made a noise by stating that Lord Nugent and the Duke of Buckingham, rummaging in that library, found three original Juniuses in a pigeon-hole. A literary flurry followed, the only result of which was, that the magazine got a very handsome assistance in the way of advertisement. But there was some truth in the matter, along with much gossip. The three letters are facts, and about to be published in London, in the Grenville Correspondence.*

But the search after Junius has not been confined to that circle. Almost every one of the remarkable writers of that day has been put forward as the author of the letters. Exclusive of the above, we have had in the ring:—John Wilkes, John Horne Tooke, Macaulay, Boyd, Burke, Barre, Hood, Grattan, Francis, Maclean, Glover, Delolme, Earl of Shelburne, the Duke of Portland, Sir W. Jones, Gibbon, Sam Dyer, General Lee, W. Gerard Hamilton, J. Roberts, Lord Ashburton, Lord Camden, James Hollis, Dr. Wray, Horace Walpole, Lord Loughborough, W. Greatrakes, Rev. P. Rosenhagen, John Kent, Bishop Butler, Lord Chesterfield, Lord George Sackville, Dr. Francis, Dr. Wilmot, Thomas Lord Lyttelton, and others. We believe somebody in the crowd called out Dr. Johnson; and another earnest inquirer said Peter Pindar! If ghosts ever laugh, "Lord Umbra" must have often made merry over such a rabble of counterfeit presentments.

Of all these, Edmund Burke was the only man whose peculiar powers came up to the standard of Junius. He had

* We have seen these, and our remarks on them are in the last chapter of this book.

the perfervid mind and vehemence of the secret writer, and, with all the philosophy and statesmanship which have secured his fame with posterity, he was considered a man of the most rancorous feeling. People said, with Archbishop Markham, that his house was a nest of adders, and his behavior in the House of Commons that of a wolf, or other wild animal in the midst of a flock of sheep, showing his teeth and snapping at every one about him. He was also considered somewhat crack-brained, by his contemporaries, who would always fly before dinner from the echoes of his exalted brogue. Wilkes said he talked like a man accustomed to live on potatoes and whisky, and Gibbon declared he was the most rational madman he ever heard, while an epigram, in the public prints, set forth that the Irish toads and snakes had no venom because it was all concentrated in Burke.* The latter was therefore talked of as a man truculent and talented enough to be the writer of the letters, some of which, in the miscellaneous series, cunningly tried to encourage the opinion, as we shall see. But Burke had not the heart of Junius. He was generally fierce with ratiocination—a thing which the other scorned as something of that "Persian apparatus" which strong haters dispense with. Burke generalized, and had an eye to the effects of eloquence ; but Junius came to particulars and persons, with the bloody sincerity of Burns' Highlander—

Wha has na thought but how to kill
Twa at a blow.

* John Williams (Antony Pasquin), the scurrilous lampoon writer so terribly flagellated by Gifford in the "Baviad" and the notes, was the author of that ferocious conceit.

Burke himself has set the question at rest; he denied the authorship to Dr. Johnson, Charles Townsend,* and Dean Marly, telling the latter he could not write like Junius; and if he could, he would not. We perceive Mr. Prior, in his last edition of Burke's life, has left out his argument, that the Irish orator was Junius. He might have allowed it to remain, seeing it is as good as any offered by the rest of the Junian theorists. Gibbon has had his advocates. But his blood was too cold to boil in the strife of contemporaries, and he always thought more of his Nestorians and Monophysites than of the Whigs and Tories. Lord George Sackville was put forward, on account of his well-known military discontents. But his style was as bad as his soldiership; and his pretensions must go to the rear with those of Lord Chesterfield, Horace Walpole, Lord Temple, and that somewhat costive celebrity, William G. Hamilton, whose memory is preserved by a nickname, and the curious history of his attempt to put a man of genius to his own selfish uses.† General Lee was once thought to be Junius. He was "Junius Americanus," who wrote several letters in the years 1769 and 1771, and also wrote the preamble of the Bill of Rights for the citizens of London. Junius, in a private letter to Wilkes, says, that his own namesake

* "Burke's Correspondence," edited by Earl Fitzwilliam and Gen. Bourke, vol. i., p. 267, Oct. 17, 1771.

† In "Burke's Correspondence," we have an account of the government pension with which Hamilton expected to render poor Burke his sole industrious literary mentor and drudge for life, and the shrewd refusal of the latter to be made use of by such a taskmaster; a man, in fact, of more tyrannical tastes than any Roman emperor of them all. Vitellius himself would be content with the brains of nightingales and thrushes, while Hamilton affected to nourish himself with those of an Irish orator

(from whom, however, he differs on many points of opinion) is plainly a man of abilities. In 1813, Dr. Girdlestone published in London an odd little book on Lee's claims; and it is merely mentioned here for the amazing portraits of the general and his dog—a pair of anatomies—which ornament the frontispiece.

Heron (the antiquary Pinkerton we believe), who published his edition of Junius, with a preliminary essay and notes, in 1801, says he thinks Junius was Lord Ashburton. He speaks of him in a manner worthy of the subject, and gives a truer estimate of his character than any we have had since 1801. He recognizes the great eloquence of the letters, their elegance and force, and the general evidence they afford of a lofty and cultivated intellect, strengthened by exercise. Reading his essay, you are sure he does not mean any clerk. It is the fit prologue of some lordly entrance—the trumpet of the true Junius. But there is some appearance of constraint in this essay and the notes. He contends for no candidate, merely saying he thinks it probable Junius was Lord Ashburton, and so dismisses the matter in a sentence. He pronounces the name, and passes on. After coming repeatedly (as we see by the notes to the letters) in contact with the man who completely suits the terms of his essay, he mentions one with whom he has not come into contact at all! We are convinced Heron shrunk from expressing his real thought. There is something else provoking suspicion in his book. It is very remarkable that, though he gives sketches of the chief men of that Junian time, he leaves out the greatest figure of all—Lord Chatham. This looks odd; but there is something still more curious connected with it. In one part of his book he promises to give, further on, a sketch of the earl and of his son (though what business the son had in such a connection it is hard to discover); but no such things are to be found: he omits them. What could have led him to be silent concerning the biography of the great man, and leave such a *lacune* in his book? He very probably applied to William Pitt on that subject. Could Pitt have said anything to dissuade or discourage him? Questions and surmises of this kind are, of course, vague, and of little positive value; but inquirers into the matter should pay particular attention to everything that concerns Lord Chatham, and mark, furthermore, how often his claims, so to express it, seem to be evaded and slurred over.

Among the latest attempts to lighten the darkness of this mystery, has been that of Mr. Britton, who, looking over the array of claimants, and thinking the force of single hypothesis could no further go, resolved to consolidate two or three of those already made, and so presented Junius as "three single gentlemen rolled into one," to wit: Lord Ashburton, Lord Shelburne, and Col. Barre. More recently still, a writer in the *North British Review*,* said to be Sir David Brewster, revives the old idea that Lachlin Macleane was the man. But Macleane was a mere man about town, and struggling with his gambling debts and other dirty difficulties at a time when Junius was fluttering the king, peers and commons of England, with a lordly and tyrannical scourge. It may be added, that the letters con-

* *North British Review*, vol. x., November, 1848.

tinued to come after Macleane had been made Collector of Philadelphia.

In the "Rockingham Memoirs,"* lately published, the noble editor is not afraid to contribute an opinion to the Junian controversy. It is like Mr. Britton's—of the composite order. He goes back to the exploded idea, so positively maintained by the "learned monster," Dr. Parr, and by others, that Charles Lloyd was Junius; but not solely so. He believes George Grenville himself wrote the first letters of the series, and afterwards employed Lloyd to take the materials of those epistolary thunderbolts to Mr. Philip Francis at the War Office, to receive the filing and finishing of that remarkable juvenal! When a duke writes criticism, he should be treated with respectful consideration. But, after all, we must admit he only makes another incredible sort of trinity, a draggle-tailed hypothesis, to speak leniently.

In a late *Quarterly Review*, we see another adventurous theory of identity, with the merit, at least, of originality. The article commences very well, and the following is worthy of all acceptation: "The author of the letters, it has been well observed, must be sought for in narrow limits. He could not have been one of the obscure professors of literature to be found by thousands in our own day. He must have moved in the highest ranks of political life—he must have been contemptuous of the emoluments of authorship. That these compositions, over a period of five years from first to last, should have been the only effort of the alert and energetic intellect which produced them, is most

* "Memoirs of the Marquis of Rockingham," edited by the Duke of Albemarle.

unlikely. When Junius is really discovered, we shall probably see him disappearing like a storm-cloud from one point of the political horizon, to burst with thunder and lightning in another."* What follows this very excellent opinion? What formidable English genius stalks in at the heels of such a prologue? Why, a callow debauchee, Thomas Lord Lyttelton—a feeble imitation of Lord Rochester—in the twenty-third year of his age. We do not remember to have anywhere read such an instance of the *bathos*, or sinking, in prose. The power of your tyrannical theory over the poor Frankenstein that fashions it, could not be shown with more furious felicity. Taking a calm general view, the writer sees clearly, and with judgment; but when he comes into his hypothesis and jumbles himself up with dates and coincidences, he is but a lost man, for seventy mortal pages together, full of pale-colored and unconvincing parallels and passages that lead to nothing of the identity he desires to establish. It is really too bad to see Junius disappearing in the grandeur of a thunder-cloud, at one point of the horizon, only to find him emerging elsewhere from a brothel, with a semi-fuddled Lytteltonish expression of countenance, and "waking the night-owl with a catch," at two o'clock in the morning!

But it was no part of our purpose to discuss any of these claims, and we have gone out of the way in alluding to them. Except two theories on which this argument shall turn, the rest seem really to be the mere rubbish of so much falsified pretension, not worth any further argument.

* *British Quarterly Review*, vol. xc. December, 1851.

The efforts to discover Junius seem to have been inadequately made. The political ground over which he and his contemporaries moved, has not been sufficiently surveyed by the majority of the investigators. They have kept their eyes within the space of five years covered by the letters, forgetting that it is hard to recognize any man, the man you know best, by a piece of his body—by a fragment of his life, and that the antecedents and motives of such striking displays must enter into any estimate likely to lead to a just conclusion. Mr. Taylor, whose book, published over forty years ago, seems to have been a great authority, has shown himself very unfit for his task. He first said Dr. Francis was Junius, and proved it. He then corrected himself and argued for the son, Sir Philip, and he confesses that it was by accident he met with "Almon's Anecdotes" of Lord Chatham, a book that furnishes him with the greater portion of his self-refuting argument. The idea of coming at the secret by accident—of circumventing such a wizard as Junius by unforeseen advantages, is ridiculous. As for the history, or rather the biography of that Georgian period, and the contests between Whiggery and Prerogative, Mr. Taylor seems to have little regarded them; and the great majority of the querists and critics that have come after him do not appear to have had a much larger degree of information respecting them. Mr. Taylor especially relied upon the virtue of parallels and coincidents. This fashion has been extensively followed, and, certainly, if the hidden writer could be conjured forth by such legerdemain, we should, at this moment, have a score or two of Juniuses Unmasked scowling up and down the field of our literature.

The late Sir Harris Nicholas expressed some acute and judicious opinions respecting Junius. He thought the question had never been properly investigated, and that the failures are the reproach of criticism. He says, one cause of want of success was the tendency to rely too much on the statements of the secret writer, which he would make "for the purposes of argument or illustration—to give greater force to his attacks, or divert attention from himself." With these objects, he evidently feigned representations of his own character, situation and feelings, simulated the approbation of men and measures, attacked and defended individuals, etc. "To deny that Junius was a consummate actor, even if a stronger term would not be still more applicable, would be to deny that he wrote from political or party motive, and that he availed himself of the weapons which then disgraced party warfare. It is not, therefore, in studied phrases, elaborate metaphors or well-turned periods, nor in the attacks upon, or praise of, individuals that the author is to be traced."* Sir Harris, of course, meant, he is not to be traced in these alone; for they must be considered in every investigation of the subject. He advised a careful and patient search for internal evidence, such as he had proposed to himself in all the letters of Junius, believing that the materials thus to be gathered would enable the inquirer to build up a true hypothesis, and come at the secret writer by analysis. But there is a quality of deception in Junius which makes that method useless. We cannot rely on anything he says; we know he would carry

* "Bohn's edition of Woodfall's Junius," vol. ii.

a shading of simulation along his most earnest lines, and cannot distinguish the truths from the fallacies. Besides, every individual would have his own peculiar manner of feints and ambages. Sir Harris's plan would never answer. No one can analyze a conundrum. The attempt would only lead to a bewilderment of the faculties and nothing distinctly visible in the end; as was, indeed, the case with Sir Harris himself, who, when he had analyzed for a good while, said he could not arrive at any Junius. His analysis had left him in a state of infidelity to any of the creeds. He swept the board clear of them all. He failed, in fact (if he did not designedly turn away from his conclusions), because he kept his attention too closely fixed in the maze of the letters, and did not sufficiently recognize that we must work externally as well as internally. To reach Junius, we must circumvent him, by a just knowledge of his ground and surroundings, as well as countermine him through his literary peculiarities.

The worthiest of the Junian critics point to one in high station; and Junius must be looked for among the men of most mark and likelihood. The search for him has exhibited an approach to the truth. The crowd of competitors has been gradually diminished, and only two or three can claim a serious thought. In spite of the late advocacy of the Lytteltons, Macleanes, and Temples, it is allowed that the sentiment of the literary world, as expressed or implied in works of character and standing (to wit: the Chatham Correspondence, Lord Campbell's Chancellors, Lord Mahon's History of England, Mr. Macaulay's essays or letters, Bohn's edition of Junius), leans to Sir Philip Francis, and certainly influences the tone of criticism in the periodicals and society. Up to 1814, it was Grenvillite; since then it has been Franciscan. Francis certainly presents a number of coincidences, probabilities, and seemings, wonderfully convincing to all easy and unstudying investigators—the great majority. Their arguments have their value, no doubt, and it consists in the fact, that anything which brings us to Francis, only leads us the nearer to the true Junius. It is curious to see how that young clerk and his advocates are at issue. He did all in his power to preserve the secret of the best friend of his life; while they, urging on his claims, tend with a necessary fatality to thwart his object. The slight amount of controversy in these pages shall be mainly used against the Franciscan advocates. The latest of these, Mr. Bohn's editor, goes further than the rest, and puts forward something new; and, respecting him, we cannot help saying, he seems more likely to have decided without bias than Lord Mahon, the editors of the Chatham Correspondence, or those taking the tone from them. This, no doubt, may be a baseless suspicion; but we shall continue to entertain it, nevertheless. The step made by him, in advance of the rest, is the admission that Lord Chatham had a hand in the letters; that he was the ally or auxiliary of Junius. He could not avoid this conclusion. Tracing the arguments offered on behalf of Francis, the inquirer soon becomes aware of something he was not looking for in that direction. In the curious movements, and a certain appearance of reference and restraint, discoverable either in the Franciscan arguments or the *rôle* of Sir Philip himself, he gets a suggestion of the truth, as Leverrier and

Adams got theirs, by marking the behavior of Uranus; and we are carried at last, by sure calculation, to recognize the long-shrouded perturbator. Sir Philip is necessary to the truth of this mystery, and he and Junius are as inseparable as the ghosts of Paulo and Francesca.

All these considerations marshal us the way we ought to go. With little respect for the microscopic modes of inquiry adopted, with whatever intent, by Lords Campbell and Mahon, Mr. Macaulay, Sir David Brewster, and the crowd of writers and critics, poring, with the sagacity of Malvolio, over the great Cs and Ps of the letters, and looking to phrases, exclamations, dates, coincidences, men in cloaks and bag-wigs, library pigeon-holes, and so forth, going over the same track of doubts and hearsays, and wearying all minds with nothing to the point, we shall indicate the outlines of the Junian shape, and leave the *impedimenta*—the little collateral and complementary matters—to make the best of their way after the main argument. If we shall point to the *Who*, sufficiently plainly for general, common-sense recognition, we may very fairly leave the *How*, and the *Where*, and the *Why* to be more nicely arranged by the subsequent efforts of criticism. We hold, then, with a strong assurance, that, to find the extraordinary man shadowed forth in the "Letters," we must look for him among the most noted and overbearing politicians of his era—not as an echo, but an original; look for him among the very foremost intellects of that stirring time, when the battles of British opinion were shaking the world, and changing the destinies of continents and empires. The track of some powerful biography would, naturally, be likeliest to lead us to the end we have in view;

and, therefore, making the fittest premise of such an argument as this, we shall try to follow, through an almost continual storm of opposition and party strife, the imperfectly-recorded career of one forever busy with his tongue and pen, subtle, intriguing, abusive; the terror and admiration of king, lords, and commons; various and voluble—the Roscius as well as the Cicero of his age; a veteran gladiator, well skilled in all the currents of a heady political fight, and seldom or never out of one—William Pitt, First Earl of Chatham.

CHAPTER II.

ANTECEDENTS OF JUNIUS — THE POLITICAL CAREER OF WILLIAM PITT, EARL OF CHATHAM.

Trace to its cloud this lightning of the mind.
BYRON.

The mind of the writer must have been nurtured to this cast and tone of passion.
HERON (1801).

THE biography of William Pitt is a meagre one, considering his great renown as the noblest of British statesmen and orators. He was born in 1708, and educated at Eton school, whence he went to Oxford. At college, he made a respectable progress in his classic studies, and read much in English, thus forming the tastes of his life, during which he preserved his partiality for the Roman authors and the polite literature of England. His letters to his nephew, Thomas Pitt ("Chatham Correspondence," vol. i.), show the influence of such studies on his mind, and how familiar he was with the amenities of mental culture, and the *belles lettres*. Tacitus and Polybius were his favorite authors, and he was in the habit of copying portions of Thucydides, to form his mind after such a noble model. At an early age, and before he had taken any degree, he traveled on the continent, "where," says Lord Chesterfield, he generally improved his mind. On his return he accepted a cornet's commission in the Blues, entered parliament for the family borough of Old Sarum,* at the age of 27, and began his career, as he ended it forty-three years later, in opposition. His first hostility was against Sir Robert Walpole, under the banner of the great commoner, Pulteney, whose course of life, as it resembled his own in some respects, perhaps gave it its first directing impulse. The earliest known speech of Pitt was a good deal in that equivocating vein, discoverable in many parts of his future biography. Like Pulteney and the other patriots, he had attached himself to the heir-apparent, and seconded a motion for a congratulatory address to the king, George II., on the marriage of the rebellious Frederick, Prince of Wales. The royal couple disliked their son, and perhaps not without reason, fairly wishing him out of the world, at times, as Lord Hervey tells us, in his memoirs. Pitt's speech was laudatory of the prince, and conveyed an amount of irony which the king would feel and remember. In less than a year Walpole deprived the "terrible cornet of Horse" of his commission, seeing he could not muzzle him, and Pitt then became groom of Prince Frederick's Bed Chamber. His sister, Mrs. Ann Pitt, also became attached to the apartment of the Princess of Wales. It is easy to imagine how the formidable man, who so often

* Twenty-five years ago, this venerable place might have pleaded such a fact against the general sarcastic outcry which turned Gatton and itself into a sort of twin-proverb. It will be long enough, very probably, before the Manchesters, and other large cities of England, will equal those much-abused close boroughs, in contributing to the statesmanly renown of that county.

and so bitterly, masked or unmasked, assailed George III., very often dandled him in his arms as a child, and carried him cock-horse to Banbury. Pitt's temper, naturally haughty and vehement, was not improved by his dismissal, and he became very fierce and abusive in his place, in the House of Commons. Horace Walpole, brother of Sir Robert, provoked him by calling him a young man, and drew upon himself the rebuke which Dr. Johnson has so solemnized. There are not many traces to be found of Pitt's early parliamentary career. But it is certain that the king and the court party disliked such a loose-tongued partisan of the prince, and that he and Lyttelton and Cobham had formed a sort of compact, to stand or fall together. In 1742, a debate occurred, in which he grappled with his most enduring antagonist. Horace Walpole, writing to Sir Horace Mann, says: "We have had another great day in the House, on the army in Flanders, which the opposition were for disbanding; but we carried it by 120. Murray spoke for the first time, with great applause. Pitt answered him, with all his force and wit of language, but in an ill-founded argument. In all appearance they will be great rivals."* They were rivals before that day. On the death of George I., the boys, being at Oxford together, wrote each a prize threnody on the occasion, and Murray, the senior by about three years, was the victor. On the next day of the aforementioned debate (December 10th), Pitt not only attacked the Hanoverian army, but the Elector himself, in a strain of

"Walpole's Letters to Sir Horace Mann," vol. i., p. 264. Pitt, mindful of his college days, was, doubtless, eager to be at Murray in any sort of argument.

sarcasm which astonished every one. Next year, after the battle of Dettingen, he declared, in one of his speeches, that the ardor of the English soldiers was restrained by the cowardice of the Hanoverians, and called the affair an *escape*, not a *victory!* He also affected to think the king had run no risks at all in the field. The intrepid air of the man, in saying all this, used to make some of his hearers tremble; and we see in it some of the first genuine flashes of the Junian spirit. The king hated his very name; while the people called him "true Briton," and lauded him to the skies for his attacks on those electoral interests, so expensive to the nation.

In 1744, on some ministerial changes, Pitt's friends went into office, and he looked for the place of Secretary of State; but he found the king's antipathy strongly opposed to his advancement. Being appeased by the Duke of Newcastle, and encouraged with promises, he thought fit to moderate the rancor of his tongue in opposition. He began to advocate what he had formerly opposed, supporting an increase of the army and the foreign subsidies, with forcible arguments. In 1745, he advocated the measures which enabled fourteen Whig lords to raise each a regiment of horse—the Duke of Bedford, Lords Gower and Halifax, says Horace Walpole, being "at the head of the job." These colonelcies of horse, projected at a time when rumors of Prince Charles Edward's *raid* were in the air, give one a significant idea of the chieftainship which then divided, or wished to divide, the government between them, and colored all the political history of the time. But, in spite of Pitt's milder demonstrations, his majesty was obdurate; the door of the office sought was not, for twelve years, to be opened to that disconsolate Whig Peri at the gate, looking wistfully through the bars. His parliamentary Georgics, in fact, were not well calculated to bring him anything better than a harvest of popular huzzas. His friends, the Pelhams, once more tried earnestly to bring him in, and Lord Cobham, for himself and his following, agreed with the Duke of Bedford to support the foreign policy of government, on condition that Pitt should be made Secretary of War, and the Grenvillites and the rest otherwise placed. But the king resisted his ministers, and refused to have anything to say to the terrible man who abused his Hanoverians, and said he himself was in no danger at Dettingen. The Pelhams then resigned, whereupon George II. turned obstinately to Lords Bath and Grenville, bidding them take the helm, and save him from the coalition. The reader will perceive how the government of that time resembles the condition of things twenty years later, and how George III. was obliged to manœuvre, like George II., looking to the Earl of Chatham, as his grandfather had looked to the other great commoner ennobled—Pulteney, Earl of Bath. But Lords Bath and Grenville were deterred by the forces against them, the king was obliged to give way, and Pitt came into office with a high hand, taking it, as it were, by storm. It was, however, but an Irish office—the king still insisted on that—the Vice Treasurership of Ireland. In a little time he was made Paymaster of the Forces —a department which was suitable, in some degree, to his genius, and certainly facilitated the knowledge of military matters, and the business of the War Office, which he afterwards put to such account, during his immortal secretaryship, and which Junius, too, could make use of in a manner so puzzling to most people. Thus, after ten years' fighting—quite a Trojan siege—he found himself in possession of the place, or rather within the outer walls. During his struggles in the cold shade of opposition, Pitt had been comparatively poor, but his circumstances were now improved by his marriage, and a legacy of £10,000, left him in admiration of his eloquence and patriotism by Sarah, Duchess of Marlborough, a fine-spirited woman, with all her faults, who affected the high Roman tone of "the country party," and sighed to think that England was going to destruction—buying up estates at a bargain all the time, and adding acre to acre long after her eightieth year.*

The old king held out astonishingly, he showed no signs

* The brave duchess had quite a passion for leaving legacies, or making gifts to great men of the Whig tone of patriotism. She left £20,000 to Lord Chesterfield; gave £1,000 to Lord Marchmont, and another £1,000 to Pope—a gift spoken of by Bolingbroke in a letter to Marchmont ("Marchmont Papers"). It is not pleasant to remember that, after receiving the money, the poet should have left behind him (in his Epistle to a Lady, that cruel portrait of her Grace, as Atossa. She survived him for a short time, and might have seen the lines, in which case her opinion of him would not have been more favorable than Bolingbroke's. That "guide, philosopher, and friend" declared, after Pope's death, that the poet had dealt treacherously with him in printing the "Patriot King" without his knowledge, and against his wishes. After all, Pope might have looked on the gift as a sort of bribe. The duchess was greatly afraid of a man who had secured the ear of posterity, conscious that the brave disorder of her biography would tempt him to put her in his Portrait Gallery. It is probable Pope had made the verses before he got the money, and could not find it in his heart to destroy them. He might also think she would never see them—an argument suitable enough to the tone of his moral philosophy.

of dying. After that gleam of favor in 1746, Pitt supported the measures of government, as in duty bound to do; and, in time, the Cobhams about him changed into the Grenvilles, a rising family of ambitious brothers and sisters. Pitt still looked to higher office, and, writing to the Duke of Newcastle, then with the king at Hanover, earnestly expressed his longing "to efface the past by every action of his life." In 1751, when his former friends of the Prince of Wales' opposition denounced the Duke of Newcastle's Bavarian subsidy, and his commercial treaty with Spain (involving a Spanish right to search English vessels on the coast of South America, which Pitt had formerly repudiated), the latter was the chief defender of the ministerial policy in the Commons:

> He ceased to make a fiddle faddle
> About a Hessian horse and saddle!

In this and other questions, he was ready with his dexterous palinodes, which, indeed, might be found the more reasonable for the exaggeration of his preceding opposition; though, doubtless, he must have groaned in soul to think what negotiable popularity he was sacrificing to his dream of ministerial power. The interpellations and taunts he was forced to endure in the House, tried his proud spirit severely, and led to a number of gladiatorial passages, in which he showed a wonderful science and command of his weapons. In 1752, the Prince of Wales was dead. Three years afterwards, Mr. Pelham, the premier, died, and then, the poor king, knowing the elements of the Whig power surrounding the throne, said, with a troubled prophecy:

"Now, I shall have no more peace." Newcastle was made prime minister, and to him Pitt stuck dutifully, though with very little respect for his Grace's style of statesmanship.

Still, the door of royal favor remains shut. Pitt is impatient, subservient, and despairing. He tells the Duke of Newcastle he had flattered himself the interests of his Grace were concerned in bringing forward a man of his own raising. He longs for some softening of his Majesty's mind towards him, and then, to alarm the duke, says his wishes all tend to a quiet retreat. In a letter to Lord Hardwicke, he says: "The weight of irremovable royal displeasure is a load too great to move under, it must crush any man, it has sunk and broken me."* We may conceive his discontent and smothered anger when he could write in such a strain as that—his humble language contrasting with the haughty assumption that it is the king who is his adversary. Pitt's talk of retirement in these querulous epistles was all pretense; his watchful *arriere pensee* was still shaping out some powerful future. He had married the Lady Hester Grenville, and become the greater part of a strong family confederacy. He had, also, an understanding with Fox, that, in the ministerial changes, which they would do all they could to bring about, Pitt was to be Secretary of State, and Fox at the head of the Treasury. Meantime, the former began to treat the administration roughly, and ever and anon, refreshed his powers by an assault on his ever present rival, Murray. Fox, writing to Lord Harting-

* "Chatham Correspondence," vol. i., p. 105.

ton, Nov. 28, 1754, says of one of Pitt's speeches: "Every word was Murray, yet so managed that neither he nor anybody else could or did take any public notice of it, or in any degree reprehend him. I sat next Murray, who suffered for an hour." Mr. Fox does not attempt to describe the management or manner of this attack; perhaps, it would have taxed his less subtle intellect to do so; for, though Fox was cunning, Pitt was deep. But we cannot help thinking it displayed something of that equivocal art, visible in certain of the miscellaneous letters, and to be spoken of more particularly in some of the succeeding pages.

The Paymaster and Mr. Fox used, at this time, to meet by night, like conspirators as they were, to discuss and arrange their plans for the seizure of office. The king, feeling himself undermined, refused to allow Fox to have the leadership of the House of Commons, and also refused to hear of Pitt for the Secretaryship of State. Newcastle, dreading the concerted action of the plotting pair, resolved to separate them. Fox was taken into the Cabinet, and Pitt was left as he was—neglected, mortified, and exasperated. But he prepared a stroke of revenge. In 1755, the king returned from Hanover with a subsidiary treaty; and, forthwith, orders to pay large sums of money to Hessians and Russians, were sent to Mr. Legge, Chancellor of the Exchequer. The latter, supported by Mr. Pitt, refused to pay them, and a notable *eclat* was the result. When parliament met, Pitt, declaring aloud that the English people should have prevented with their bodies ("a physical force" expression in the genuine style of Junius) the going of the king to Hanover, came out in all his British glory, thundering against the Electorate, the subsidies, and all the rest of the royal predilections, and also denouncing the general imbecility of the administration. Horace Walpole (what would the world do without that cynical philosopher, so full of affectations and prejudices, who furnishes us so opportunely with intelligence to be found nowhere else, and fills up so many *lacunes* of political and personal history?), describing one of the parliamentary mellays of 1755, sets before us, in a letter to Gen. Conway, some of the characteristics of the Junian literature: "You will ask, what is beyond this (a speech of Gerard Hamilton's)? Nothing, but whatever was beyond whatever was, and that was Pitt. He spoke, at past one, for an hour and thirty-five minutes. There was humor, wit, vivacity, fine language, more boldness, in short, more astonishing perfection, than even you, who are used to him, can conceive. He was not very abusive, yet very attacking on all sides. He ridiculed my Lord Hillsborough, crushed poor Sir George (Lyttelton), crucified the Attorney (Murray), lashed my Lord Grenville, painted my Lord of Newcastle, attacked Mr. Fox, and even hinted up to the Duke of Cumberland himself."* This assailing of the whole line will remind the reader of "Correggio" (Letter 4), "Lucius" (Letter 35), "Atticus" (Letter 48), and "Domitian" (Letter 87)—all in the miscellaneous series. The end of this House of Commons war was, that Fox was made Secretary of State, and Pitt, Legge, and Grenville, were dismissed.

Thus was the high-spirited and ambitious athlete once

* "Walpole's Correspondence," vol. i., p. 308

more thrown heavily in the ring. But circumstances were about to avenge him. Everything had been falling into confusion in the helpless hands of Newcastle; nothing but domestic discontents and foreign disasters, the loss of Minorca, the cruel and cowardly shooting of Byng, and the people, as in the days of Swift, ready to hide themselves in the ground at the reports of French invasion. Towards the close of 1756, the duke shuffled from the helm, and left George II. to fall into the hands of the dreaded Pitt. The latter now told Fox, *point blanc*, that he would not act with him as minister, and, flushed with a consciousness of strength, said to the Duke of Devonshire: "My lord, I can save this country." The latter duke now became first Lord of the Treasury, with Pitt as Secretary of State, Lord Temple, First Lord of the Admirality, and George Grenville, Treasurer of the Navy—the three brothers holding, so to speak, the bolts, and exercising the sinews of war. But the king still struggled against his fate, and the excluded politicians rallied round the royal closet. Temple opposed with vehemence a vote of thanks to his majesty for bringing over some Hessian troops, and the king's antipathy to the whole family was, if possible, increased. The language of one of them (Pitt) was, he said, beyond his comprehension, and the other (Temple) was a rude, insolent man. Regardless of the plans for the restoration of the public confidence, proposed by the new ministers, he vehemently desired the return of the Duke of Newcastle—he only wanted to turn out the scoundrels. "I think," said George II. to Lord Waldegrave, in allusion to his grace, "he is apt to be afraid; therefore, go and encourage him.

Tell him that I do not look on myself as king while I am in the hands of these scoundrels, that I am determined to get rid of them at any rate, and he may depend on my favor and protection."* But the duke shrunk from the perils of the crisis. Still the king struggled to liberate himself, and, urged by the Duke of Cumberland, fiercely broke up the ministry, and dismissed Pitt, Temple, Legge, and their friends. This was in 1757. The whole kingdom was in a ferment, and the people in general were loud and decided in their encouragement of Pitt and the rest. The king and his friends, on the other hand, made desperate efforts to form a ministry. Lord Waldegrave, a very honest courtier but a very poor statesman, tells us how George II. wanted to make even him Prime Minister, in spite of his protestations! All the court contrivances, however, were discomfited, and, after a confusion of three months, Pitt came back again, and planted his hated flag upon the floor of the royal closet. It was a great triumph. But the fate of difficulty and clogging compromise was ever to follow him. He had the poor Duke of Newcastle—whom he would have excluded—for a colleague, as first Lord of the Treasury, and Lord Granville, whom he had styled flagitious, was President of the King's Council.

Pitt, at last, held the place he had been looking up to, for twenty years. But now that he was in it, he found it a perilous and rugged platform, surrounded by jealous adversaries, who only tolerated his overbearing superiorities from fear. He was obliged to strain every nerve to keep

* "Lord Waldegrave's Memoirs," p. 96.

his footing, and must have intimately felt the truth of that sentiment versified in a succeeding day, and applied to a spirit as self-willed and full of ambition as his own:

> He who ascends the mountain tops shall find
> The highest peaks most wrapt in clouds and snow;
> He who surpasses or subdues mankind,
> Must look down on the hate of those below.
> Though, high above, the sun of Glory glow,
> And, far beneath, the earth and ocean spread,
> Round him are icy rocks, and loudly blow
> Contending tempests on his naked head,
> And thus reward the toil which to these summits led.

The secretary well knew the nature of the men and things about him. He knew that, for all his efforts to achieve the glory and good of England, there were thousands, and those among the highest in the realm, who would repay him by pulling him down and driving him into retirement; and the consciousness of this gave his words and acts a dash of that impulsive willfulness which, at a later period, procured him the name of a lunatic. Temple asked, in 1759, for a ribbon of the Garter, and the king refused. Pitt, strongly moved, added his own requests to those of his brother-in-law, and at last wrote to the Duke of Newcastle: "Unconscious as I am of the want of diligence and fidelity, in sustaining the vast and dangerous load his majesty has been pleased to lay on my shoulders, I will forbear, now and forever, entering into a subject where I may possibly judge amiss, and wherein, above all things, I most wish not greatly to err. * * * All I mean at present to trouble your grace with is, to desire that, when next my reluctant steps shall bring me up the stairs at Kensington, and mix me with the dust of the ante-chamber, I may learn, once for all, whether the king continues finally inexorable and obdurate."* In spite of the heavy style—deliberately chosen—that marks much of Pitt's official correspondence, and which appears somewhat in the foregoing, strong shapes of expression, such as that about "the dust of the ante-chamber," show the nature of the writer, and remind one of his sarcastic House of Commons displays; while that bold assumption, that the king himself is his enemy, together with the threat of throwing down his load in some possible *terrivy* and leaving everything at six and seven, foreshadows the willful desertion of 1767 and 1768, the fierce accusations of 1770, in the House of Lords, and the resolute language of Junius in lofty castigation of George III.

Four years passed away in a war of sea and land fights and triumphs in every quarter of the globe, such as, from a condition of danger and depression, raised England to an unexampled pitch of authority and renown. The conquest of Canada, Cape Breton, St. John's, Senegal, Pondicherry, Goree, Dominique, Belleisle, Martinique, Granada, St. Lucie, St. Vincent, the Havana, the crushing of the French power in India, the demolition of the French fleets in their harbors or on the high seas, the statesmanship and guineas which strengthened the King of Prussia against a swarm of enemies, and the diversions which left the House of Bourbon covered with defeat on the continent of Europe—all these things were due to the victorious genius of the only real War Minister England has ever had, and they form one of

* "Chatham Correspondence," vol. i., p. 434.

the brightest chapters of British history. Pitt had a haughty consciousness of his glory, and of what he deserved of his king and country. But how short was his tenure of that power which became him so well! Small and feeble men, corrupting the morals of the nation, and lowering it into contempt, enjoyed long leases of power with its emoluments and the favor of the sovereign. But the man whose ministry was the most splendid in his country's annals was scarcely warm in his seat when he was hustled out of it. In his life of seventy years, ever struggling to win that prize of his high calling, and sacrificing his ease, and very often his self-respect, in the pursuit, he was allowed but *four* in which to breathe the native atmosphere of his mind, and exercise his inborn faculties of statesmanship and command. But four years. The rest was, subserviency, intrigue, duplicity, anger, hypocrisy, disappointment, and the perverse energy of the passions. Perhaps we cannot truly estimate how all this must have embittered the nature of William Pitt—that strong, splenetic nature, so full of impulse and ambition, and so keenly gifted with the capacity of suffering. We are so accustomed, in the absence of parliamentary reports, or any means of getting a correct idea of that high-reaching character, to judge of him by some stupid official correspondence or other inadequate presentment of the man, that we do not, at a general glance, discover the angry heart of a disappointed statesman in such a crisis. But still we can fancy how a spirit born to rule, such as his, must have felt the briefness of his ministerial power, and the insulting opposition that labored to mar it, and soon forced him to surrender it.

His great ministry—his *Quadrennium*—drew to a close with the life of George II., who bequeathed to his successor, along with his crown, a sincere antipathy to William Pitt.* George III., urged by the teaching of his mother and the advice of his friends, was resolved to rid the crown of the troublesome Whig oligarchy or oligarchies, which, for seventy years, had borne sway in England, instead of the Stewarts. The monarchy, surrounded by the great Whig families, presented something of the feudal appearance of former dynasties in the midst of the military fiefs. The Newcastles, Argyles, Devonshires, Bedfords, Graftons, Richmonds, Cavendishes, Dorsets, Grenvilles, and so forth, with their peers and followers, stood round the throne, asserting a hereditary right to the business of government, and looking on the country as on the brink of ruin, unless the great Whig families should have the privilege of saving it. Those lords who had raised regiments in 1745, would naturally think themselves the bulwark of the Protestant succession, and highly deserving of everything the nation could bestow upon them.† They would allow the king to reign—to have

* A trifling incident may also help to show what the court people thought of the great minister. When George III., a few months after his marriage, went in procession with the queen to the London banquet, the populace, recognizing Pitt's carriage and liveries among the rest, crowded round them with acclamations, hugged his footman and kissed the horses! The royal folks, no doubt, felt as the king of Scotland once did towards Johnnie Armstrong, and the affair was called by the courtiers "the abominable behavior of Mr. Pitt."

† Horace Walpole says, that the Dukes of Bedford, Bolton, and Montague, Lords Harcourt, Halifax, etc., got permission to raise regiments, which were paid by government. But he says it is certain, that not six regiments were ever raised, or four employed. He gives a pretty broad hint that several of the lords were paid for soldiers that they never enrolled.

the sword of honor and the crown; but the government, that is, the emoluments of government, were to belong to some prevailing section of themselves. Those chiefs employed their pocket lists as their feudal ancestors employed clansmen or men-at-arms; and we have William Pitt himself borrowing the Duke of Newcastle's majority, to carry out some points in his war-policy. Lord Waldegrave, in his "Memoirs," describes, in a few words, the general character of the government at that period: "When the Hanoverian succession took place, the Whigs became possessors of all great offices and lucrative employments, since which time, instead of quarreling with the prerogative, they have been the champions of every administration. However, they have not always been united into one body, under one general, like a regular and well-disciplined army, but they may be more aptly compared to an alliance of different clans fighting in the same cause, possessing the same principles, but influenced and guided by their different chieftains."* George III. desired to change all that, as much as possible, and restore the crown to something of its ancient influence; and though it is not the fashion, at this time of day, to extenuate the willful policy of that king, or the statesmanship of his ministers and favorites, yet we should be disposed to give his cause a fair hearing, when we estimate, at this cool distance, the nature of that bewildering opposition which worked so arrogantly and selfishly against him. The rapacious and overbearing Whig chiefs, scheming against one another, and appropriating everything

* "Waldegrave's Memoirs," p. 18.

within their reach,* were forever talking of liberty and the constitution, and it is not to be wondered at, after all, if the poor young king grew sick of such a jargon, and longed to revert to a purer system of monarchy (and, perhaps, not a more turbid system of constitutional government), in which he may feel himself somewhat more of a king than a *cochon à l'engrais*, and have none of those insolent Whigs coming into his closet and scolding him into convulsions, or the milder necessity of eating nothing but potatoes ("Royal Farmers"), for a week. Looking round him, he saw in William Pitt one of the most formidable exponents of that Whig predominancy he disliked so much, and felt that it could not be diminished while the Great Commoner continued in the van of power, overawing the royal mind by his superiority, and controlling everything with the voice and port of a dictator. Pitt, on his side, believed in 1688, and the principles which placed the house of Brunswick on the throne; and he also firmly and potently believed that any attempts against himself and his statesmanship would be calculated to damage these in some measure. He was always disposed to act with his alliance and on the recognized Whig system. But it must be understood, that he always supported these with the more earnestness and vivacity, that they seconded his own high views of national glory and prosperity—in other words, aided his ambition.

* Lord Hervey, in his "Memoirs," says that, having once observed to George II. that he supposed his majesty found great relaxation in his frequent visits to the country, the king replied: "Yes, my lord, I am very glad to get away into the country; for I see so many hungry faces around me in London, I am afraid they will eat me up at last."

In the beginning of his reign, George III. began to put his policy in operation—a shrewd little policy of dividing to conquer. He manœuvred to break the family alliances and other coalitions which might presume to dispute his cabinet with him. He followed out this idea with wonderful pertinacity and a fatal sort of success, in the midst of perilous confusions, through tempests of vituperation, and in spite of the most desperate looking national disasters. He agitated so vigorously, that the first nine years of his reign witnessed seven ministries, or rather premierships—the former being, perhaps, too definite a phrase for that scrambling succession of administrations, curious evidences of the chaotic state of things then existing. They were no clean clearings-out, and compact comings-in—no more marching in bands was permitted. Everything was done in a bit-by-bit, patchwork way, so as to have men of various leanings included, and thus guard against a monopoly of ministerial power by any too-powerful subject. It is rather puzzling to try and distinguish the wavering outline of these ministries. Pitt's ministry slid into Bute's, and that somehow into Grenville's; after this occurs a huddle that seems about to change into the Bedford or the Pitt, again; but it is the Rockingham that comes; and soon another shuffling takes place, and we have a shape of government—"if shape it may be called, that shape had none"—it is the ministry in the truckle-bed from which Lord Chatham flies away disgusted and enraged; and as we look at it, it is the Grafton ministry; then that, too, changes, in the twinkling of a zodiac, and lo! it is the good-humored and fatal Lord North, patting his portly person, and unconsciously making the most perilous and important chapter of modern history.

In the attempt to get rid of the expensive and overbearing William Pitt, the Earl of Bute was a prime instigator. There are letters in the "Chatham Correspondence" which seem to show, and are intended to show, a cordiality between the favorite and the minister, and we have seen statements that Bute's influence with the court party was far less than the world supposed; leading people to the idea that Lord Chatham, who must have been well informed on that subject, could not have entertained any violent antipathy to the Scottish Sejanus. But that Bute had a hand in Pitt's dismissal is as sure as he had a potential voice in forming the biases of George III. With a presence in history, almost as shadowy as that of *Nominis Umbra* himself, and "with no more biography than a fly," as Chancellor Thurlow used to say, how wonderfully that fastidious and somewhat feeble man has contrived to make himself talked of in the world! Bubb Doddington, in his "Diary," reveals the Earl's *animus* towards Pitt. Under date of 29th December, 1760, the diarist says Bute called on him and expressed a wish that Lord Holdernesse should quarrel with his colleagues, and throw up his office in seeming anger, in order that he (Bute) may go in without appearing to displace any one. From the same source, we learn that Glover, the poet, spoke to Doddington, in admiration of Bute, applauding his conduct and the determination of the king, and saying they would beat everything yet. This gives a glimpse behind the scenes; shows the plotting character of the young king's court, and the efforts of his "friends" to get rid of the Secretary.* The Princess of Wales, too, who lived on very friendly terms with the Earl of Bute, was a great part of these intrigues; and we can easily conceive how Pitt's contemptuous rage against those personages would be expressed in the bitterest language of Junius. His ministry drew to its close in 1761. The king was always sighing, like Falkland, for the blessings of peace, and thus formed the general fashion of deprecating the continuance of the war. In the autumn of 1761, the minister, who had organized victory before Carnot was born, finding that France and Spain had signed a family Compact, wanted to attack them promptly, and bring them to their senses by one or two of his *coups de tonnere.* But the feeling was entirely aginst him; the real enemy was not Bourbon, but Pitt. It was a courtly grief of the first magnitude to see him towering like a colossus, under whose huge legs his colleagues and others were doomed to creep about and find themselves dishonorable—staves. A majority of the Cabinet outvoted him, on this question of war, whereupon he haughtily resigned, declaring, with a scarce disguised contempt, to the people about him, that "he would not be responsible for measures he was not permitted to guide." Dutiful politicians of all sorts threw up their eyes and hands in amazement at such language, which, they said, was only fit for the Grand Turk, and Temple quitted office with his brother-in-law. Newcastle also, the nominal head of that ministry, resigned soon after, casting on the long-

* No one, reading the concluding page or two of "Doddington's Diary," can have the slightest doubt that Lord Bute did everything in his power to bring about a change such as would remove Pitt.

enjoyed domains of office, as he quitted them for the last time, a glance like that of Boabdil, when he bid a last adieu to the pleasant seats of Granada. Then the court party triumphed, and the shy, saturnine Lord Bute succeeded in grasping what, with the king's aid, he had plotted for—the premiership of England—a brief possession.

George Grenville refused to follow the fortunes of his family and provoked the future sarcastic opposition of Pitt, by getting into the place lately held by the latter. In 1762, the Duke of Bedford, a strong opponent of Pitt's belligerent policy, went to France, and there concluded the treaty of Paris, signing away, with a stroke of his pen, conquests which had cost the late Secretary so much travail of soul to achieve. Meanwhile, a storm, directed by the latter, whether in parliament, or through channels of the press of which we have no certain knowledge as yet, blew against Bute and the court policy; a boot-jack and a petticoat (this last representing, by synecdoche, the Princess of Wales) were burnt together in the streets; and, then, the obnoxious minister bent, sighed like a reed, and passed away behind the scenes to come no more forward in history. He had achieved great things, however, in driving out Pitt and Temple, and shutting the gates of Bellona, for whose worship the former was the only adequate high priest. Still, these royal victories were as disconcerting as those of Pyrrhus. Popular feeling and the Pittite phalanx were at work, and his majesty, seeing that, without a strong ministry, different from that of the long-headed arithmetician then at the head of the cabinet, the business of the country would be at a deadlock, now seemed willing to have Pitt back; but without his tail. The Great Commoner always treated his majesty, as yet, with scrupulous and obsequious courtesy, and George III., shrewdly guessing that, while feebler politicians would cling for support to their alliances, the genius of Pitt would urge him to stand and move alone, was the more anxious to treat with him and tempt his ambition. Bute sent Beckford to him and afterwards called, himself, upon him. Then, on August 27th, 1763, Pitt was brought to the young king, who had been properly drilled for the interview. The Hardwicke MSS. profess to give an account of it, and the "Grenville Papers" furnish another, and the average truth of this indistinct and shuffling business would seem to be that the king, consenting that Pitt should be premier, wished to retain some of those already in the ministry, while he delivered himself from the irksome control of Bedford and George Grenville. He would open the door a little way, on his cunning plan. But Pitt desired that it should be flung back, on golden hinges turning, to admit his allies, saying—very probably with a sarcastic affectation of humility habitual with him—that he was but a little knife, and if his majesty would use it, he should not blunt the edge. The king seems to have listened with a deference and even an assent which, in Pitt's opinion, looked like acquiescence, when the ex-minister spoke of the necessity of a radical change of men and measures. This interview took place on Saturday; and another took place on Monday. Meantime, his majesty reported the colloquy, and received counsel of his mother and his friends. In the second interview, Pitt spoke, as before, of removing those who had brought about the late disadvantageous peace, and employing those who had credit with the nation. Alas! it was of the latter the poor king was especially apprehensive; and, as regarded some of those whom Pitt would remove, he could only say, and repeat, that his honor was concerned; and so brought the interview to an end. Pitt always asserted that the king had deceived him in these interviews; that he had retracted in one, the assent he had given in the other, and that there was "something behind the throne, greater than the throne itself."

Meantime, the pamphleteers and newspaper writers were skirmishing at a vehement rate. Lord Temple, an irascible man of honorable principles and moderate capacity, feeling that a royal dislike of his connection had caused the failure of the late negotiation, encouraged a war of the press against the government. He was the friend of every man who could point a quill against the court and the Earl of Bute, and the chief supporter of Wilkes, conductor of the most renowned journal in history. Macaulay, in consideration of his heartiness in hounding on the demagogues, calls him the "malignant Temple"—a verdict too much in that writer's exaggerated style. Pitt, at this time, took marked occasion to express, in the House of Commons, his disapproval of the doings of Wilkes, hinting that Temple was considered the great patron of such vituperative warfare, and at the same time, oddly enough (but perfectly in character), protesting he would act, live, and die in union with his noble brother. His disavowal of Wilkes had its effect, and advances were still made to him.

In 1764, he detached himself from his alliance with the

Duke of Newcastle, and expressed to this nobleman his determination to act for himself in future. Having seen, he said, his war policy lately given up in a full house, he would have no more centres of union.*

In 1765, at a time when rumors of dangerous mobs and mutinies were flying about everywhere, the Duke of Cumberland, by command of his majesty, undertook to negotiate with Pitt and Temple, or rather with the first, hoping some chance may push the latter out of the question. And now commence those movements and occurrences from which, looking closely at them, we can immediately gather the identity of Junius and Lord Chatham.

The negotiation failed, because the king stipulated that Lord Northumberland and Mr. Stuart Mackenzie, the latter, Lord Bute's brother, should remain in their places; and this was not agreeable to Lord Temple. Another negotiation followed, with the same result. Then Pitt, as is very evident from what we know of the sayings and doings of that period, began to find Temple a sort of clog and hinderance to that compromise, which, in the ambitious commoner's opinion, was called for by the occasion. The king tried his courtesies and conciliations on Pitt. He had found Bedford intolerable; and George Grenville himself would grumble about a trifle given or proposed for Sir William Breton, or any one supposed to be connected with Lord Bute. Indeed, when it was a question of giving away any good thing to them, Grenville could hate the Scotch like a Wilkite. All this, and his penurious behavior respecting

* "Chatham Correspondence," vol. ii., p. 297.

the king himself, influenced his majesty in his advances to Pitt. But matters proceeded slowly and warily. The king distrusted the veteran astuteness of the Great Commoner, and the latter nursed an angry recollection of that unsatisfactory interview.

In the mean time, George Grenville (who will be remembered with Erostratus), having received an extremely correct plan of taxation, shaped and passed his Stamp Act, and so set the world on fire.*

This Bill was opposed by Mr. Pitt, who, with his usual sagacity, though he could only recognize Grenville in the matter, said it was marked with the mean and narrow genius of the originator. Negotiations continued; but believing his pear to be almost ripe, he held back. He would not enter the ministry, bound up with any party cabal. On 24th of February, 1765, writing to the Earl of Shelburne, he says, rather sharply, that the king's pleasure and gracious command alone shall be a call to him: "I am deaf," he adds, "to every other thing. I will not say more, lest I say too much."† In this holding off of Pitt, the Duke of Cumberland, coöperating with the Duke of Newcastle,

* The "Grenville Papers" contain a curious statement respecting this renowned Act, which did not originate with Mr. Grenville. Mr. Henry McCulloch, of Turnham Green, wrote a letter to Mr. Jenkinson in 1763, accompanied by two bills or proposals; one respecting a duty on vellum and paper, which, at *6d.* to *18d.* per sheet, would bring £60,000 a year from the American colonies; the other for creating and issuing bills of credit, called Exchequer Bills, for the use of the colonies. The reader is, doubtless, thinking of the saying attributed to the Chancellor Oxenstein. The statistical and financial renown of the McCullochs, is, after all, greater than the world supposed.

† "Chatham Correspondence," vol. iii., p. 12.

succeeded in arranging matters with the Marquis of Rockingham; and the *Lutestring* Administration, calculated for a season's wear, was brought into precarious existence. The Rockinghams were extremely desirious that Pitt should rouse up his power and come among them; and Edmund Burke, writing to Flood, on 18th of May, 1765, says: "Nothing but an intractable spirit in your friend Pitt can prevent a more admirable and lasting system from being put together, and this crisis will show whether pride or patriotism be predominant in his character, for you may be assured he has it now in his power to come into the service of his country, upon any plan of politics he chooses to dictate, with great and honorable terms to himself, and every friend he has in the world, and with such a strength of power as will be equal to anything but absolute despotism over the king and kingdom. A few days will show whether he will take this part, or continue on his back at Hayes, talking fustian." Pitt, however, continued inexorable, and bowing gravely and negatively, with a grand stage bend, over the horrible perplexity of the Rockinghams, assured them that confidence was a plant of slow growth in an aged bosom; a declaration which he probably meant should go a little further and higher than the treasury bench. On the same occasion—the opening of the Session of 1766—he denounced the American policy of ministers, and the Stamp Act. This brought up George Grenville, who retorted by saying, the colonists were encouraged in their disaffection by factious men at home—by the speeches of Pitt himself in that house. In a few months, the Rockinghams, in spite of the subtle efforts and partisan arrangements which so curiously mark the political history of that time, and which inevitably remind the irreverent reader of the Noodles, Coodles, Doodles and Foodles of Bleak House, went down—only to make way for something more bewildered and tragic still.

The king now proceeded to the completion of his shrewd designs. He professed to give Pitt the privilege of making his own ministry, and thus, taxing the generosity of the Great Commoner, constrained him more effectually than he could ever hope to do in any other way. His majesty showed a palpable desire that Temple should be dispensed with in the new arrangements, and in a significant letter to his first minister, now (July, 1766) Earl of Chatham, tells his lordship that the aforesaid nobleman has been with him, and expresses a wish to give the earl a report of the interview, in order to prepare him for a conversation with his brother-in-law. "I opened to him," says George III., "a desire of seeing him in the Treasury, and, in conjunction with you, chalking out such an administration as can be formed, considering the unhappy divisions that subsist between men, yet taking the present administration as the basis to build upon, with such alterations as may seem necessary, I am sorry to see, though we only kept in generals, that he seems to be inclined to quarters very heterogeneous to my and your ideas, and almost a total exclusion of the present men, which is not your plan. I concluded with saying, I should only agree to such a plan as you could with pleasure be a part of, not to one wherein you had not a principal share."* This gives a clear idea of the king's

* "Chatham Correspondence," vol. ii., p. 443.

mode of arrangement. The drift of the letter—the desire to have the first word, to put Chatham's views at variance with those of Temple, and, above all, to flatter the former with the appearance of acting closely and confidentially with the king—is very palpable. Everything succeeded to his majesty's wish. Temple had an interview with Pitt, in which they differed so much that the former went off in displeasure, declaring to Lord Northington that the desire to have him in the ministry was only a farce, and to his sister, that he would not be stuck into it as a cypher, surrounded by other cyphers, at the will of the premier. The family alliance was now broken. Temple was out of the way, and Chatham seemed disposed to act amicably with the court party. But an angry Nemesis was about to dash his majesty's astute policy, and some of his worst troubles were now on the point of beginning.

From a consideration of the foregoing, we can perceive how closely the spirit and political profession of Pitt coincide with those of Junius. Pitt's career was a continual fight with the powers of the court and government in support of the Whig principles and influences, advocated by the secret writer. The aggressive and haughty animosity visible in Junius, his irrespective manner of assaulting the gravest and highest persons in the kingdom, is undeniably Pitt's, as may be seen even in our scanty statement of antecedents. The moral and intellectual features of both are the same.

But these antecedents, significant as they are, furnish but half the circumstantial evidence which, without any effort, but with irresistible force, tends to establish the theory or statement of these pages.

CHAPTER III.

LORD CHATHAM'S DESPERATE ATTEMPTS TO CONSTRUCT HIS HELPLESS MOSAIC MINISTRY—HIS STRANGE RETIREMENT AND THE CONSEQUENT CONFUSIONS.

But, now that I am forced to leave the ship, after having resigned, not abandoned, the helm, I am desirous of seeing, from the land, the wreck of my successor.—CICERO, TO ATTICUS.

He, indeed,
Retired into the desert, but with arms.
MILTON.

GEORGE III., unprophetic of the event, took a good deal of trouble to bring Chatham into the cabinet, as a sort of palladium of his cause. But the introduction was as big with disaster as that of the Greek horse of old, into Troy. The new earl went into office without his party, and found himself strangely allied with that which he most hated—the court party—and controlled by the king's wishes in the formation of his ministry. But he was not more embarrassed by such an alliance, than by the displeasure of his late friends and their determination to give him no assistance. The first difficulties were ominous of the fate of the administration; and, if Lord Chatham ever had any hopes of success, he appears to have bid adieu to them very soon.

Everything was calculated to discourage him. His peerage and pension lowered him in popular estimation, and, whenever he remained at home with the gout, the joke of the day, reported by Lord Chesterfield, was, that "he had indured himself by a fall up stairs."

In endeavoring to form his administration, the earl had as many difficulties to meet as Nehemiah had of old, beset by the Horonites in building the wall; though, there the resemblance ends; for the Hebrew never thought of pulling down his wall after he had got it up. The new premier made offers to a great many, but, says Almon, "the superiority of mind which had denied him the usual habits of intercourse with the world, gave an air of authority to his manner and precluded the policy of a convenient condescension to the minutiæ of politeness and fascinating powers of address. He made an offer of Secretary of State, to Lord Gower, whom he had refused, when proposed for the office by his brother, Lord Temple. He made offers to Lord Scarborough, Mr. Dowdeswell, and several others; but in such terms of *hauteur* as seemed to provoke, though unintentionally, the necessity of refusal. To the first an abrupt message was sent, that he might have an office if he would; to the second, that he could take such an office or none. The offers were all rejected. He then waited on Lord Rockingham at his house in Grosvenor Square. But Lord Rockingham refused to see him."* Something must be allowed for the Grenvillite coloring of all this; but, it is true in the main. Lord Chatham played like a gamester

* "Almon's Anecdotes of Lord Chatham," vol. ii., p. 29.

who knows luck is against him. In the Chatham Correspondence we have him writing to Mr. Dowdeswell, to offer him his choice of the first seat at the Board of Trade, or the place of Joint Paymaster, and asking for his answer in the course of the day. Mr. Dowdeswell refuses either, in terms which certainly indicate some discontent with the condition accompanying them.* His Lordship, who had always, in fact, more of the *fortiter in re* than the *suaviter in modo* in his nature, would be apt to show very little of the latter at such a tormenting crisis.

At last that difficult ministry of 1766 was set up. But people observed, with a puzzled curiosity, that the framer chose a mere side office for himself—that of Lord Privy Seal. His colleagues were the Duke of Grafton (who, just before the Rockinghams had given up the ghost, deserted them, declaring he would work in the trenches, with spade and mattock, under a leader like Lord Chatham, and who was now first Lord of the Treasury), Charles Townsend, Chancellor of the Exchequer; Lord Shelburne and Mr. Conway, Secretaries of State; Lord Camden, Lord Chancellor; Lord Northington, President of the Council; Viscount Barrington, Secretary at War; the Marquis of Granby, Master-General of the Ordnance. The minor personages of the administration indicated as strange a mixture as the foregoing; and the character of the whole has been made familiar to all historic readers by Edmund Burke's description of it: "He made an administration, so chequered and speckled; he put together a piece of joinery so crossly indented and whim-

* "Chatham Correspondence," vol. iii., p. 29.

sically dove-tailed; a cabinet so variously inlaid; such a piece of diversified mosaic; such a tesselated pavement, without cement—here a bit of black stone, and there a bit of white stone—patriots and courtiers, kings' friends, and republicans, Whigs and Tories, treacherous friends and open enemies, that it was a very curious show, but utterly unsafe to touch, and unsure to stand upon."* The orator then goes on further to compare it to a truckle-bed, in which the officials were pigging all together, heads and points; and, in the metaphorical abundance of his description, certainly exemplifies the confusion he is describing. There never was, in fact, such a strange ministry, before or since; and we think these pages can show that there never was such a strange premier, before or since.

In this state of things, the whisperings and buzzings of party intrigue filled all the air. Everybody knew the rickety condition of the ministry, and looked every day for some change in it. At the close of 1766, in consequence of the removal of Lord Edgecombe from a Bedchamber, or a White Stick, there was an earthquake. The Duke of Portland, Lords Scarborough, Besborough, and Monson retired from the ministry, as did, also, Admirals Keppel and Saunders. Lord Hardwicke, about this time, says: "The Grenvilles are very confident the Duke of Bedford, and his party, will have nothing to do with Lord Chatham." And, again: "For my part, I do not see my way through the chaos, nor how it is possible to reconcile so many jarring interests. The new peer treats them all as Lord Peter does

* Speech on American Taxation—BURKE's *Works*.

Jack and Martin."* On the 9th December, Lord Chesterfield writes, in a letter to his son: "Eight or nine persons, of some consequence, have resigned their appointments, upon which Lord Chatham made overtures to the Duke of Bedford and his people; but they could by no means agree, and his grace went, full of wrath, to Woburn. People wait to see whom Lord Chatham will take in; for some he must have, even *he* cannot be alone, *contra mundum.* Such a state of affairs, to be sure, was never seen before in this or any other country."† Meantime, Lord Peter, assuming a bold air in the House of Lords, told them he would destroy faction, and could look the proudest connection in the face. "The nobility are not to be brow-beaten by an insolent minister!" cries the Duke of Richmond. "Such language was never before heard, westward of Constantinople!" says the amazed Secretary Conway. On the motion of the premier to examine the charter of the East India Company (introduced at the same time by Beckford, in the Commons), he found the parties he had defied, or neglected, combining against him—the Bedfords, the Rockinghams (happy to return the compliment, and Burke unprophetic of Warren Hastings), the Grenvilles, the Yorkes, the Portlands, the Devonshires, the Dowdeswells, and some of the Butes, all yelping at him, and hardening their faces against him on every side.‡ What with the desertions, the general

* "Chatham Correspondence," vol. ii., p. 29.

† "Lord Chesterfield's Letters," vol. iv., p. 442.

‡ "There are," said Lord Northington. "four parties: the Butes, the Bedfords, the Rockinghams, the Chathams; and we (the latter) the weakest of the four."

league of opposition, the failure of his humiliating overtures, particularly to the Duke of Bedford, and, perhaps, his secret self-reproaches for that desertion of Temple—so vilely requited, too—Lord Chatham felt the full desperation of the crisis. We must regard it attentively, for it is the point from which can be plainly traced the bifurcation—not to say parallel—represented by the fierce and truculent literature of Junius on one hand, and the wild, strange conduct of Lord Chatham in retreat, together with his terrible onslaughts in the Lords, on the other.

The Privy Seal stood alone. Not as the Secretary stood before, but as a political Lear, exposed to the storm which blew and rumbled all about him, and mustering fancies as fierce as those of the angry old king, when he thinks of shoeing his horses with felt, and stealing murderously on his enemies. Tormented in the feet by the gout, and still more in the head, by the retrospect and prospect of his disappointments, he flung the direction of public affairs from his hands, and left the government like a ship without a helmsman. He saw the difficulties of his former ministry renewed and exceeded, without any promise of the glory which could once console him. He had no reliance on the king. He had not been ten days in the cabinet, when, as he afterwards said in the House of Lords, "he felt the floor rotten under his feet!" Towards the close of 1766, the baited and baffled man went away to Bath, and other country places, giving out, that his infirmities obliged him to retire; and that, therefore, his colleagues need not calculate on any regular assistance from him. This was a decided step. The ministry soon felt the absence of their head. They fell into confusion, and kept calling on him for help and direction. He gave them none; he hardly vouchsafed any answer. Pursued by the piteous or spiteful reclamations of those he had thrown to pig together on that astonishing truckle-bed, he remained inexorably in his retreat. He lived, and made no sign. The political world was in amazement, as we can gather from correspondences and memoirs relating to that period. Meantime, the people he had left behind helped, by their sayings and doings, to keep his wrath warm. Burke, speaking in 1774, and referring to 1767, says: "Whenever Lord Chatham fell into a fit of the gout, or any other cause withdrew him from public cares, principles the contrary of his own were sure to predominate. When his face was hid for a moment, the whole system was on a wide sea, without chart or compass. * * Deprived of his guiding influence, they were whirled about, the sport of every gust and easily driven into any port; and as those who joined with them in manning the vessel, were the most directly opposed to his opinions, measures, and character, and far the most artful and powerful of the set, they easily prevailed so as to seize upon the vacant, unoccupied and derelict minds of his friends, and instantly they turned the vessel wholly out of the course of his policy. As if it were to insult as well as betray him, even long before the close of the first session of his administration, when everything was publicly transacted, and with great parade, in his name, they made an act, declaring it highly just and expedient to raise a revenue in America." Again, Lord Charlemont writing to Mr. Flood on the 19th February, 1767, says: "No one in opposition can get up without directly abusing Lord Chatham, and no friend ever takes his part." On the 9th of April, following, the same nobleman describes the state of the administration: "Lord Chatham has not been allowed to see any one, nor to receive letters. He is still minister; but how long he may continue such, is a problem, that would pose the deepest politician. The opposition grows more violent, and seems to gain ground. The ministry are divided into as many parts as there are men in it, all complaining of his want of coöperation. Charles Townsend is at open war, Conway is angry, Lord Shelborne out of humor, and the Duke of Grafton by no means pleased."

In December of the same year, Lord Chesterfield, writing from Bath to his son, says: "Lord Chatham's physician ignorantly checked a coming fit of the gout, and scattered it over his body, and it fell particularly on his nerves, so that he continues exceedingly vaporish. He would neither see nor speak to anybody while he was here. For the last eight months, he has been absolutely invisible to his most intimate friends."* This extraordinary conduct of a man merely vaporish, must excite the suspicion of the reader, who will observe that, about eight months before the writing of this letter, the first of the Miscellaneous Series of Junius appeared, making a curious feint against Lord Chatham, and then opening on that rebellious helpless ministry and the Court, in all moods of the bitterest hostility! We should think it would be rather unpleasant for any of those "intimate

* "Lord Chesterfield's Letters," vol. iv., p. 463.

friends," to walk into the workshop of Brontes in the act of making his thunder and launching it.

Still the retreat of Lord Chatham agitated the king and the ministry, and puzzled everybody. Lord Chesterfield writes in January, 1768: "Lord Chatham is at his repurchased house at Hayes, but sees no mortal. Some say he has a fit of the gout, which would probably do him good. Many think his worst complaint is the head, which I am afraid is too true." A great many suspected, indeed, at that time, that the complaint of the gout and general debility, was a mere pretense. Lord Camden, writing to the Duke of Grafton, a few months before the last-mentioned date, seems to think the earl's illness exaggerated: "The whole country in the neighborhood," he says, "report him much better, but his knocker is tied up, and he is inaccessible. I read a letter from Lady Chatham, yesterday, who is so fearful of owning my lord to be better, that she retracts it while admitting it in the same sentence, and conveys hopes of his recovery while she forbids them. I verily believe he is considerably mended."* These lines, written by the friend of Lord Chatham, are remarkably significant. The world could not be brought to believe that the gout could torment any man in that terrible manner, for eight or ten months at a stretch. But then, what was he about, all that time, with his knocker tied up? A question to be asked. Some said, carelessly, with Lord Chesterfield, that he must be touched in the head; but this easy and favorite mode of explanation in such cases, did not at all satisfy

* "Campbell's Lives of the Lord Chancellors," vol. v., p. 272.

those who knew the earl best. Besides, that was an old story. They said he was mad in the *Quadrennium*, too.

As his lordship will not be brought out by entreaties, they try other means. Lord Bottetourt, seeing how matters stood, and very probably instigated by ministers, demanded the decision of the Privy Seal in a matter which interested him—the question of the Wormly Copper Mines. He prepared a motion, to the effect that, if Lord Chatham would not do the business of his office, others should be appointed to do it. Commissioners were accordingly chosen on February 2d, 1768—Messrs. Richard Sutton, William Blair, and William Frazer. Lord Chatham knew that all this, particularly the appointment of such mean men, and one of them, at least, a Scotchman, was meant to insult and annoy him; and, on February 16th, Junius speaks of it as a gross affront, and says, that Lord Chatham should have too much spirit to put up with it; that any man of spirit could no more lend his office than he could his mistress to the purposes of prostitution; much less would he descend to take either of them back again with the public mark of infamy upon them.* This mode of expression is such as none but one personally insulted would employ.

Still, the retired minister is besieged with importunities from the greatest men in the kingdom, who, curiously enough, do not seem to have the slightest idea they are addressing a lunatic. They pay no attention to that report, but write, write, write. The king, who knows his man, writes repeatedly, as we see in the "Chatham Corre-

* Miscellaneous Letter xii. No Signature.

spondence," published eighteen years ago, by the great-grandsons of the earl. For two long years—such was the astonishing period of that strange retreat—his majesty continued, ever and anon, to address his inexorable Privy Seal, impatient, incredulous, and scarcely concealing his royal displeasure. On 30th May, 1767, the king writes the following significant sentences to the recluse, whom he evidently suspects of hypocrisy: "Though your relations (the Grenvillites), the Bedfords, and the Rockinghams, are joined, with the intention of storming my closet; yet, if I was mean enough to submit, they own they would not join in forming an administration; therefore nothing but confusion could be obtained. Your duty and affection for my person, your own honor calls on you to make an effort. Five minutes' conversation with you would raise his (Grafton's) spirit, for his heart is good; mine, I thank heaven, wants no raising. My love to my country, as well as what I owe to my own character, and to my family, prompt me not to yield to faction. Though none of my ministers stand by me, I will not truckle."* My Lord Privy Seal is to take notice of that, and remember it! No one shall make the king submit, or force the door of his closet. Again, on the 2d June, his majesty writes to Lord Chatham, and, after telling him plainly the ministry must fall to pieces, if he will not come out, goes on thus: "If, after this, you again decline taking an active part, I shall then be under the necessity of taking steps that nothing but the situation I am left in could have obliged to."† In another

* "Chatham Correspondence," vol. iii., p. 260.
† Ibid., vol. iii., p. 267.

letter of exhortation, speaking of the crisis, he says, it would "almost awaken the great men of former ages, and should, therefore, oblige Lord Chatham to cast aside any remains of his late indisposition."* George III., a shrewd man, who knew the secret political springs, and who, we repeat, knew Lord Chatham, *intus et in cute*, would never have written these letters to a man in the slightest degree touched with insanity. To such royal letters of exhortation, doubt, or defiance half-concealed, the stern and wily recluse would always reply by prostrating himself—nothing less!—at his majesty's feet, and begging for mercy and forgiveness in the most affected and afflicted strain of oriental submission. In this respect, those letters of the sometime William Pitt are absolute literary curiosities, worthy the attention of a future D'Israeli. The man is always complaining of debility; always prostrating himself. But out he will not come; not for an hour, not even to see any one in his own parlor. The king, at one time, begs to know what sort of a physician he has got. This was Dr. Addington, whose son, aided by the friendship of the second Pitt, became afterwards Prime Minister; and people were in the habit of saying that the "mad doctor" was likely to make the earl as mad as the generality of his patients. His majesty slyly informs the Privy Seal—the priviest of the kind, probably, on record—that he will send his own medical attendant, Sir Clifton Wintringham, to see and prescribe for his lordship. This was coming alarmingly to the point, and the sick man makes the greatest haste to prostrate himself, and protest he would rather be excused; his family physician

* "Chatham Correspondence," vol. iii., p. 277.

understands his case best (we are very sure he did), and he hopes his majesty will not think any more of sending Sir Clifton Wintringham.

But the king was not yet baffled. In the letter already quoted, of 30th of May, he wrote to the obstinate hermit to intimate, that as the Privy Seal could not come to the king, the king would go to the Privy Seal. That, indeed, was terrible. His majesty may bolt in with his "What? what?" and catch the poor incapable "Brutus" girding violently at the ministry, in the matter of Corsica, and appealing fiercely to heaven; or, "Atticus" swearing he will not tamely submit to be sacrificed! Away, therefore, flies a messenger to the king, who is thanked with prostration, requested not to think of conferring that overwhelming honor, and assured that the wretched Privy Seal will make an effort and see the Duke of Grafton, if his majesty desires it. With an imposing array of crutches and flannels, accordingly, Chatham gave his grace that compulsory interview; and we may imagine the benefit the latter would be likely to derive from it. The duke's opinion of the patient, when he tried to sum up and distinguish his impressions, after coming away, was, that the earl seemed "incurably nervous." There can be little doubt that the Privy Seal would be extremely fidgety during this painful *tête-à-tête* with the man whom he had been flagellating only a week or two before,* for his ungrateful treatment of the great minister who had led him by the hand into public life. After this unsatisfactory interview came the king's angry note, already quoted, of the 2d June. Still the great difficulty continued—the ministry

Miscellaneous Letter, xlviii., signed Atticus.

in a state of confusion, and the royal messengers galloping to and from Hayes. Something must be done, and the Duke of Grafton is to go down, see the earl again, and ask whether he means to keep office or to resign. His grace requests an interview; but he can no longer see the Privy Seal, and is obliged to sit and talk with Lady Chatham instead. In the "Chatham Correspondence," under date of 9th October, 1768,* appears her ladyship's memorandum of the *tête-à-tête*, which is remarkable for the diplomatic tone of it. The doubting duke questions, and the lady replies, with the caution of a witness at a trial, making very scanty admissions. To the question, whether the earl is disposed to continue minister, or resign, she answers, that her lord's health is very infirm, indeed; and to the duke's statement of difficulties, scruples, and so forth, rejoins with something of the same assurance still. In the course of her observations, she says the dismissal of Lord Shelburne had displeased the earl. She says nothing about the dearer friend, Sir Jeffrey Amherst,† dismissed at the same time. She must have thought there was no need of harping upon it, seeing that Junius had been already making the press ring with it. This interview indicates, palpably, that Lady Chatham well knew and assisted her lord's plans and contrivances of secrecy. A few days subsequently the earl sent back his seal to the king, and ceased to be a minister.

In connection with this sullen seclusion of the Privy Seal there is one demonstration which is not without a cer-

* "Chatham Correspondence," vol. iii., p. 336.

† General Amherst received his knighthood and garter on Staten Island, at the hands of General Monckton.

tain significancy. In August, 1767, about five months after the commencement of the Miscellaneous Letters, a power of attorney was procured, enabling Lady Chatham to sign letters and transact business for his lordship. This seems curious, considering that, in his retirement, he had little correspondence, or need of tiring his fingers, and that the countess had been, at all times, in the habit of acting as his amanuensis. But the demonstration was very effective; and the general idea was, that the Privy Seal was far gone, indeed, not being able to hold a pen. Still, as we have shown, there was a great deal of doubt abroad, respecting the condition and motives of that malcontent minister, and reports wandered about, at variance with the impression of his debility. Lord Chesterfield, in one of his letters, after saying that Lord Chatham refused to see him, or anybody else, states that he saw him in a post-chaise, "looking very well."

In another communication, we read of an architect employed at Hayes, about that time, who, making his unheeded way about the premises, came upon his invalid lordship, looking, as he looked in the post-chaise, "very well." He told what he saw when he went to town, and that greatly displeased Lady Chatham. Tom Whately*

* Lord Mahon quotes a letter from Mr. Whately to Lord Lyttelton, in which the writer draws a doleful picture of the earl's condition. "His depression and dejection are very great—so much so that he insists on being alone in his apartment, leaning his head on his hands (Tom must have peeped at him through the keyhole), ordering that no one shall remain in, or come to, his room, and giving notice that he shall knock, if he wants any one or anything." A very significant kind of dejection and depression, no doubt!

scouted such a report—said the man must have made some mistake—was not to be credited, in fact. Tom was trying, apparently, to "take care of himself." The reader remembers what Lord Camden said of one of Lady Chatham's letters. Her interview with the Duke of Grafton is also strongly significant of something to be guarded. All these things, and others of the same kind, which cannot find room here, lead us inevitably to the conclusion that it was neither insanity nor podagra which kept Lord Chatham in that wonderful condition of retirement.*

There is another consideration too curiously suggestive to be omitted in such a disquisition as this. It is drawn from Horace Walpole's observations on this crisis, contained in his "Memoirs of the Reign of George III." This amusing philosopher and politician, who was no friend of Chatham (nor, indeed, of any one else; for, as regards General Conway, to whom he seems to have been the most attached, he lets us, with an extraordinary frankness, perceive what a mercenary thing his friendship was), does not trouble himself to dive after what does not appear near the surface, but satisfies himself with saying the grim earl was mad:

> Mad called he it, for, to define true madness,
> What is't but to be nothing else but mad?

In the second and third volumes of these Memoirs, *passim*, we light on a dozen places in which he terms the earl mad

* Horace Walpole says ("Memoirs of George III."), that when Lord Chatham came unexpectedly to the king's levee, in July, 1769, the courtiers were surprised to see him looking so well and so fat. (Vol. iii., p. 373.)

or wild. He says, that "even before his administration was formed, he had already commenced that extraordinary seclusion of himself, which he afterwards carried to an excess that passed, and no wonder, for a long access of frenzy." And again: "As if there were dignity in folly, and merit in perverseness, as if the way to govern mankind was to insult their undertakings, the conduct of Lord Chatham was the reverse of common sense, and made up of such undissembled scorn of the world, that his friends could not palliate it, nor his enemies be blamed for resolving it into madness." We are interested in some of the *traits* of this madness, particularized by Walpole. In 1767, the house at Hayes was out of Lord Chatham's possession, and he was restlessly anxious to have it back again. Burton Pynsent was in Somersetshire, while Hayes was but a two hours' drive from London. Mr. Thomas Walpole was the purchaser of the earl's late mansion and grounds, and Lady Chatham wrote to him an eager and pathetic letter, asking if he would take back the purchase-money, and let the afflicted earl, whose mind was strangely bent on this matter, return to his old haunt. Mr. Walpole very handsomely consented, greatly to the ease and satisfaction of the invalid, who, doubtless, felt that the air, in the neighborhood of the metropolis, was purer than anywhere else. Walpole goes on to tell us of the earl's doings at Hayes: "He had an impatient dislike of all noise, or whatever promoted noise, so much so, that his children he could not bear under the same roof, nor communication from room to room. A winding passage between his house and children, was built with the same view. When, at the beginning of his second administration, he fixed at Northend by Hampstead, he took four or five houses successively, as fast as Mr. Dingley, his landlord, went into them, still, as he said, to ward off the noises of the neighborhood."* Again, there was a very mad-looking caprice to have food in his own apartment whenever he had a mind to eat it, and "a succession of chickens were boiling and roasting at every hour, to be ready whenever he should call." If to love chicken, roast or boiled, be a sign of insanity, we suspect that disease is more general than the regular faculty have suspected. But we have an idea that there was more method than madness in the cookery at Hayes, as well as in the other arrangements. Walpole's gossip comes, without a doubt, from one well informed on such matters, and he would be more than ordinarily inquisitive about everything going on. in such an eccentric household as the Earl of Chatham's. The desire of the latter to remove all prying eyes, to keep his children, whose prattle and amusements he always loved with the kindest paternal nature, at a distance from him under another roof, as it were, and to be free from the distracting business of regular meals, seems to give evidence of some secret design and occupation. That prepense device of the winding passage, to isolate himself from the rest of the family, would undoubtedly be an excellent preparation for uninterrupted work at his desk, and also, for unseen communication with any agent, messenger, or faithful secretary, which such a restless and intriguing genius would stand in need of. The reader will, doubtless, be

* "Memoirs of the Reign of George III.," vol. iii., p. 41.

struck with the earl's concealments even in his own household.

We do not pretend to support our statement with gossip; though we may argue that it sometimes contains a great deal of truth, and that half history is of such stuff as gossip is made of. But we offer the foregoing facts, as we believe them to be, merely as minor considerations, dependent for any value that may be attached to them, upon the force of the main argument. If that is good, they fall into their places, with all due importance, no man holding them in disparagement any more.

The foregoing evidences are calculated to remove from the reader's mind, the mere ermined idea of the Earl of Chatham, the general impression that he was an enfeebled and dignified being, full of loftiness and ceremony, and untouched by the violent passions of common men. They show that he acted capriciously and like a madman, in the opinion of his contemporaries. They harmonize that eccentric and overbearing man with the received idea of Junius; and this preparation was necessary to a fit appreciation of what is to follow. Again (we repeat), the reader is brought face to face with the fact, too much overlooked, that while the early series of the Junian letters was coming mysteriously forth to the public eye, the Earl of Chatham was as mysteriously shut up from it. The recollection of this may excite a stronger and clearer attention to the further course of this argument.

CHAPTER IV.

LORD CHATHAM'S RESOLUTION TAKEN—THE FEINTS AND PRECAUTIONS MADE USE OF, TO BAFFLE THE CURIOUS INQUIRY OF THE WORLD, RESPECTING HIS AGGRESSIVE EPISTLES.

It shall go hard
But I will delve one yard below their mines,
And blow them at the moon.

HAMLET.

What shall I do to be for ever *un*known?

COWLEY (*altered*).

BETRAYED by his own ill-calculating ambition into an act of compromise, which cooled his friends and heated his enemies in an extraordinary degree; stung alike by the king's triumph over his consistency, and the defection or mutinous behavior of his colleagues, Lord Chatham carried into retreat a resolve to retrieve (or ruin) matters, by making war on the ministry, and every ministry subservient to the court party. Retirement could bring no calm to a man like him, who would rather wear out than rust out, and who, in the end, died in armor at his post. Conscious of his mental resources and the feebleness of those opposed to him, and knowing it was not in his power to carry on a contest on the parliamentary arena, just then, he prepared himself for a hostile movement of another character. At no time, indeed, could a man, so capable of wielding the democracy of England, feel either house of parliament a fitting stage for his powers, seeing that the rule against the publication of the debates prevented the people from knowing what he spoke, except in a garbled or curtailed shape, and generally after a lapse of time had lessened the interest of his speeches. In many of his greatest moments, he must have felt that he wanted an audience, and lamented that his voice should be so lost in that unreverberating chapel. Pitt, in a Greek *agora*, would have rivalled, probably surpassed, Demosthenes, for, as well as we can judge, he was a more impulsive and a more vituperative man, and would, therefore, have been much more popular with the *oi polloi*. In the House of Lords, the earl found his voice still more deadened, and was accustomed to sneer at the scarce witnessed and somewhat dull debates of that place. In 1770, writing to Earl Stanhope, he says: "The labors within the house are now the labors of Hercules; for the house being of late kept clear of hearers, we are reduced to a snug party of unhearing and unfeeling lords, and the tapestry hangings; which last, as mute as ministers, yet tell more than all the Cabinet on the subject of Spain, and the manner of treating with an insidious and haughty power."* The earl would often speak in a sarcastic way, of laying a thing before the tapestry—making a motion before the tapestry.† All this shows his natural longing for a larger

* "Chatham Correspondence," vol. iv., p. 55.

† The tapestry that hung on the walls of the old House of Lords, represented the Spanish Armada, defeated by Admiral Lord Howard, and others. It perished in the fire which destroyed the two houses, over twenty years ago.

audience, and a more popular appreciation; and to these he had now resolved to appeal. Baffled in his attempt to become the statesman, he determined to become the censor of the times—to make use of the press instead of the parliament, in bringing the people to bear against the power which threatened to be too strong for the chieftains and alliances.

In 1767, he was desperately ready for the new plan of aggression, so congenial to his ideas and his powers, and, we strongly suspect, the habits of his past life. Perhaps, it is not to be called new, save in the peculiar character of it. It is very probable, that, among the writers who, for the preceding quarter of a century, had agitated the public mind of England through the press, William Pitt had been one of the most frequent and effective; for it is scarcely to be supposed that the vehement blood and athletic wit, vouched for by so many of his contemporaries, would be entirely confined to the narrow arena of the House of Commons. Ever since the period of the civil wars—since the days of Marchamont Needham, Birkenhead, and Roger l'Estrange—the influence of the pamphlet and the broadside had been growing into a necessary element of government. Statesmen had made use of it, by the pens of subsidized writers or by their own. Before the general volunteer system of editors, as at the present day, it was necessary that every political section or distinguished leadership should have its staff of partisan writers; and one of the surest avenues to literary success was the capacity of wielding a quill in the agitating questions of the time. Defoe, Atterbury, Davenant, Addison, Steele,

Burnet, Swift, Prior, and Mainwaring, were among those who distinguished themselves in that way; and after them, came Smollett, Shebbeare, Johnson, Glover, Mallet, Burke, and a crowd of others, mingling the inspirations of polite literature with the fierce passions of politics and statesmanship. The highest characters of the realm had fought in these battles; Lord Somers, Chancellor Cowper, and Lord Bolingbroke had crossed pamphlets and exchanged letters. The latter lord in his "Occasional Writer," in his "Craftsman," and in other ways, had denounced Sir Robert Walpole and his Whig policy, almost as heartily as Junius afterwards vituperated Grafton and Bute. The celebrated Philip, Duke of Wharton, a man, like Chatham, of an eccentric and haughty cast of mind, had published, in his "True Briton," some of the freest and most intrepid sentiments of political liberty. Pulteney—the sometime Great Commoner, assailing Walpole in the Craftsman—Lords Chesterfield, Carteret and Harvey, Bubb Doddington, and others had worked the machinery and increased the growing importance of what has become the Fourth Estate of the English realm. Everything considered, the publication of the Junian letters as a fact, was nothing extraordinary. It was their courage and power, and above all, their pertinacity, which (apart from their uncertain authorship) distinguished them from a crowd of similar publications at that pamphleteering period.

About eight or nine months after the formation of Lord Chatham's ill-starred administration, and when the Duke of Grafton was identifying himself with the court party, and supplanting the influence of the secluded Privy Seal, appeared, on 28th April, 1767, the first of those Miscellaneous Letters in which the betrayed and exasperated statesman addressed himself to the task of beating down what he had, in an evil hour, built up, and waging a steady war of the press against the king's prerogative. The authorship of Junius in that series is recognized by every true critic. He himself declared the greater part of it to be his own. Woodfall has presented it as such, and it carries an internal evidence to the same effect as strong as any such declaration could be. In thus beginning his warfare, on a decided, continuous plan, Lord Chatham—already experienced, as we believe, in this business—had deeply pondered his means and prepared his way. He meditated something which should survive the time, make his revenges immortal, and hold up those he despised to the scorn of a coming age. His assaults should be fierce and unsparing, to meet the political turpitudes which had exasperated and defeated him; he would speak daggers, and pour out that powerful rhetoric, which George II. hated, and Horace Walpole admired, in the barest and most intelligible language of the passions. The first premise of such a course was, that the writer should be anonymous, and keep himself concealed; otherwise he would be attainted, challenged, or assassinated. A consideration of his dignity as a peer and a proud man, and of that of his family, would also oblige him to keep away from him any suspicion of an unscrupulous anger, which could stoop to the common modes of assault and vituperation—modes which were necessary to the success of his undertaking. The British peer and founder of a noble house would not have it remembered in his epitaph that he could give way to the bitter truculence of passion which, nevertheless, he should express or die. The impulses of his hostility would be all personal, gathering their distinctive character from that fact; but the main object of it would be that influence of the crown against which he had long struggled—an influence which (in the very words of Mnemon) "revived the doctrine of dispensing power, state necessity, arcana of government and all that machinery of exploded prerogative which it had cost our ancestors so much toil, and blood, and treasure to break to pieces."*

But all the world would soon recognize this as the war which Pitt had waged, and which the discontented Whig earl would still wage, and thus the secret would be compromised. In his case the most subtle precautions were necessary. He took advantage of the old complaint, and shutting himself up, at Bath and elsewhere, encouraged reports that he was tortured and crippled with the gout—a feeble, querulous old man, who would fall into hysterics at the bare mention of politics, and who could not hold a pen between his fingers. He went further, and countenanced reports that there was something the matter with his brain. In all this he certainly succeeded—that is, with the generality of people—the letters of the king, and those of the Duke of Grafton and others, furnish proof unanswerable that those who knew Lord Chatham best, never credited a word of the insanity. Still, the common impression was, that the earl was a wretched invalid—a lunatic—a lunatic with a crutch, and bawling through a grate; especially as

* Miscellaneous Letter xiii. Feb. 24, 1768.

the fierce "Poplicola," "Lucius," and the rest, took care to let the world know as much! Again, the charactery of his thoughts, his style of writing was to be considered. He had been generally affecting a loose, inflated, ceremonial mode—the very antipodes of his character and mind—curiously contrasting with the *vis vivida* of his real manner. This way of writing would tend to keep him aloof from any general suspicion of authorship as regarded the strong and pointed letters of the new writer. But there were a great many who knew his real style, who had read it in his private epistles, written under impulse, and who would be apt to recognize his peculiarities of mind and phrase in the letters. To change his true manner, or turns of thought, was out of the question. This would be to cripple those powers on which he depended for whatever effect his letters were to produce. No doubt he would elaborate these into something more correct and pointed than his ordinary modes of expression. Still he must necessarily have left them a resemblance of the author, sufficient to direct the eyes of the judicious upon him, to say nothing of the fact that his main purpose was to advocate the general courses known to be his own. But he met this difficulty, also, in a manner that disconcerted some of the acutest of his contemporaries, and has succeeded in disconcerting the world in general from that time to this. The very first of these letters, which he resolved to transmit to posterity as the literature of Junius, is a conditional, but sufficiently intelligible attack on the character of Lord Chatham. This writer against the court, the king's prerogative, and the influences behind the throne, begins by attacking that venerable Whig chief, of all men in

England, coupling with him, subordinately, his most faithful political friend, Lord Camden. This was a very successful piece of strategy. The man most certain that he knew that tone of delivery was silenced. The voice was the voice of Jacob; but the rough hand was the hand of some Esau of the press.

All this, however, should, if not at that time, at least long since, have roused a suspicion in the minds of inquirers. The reader, will, perhaps, remember a similar manœuvre related in Barham's "Life and Remains of Theodore Hook." The latter was the secret editor of the libelous *John Bull* newspaper; and in order to baffle the dangerous curiosity of those who connected him with it, he put the following notice into the journal, under the heading, *Mr. Theodore Hook:* "The conceit of some people is amusing, and it has not been unfrequently remarked that conceit is in abundance where talent is most scarce. Our readers will see that we have received a letter from Mr. Hook, disowning and disavowing all connection with this paper. * * * We are free to confess that two things surprise us in this business. The first, that anything which we have thought worthy of giving to the public should have been mistaken for Mr. Theodore Hook's; and secondly, that such a person as Mr. Hook should think himself disgraced by a connection with *John Bull.*" This answered very well for one week. The next, the *John Bull* contained the following: "We have received Mr. Theodore Hook's second letter. We are ready to confess that we may have appeared to treat him too unceremoniously. But we will put it to his own feelings whether the terms of his denial were not, in some degree, calculated to produce a little asperity on our part. We shall never be ashamed, however, to do justice; and we readily declare that we meant no kind of imputation on Mr. Hook's character."* These clever demonstrations threw most inquirers off the scent, and Hook worked on in safety. This case in point may be borne in mind, during the consideration of the Junian letters.

That Miscellaneous Series, as we have said, has been formidably in the way of those who have been led to recognize in Junius the general features of Lord Chatham, just as old *Nominis Umbra* intended it should be. We have not read Mr. Swinden's book; but the fact that he considers the greater part of that series spurious, and finds in the letter C., used by Junius in his private communications, a confirmation of the Chatham theory, does not inspire a wish to look at his proofs. Dr. Waterhouse, who published two years before Swinden, and who, in his general views, regards the mystery aright, stands helpless in presence of the Poplicolas, Anti-Sejanuses, Coreggios, and so forth. These letters have not been less hampering to the Franciscans. Mr. Bohn's editor is for putting "Poplicola" and some others out of the argument, bidding them aroint. They scowl so dreadfully on Lord Chatham, that surely they never could have been written by the young clerk of twenty-seven, whose fortunes were built up by the earl's hands, and who ever felt an affectionate veneration for his benefactor! There need be little doubt of that. But they are not to be hustled about and selected, and discarded in that childish manner,

* Barham's Life of Hook, vol. i., p. 215.

at the discretion of the theorists.. They belong to Junius, and must be fairly confronted by every one desiring to get at the heart of this concealment. The first of them is, we repeat, admirably adapted as a feint. But to a close examiner, at this distance, its exaggeration is fatal to it. That a writer whose main policy is known to have been that of Lord Chatham, should denounce him in such solemn language, for a confessedly venial fault—a fault for which the English people praised and absolved him—inevitably leads to a suspicion that there is something hollow and hypocritical in the whole demonstration.

After quoting as an epigraph, a sentence of Livy, concerning the throwing of a traitor from the Tarpeian Rock, " Poplicola" makes a general sweep against dictators, and then comes to his point with a "*Let us suppose.*" He assumes a case parallel to that of Lord Chatham (it is to be observed he never mentions him, nor uses the direct proposition—the indicative mood), and says: " Let us suppose him arrived at that moment, in which he might see himself within reach of the great object to which all the artifices, intrigues, the impudence, and the hypocrisy of his past life were directed. On the point of having the whole power of the crown committed to him, what would be his conduct? An affectation of prostrate humility in the closet, but a lordly dictation of terms to the people by whose interest he had been supported, by whose fortune he had subsisted (meaning the Grenvilles). Has he a brother? That brother must be sacrificed. Has he a rancorous enemy? That enemy must be promoted. Have years of his life been spent in declaiming against the pernicious influence of a favorite? That favorite must be taken to his bosom and made the only partner of his power. * * * He must, also, take advantage of any favorable conjuncture to try how far the nation will bear to see the established laws suspended by proclamation, and upon such occasions he must not be without an apostate lawyer (Lord Camden) weak enough to sacrifice his own character, and base enough to betray the laws of his country. But the master-piece of his treachery, and the surest way of answering all his purposes, would be (if possible) to foment such discord between the mother country and her colonies as may leave them both an easy prey to his own dark machinations (!). I cannot, without horror, suppose it possible that this our country should be at the mercy of so black a villain."* But if such a man should be discovered hereafter, he hopes the people will show that a gibbet is "not too honorable for the carcass of a traitor." This is certainly a terrible hubbub of words. But the true nature of it can easily be gathered from what follows. In the succeeding letters we see all this fierceness of blame curiously and suddenly softened and refined away, till it ends at last in mere epithets, shrugs of the shoulders, and solemn nods of the head. In the second letter, "Poplicola," in reply to a defense of Chatham, published in the *Public Advertiser*, comes remarkably down from his first fulminating attitude. (the reader remembers Hook). He had said Lords Chatham and Camden were traitors, the former of whom especially deserved hanging, for violation of the constitution (because, in a great dearth of provisions which threat-

* Miscellaneous Letter i., signed Poplicola, 28th April, 1767.

ened to be a famine, they had prevented by proclamation, the exportation of corn, for about a month); now, however, he admits the measure itself was necessary. But to maintain that proclamation was legal, that was it—*that* was what he meant! The men who did that should be hanged on a gibbet, as there was no Tarpeian Rock in London.

But the most curious feature of this matter is, that neither Chatham nor Camden did, for a moment, maintain that the act was anything more than an irregular proceeding in a period of distress. Therefore, as we see, the success of that first grand demonstration was procured with very little real detriment to the venerable earl or his friend.

Coming to the third letter, we begin to perceive the honest, bitter, persevering purpose of this literature. The Princess Dowager of Wales and Lord Bute are ferociously assailed. The writer says: "It was his (Bute's) good fortune to corrupt one man (Chatham), from whom we, least of all, expected such base apostasy. Who, indeed, could have suspected that it would ever consist with the spirit and understanding of that person, to accept of a share of power under a pernicious court minion, whom he himself had affected to detest, as much as he knew he was detested and despised by the whole nation. I will not censure him for the avarice of a pension, nor the melancholy ambition of a title. These were objects which he looked up to, though the rest of the world thought them beneath his acceptance. (This is said of the black-hearted traitor who was about to demolish the constitution, and deserved to be hanged, in the last letter!) But to become the stalking-horse of a stallion—(there is no mistaking the sincere ferocity of that expression), to shake hands with a Scotchman at the hazard of catching all his infamy, to receive the word from him—'Prerogative and a Thistle'—by the once respected name of Pitt, it is below contempt! May that union, honorable as it is, subsist forever. May they continue to smell at one thistle, and not be separated even in death."*

In the fifth letter, he turns the members of that wretched ministry into ridicule, and has a serviceable allusion to "a lunatic brandishing a crutch." Again, speaking of Lord Chatham, he says: "His infirmities have forced him into retirement, where I presume he is ready to suffer with sullen submission (of course!) every insult and disgrace that can be heaped upon a miserable, decrepit, worn-out old man."† This assertion of the earl's imbecility is significant. There is a curious appearance of sympathizing with the unhanged old traitor in it—an out-of-the-way pathos which seems rather odd in a political disquisition. There is also an affectation of a careless regard, in that somewhat gratuitous familiarity with the miserable, decrepit, worn-out old man, which must strike the reader; and, in the whole, a tone of personality, which could only have come from a man speaking disparagingly of himself. No political opponent would talk in that rather impertinent manner. Again, Atticus, who has been satirizing the ministry, all round, comes to the Privy Seal, and says: "The Earl of Chatham—I had much to say, but it were inhuman to persecute when Provi-

* Miscellaneous Letter iii. Signed Anti-Sejanus, June 24, 1767

† Miscellaneous Letter xxxv. Signed Lucius, Aug. 29, 1768.

dence has marked out the example to mankind."* The *aposiopesis* is completely Chathamic—it is the great orator, to the life—reminding the reader of that grand stare at Mansfield, in the House of Lords, then, "Judge Felix trembles!" and the full stop, with—"he shall hear from me again, some other day." In the letter the shrug of the shoulders is most eloquent—meaning, "A poor old incapable, too far gone for castigation!"

Just about this time the earl began to throw off his flannels and show himself abroad, freed from the burden of the Privy Seal. It is to be observed that the above letter of "Atticus" is dated over a week after the surrender of that Seal. What all the world knew in two days, Junius, it seems, did not know in six; and then could he have known anything about the earl, when he speaks of him as still belonging to the ministry? A question for posterity, of course. But there is a still more noticeable demonstration, regarding Lord Chatham, which reflects itself back upon those made at the beginning, and clearly shows the nature of them. In reply to a missile launched at him by Horne Tooke in 1771, Junius, whose mask is almost pushed off, is obliged to speak in praise of Lord Chatham, in order to guard his complication from discovery. It is to be remarked, that the only instances in which Junius is guilty of the inconsistency of lauding at one time, those he fiercely abused at another, occur in the cases of Lords Chatham and Camden. Tooke tells Junius in the most significant manner, that his vituperation is a result of the king's and the

* Miscellaneous Letter xlviii. Signed Atticus, Oct. 19, 1768.

Duke of Grafton's treatment of the Earl of Chatham. Junius will not seem to wince, but boldly meets the insinuation, in language which, curiously enough, has the conditional strain observable in the first letter of "Poplicola." "It seems I am a partisan of the great leader of the opposition. If the charge had been a reproach, it should have been better supported. I did not intend to make a public declaration of the respect I bear Lord Chatham. I well knew what unworthy conclusions would be drawn from it. But I am called on to deliver my opinion, and surely it is not in the little censure of Mr. Horne to deter me from doing justice to the man who, I confess, has grown upon my esteem. (The reader remembers Theodore Hooke's—"we shall never be ashamed to do justice," and, "we are free to confess"!) As for the common, sordid views of avarice, or any purpose of ambition, I question much whether the applause of Junius would be of service to Lord Chatham. My vote will hardly recommend him to an increase of his pension or a place in the cabinet. But if his ambition be on a level with his understanding; if he judges of what is truly honorable for himself, with the same superior genius which animates and directs him to eloquence in debate, to wisdom in decision, even the pen of Junius shall contribute to reward him. Recorded honors shall gather round his monument and thicken over him. It is a solid fabric, and will support the laurels that adorn it. I am not conversant in the language of panegyric. These praises are extorted from me. But they will wear well, for they have been dearly earned." *

* Letter liv., August 13, 1771.

This is designedly a badly written passage, and that part about the monument and the laurels confused and clumsy. It is full of art, and one of the most significant paragraphs in the Junian letters. At all events, this letter shows that the hostility of Poplicola and Anti-Sejanus was mere pretense; for no one could truly both abuse and praise the same man within the space of four years in such a very contrasted manner. This, and that curious falling away from his first show of opposition, lay palpably open the secret machinery of that subtlest of all letter-writers. And before passing on, we shall draw attention to a small part of that machinery, which is in curious keeping with the entire. In defense of Lord Chatham against the first attack of Poplicola, W. D. (Sir William Draper, an ardent admirer and correspondent of his lordship, whose bust, with a Latin inscription, he had placed in his garden), wrote a letter to the *Public Advertiser*. "Poplicola," in retorting on this, quotes W. D., as C. D., a seeming blunder, which, of course, led people to imagine the mask must be some one who did not recognize the initials at all—knew no one having such initials, and so fell into the mistake. He talks of C. D. all through his letter. Did Mr. Woodfall attempt to correct the mistake? Junius, with a consummate cunning, pays as much attention to the small as to the chief points of his scheme—as we shall see more distinctly in getting along.

We now come to consider another feint which, in a certain sense, is the most important of those he employed, and has largely colored the seeming of that anonymous literature. The palpable design of Lord Chatham was, that it should be attributed to the Grenvilles—to Lord Temple, in fact, or some one writing from his dictation; and circumstances remarkably favored this intention. Temple was, at that time, angrily discontented with his brother-in-law. He was the chief patron and support of John Wilkes and his North Briton—

> He was at charges for a newspaper,
> And entertained a score or two of writers.

Stung by the dictatorial airs of Lord Chatham, in the arrangement of the ministry, he went away to Stowe, where he employed Mr. Humphrey—honest Humphrey—Cotes to write the well-known "Enquiry," published in 1766, and denouncing the earl as a renegade to his obligations and principles, and the tool of the Scottish favorite.* Thus, just as he prepared himself to beat down and cry down that unfortunate ministry, Junius found close to his hand the mask he was to wear, as "Poplicola," and others. The reader remembers the words of the first letter: "Has he a brother? that brother must be sacrificed." In the "Enquiry into the Conduct of a late Right Honorable Commoner," the writer says: "He will be turned out as he has been turned in,

* Since the time of writing the foregoing, we are beset by the suspicion that Temple's people never wrote the "Enquiry"—that it was written by Lord Chatham himself. It has all the Chathamic style of animadversion, and the motto—"Plain truth, dear Pynsent, needs no flowers of speech," —is also extremely suggestive of Lord Chatham's literary felicity. We cannot believe Temple, who was *not* very malignant, would authorize any one to adopt the tone of the "Enquiry" towards his brother—one with whom he soon acted again. Without means of carrying out our own inquiry, however, we merely state our strong conviction here. This "Enquiry" was one of those things which led many to think the missile of the masked assault came from Temple's armory.

only to add, if possible, something more to that public odium and abhorrence of his name and character, which have so unanimously followed his apostasy and promotion, his desertion of his friends and his country, and the accomplishment of his long-sought wretched alliance with the favorite who laughs at his folly, despises his vanity, exalts over his weakness, and rejoices in the public execration of such a hypocrite." This is the key and tone of "Poplicola." All the world, reading that first Junian letter, agreed that "Poplicola" was a Grenvillite, employed by Temple; but they saw the pen was a new one; it had something in it which did not belong to the others. Again they saw that "Poplicola" used the very argument used by Lord Temple in the House of Lords, on the opening of the parliamentary session. Before the meeting of the houses, Lords Chatham and Camden had, on behalf of the people, stopped the exportation of corn, a matter which Camden frankly admitted was a "forty days' tyranny." On this, Lord Temple, smarting from his recent wound, towered into a liberty-loving indignation, and made a vehement speech against such a dangerous infraction of the British constitution. "Forty days' tyranny over the nation by the crown? Who can endure the thought? My lords, less than forty days' tyranny, such as this country has felt in some time, would, I believe, bring your lordships together, without summons from your sick beds, faster (mark the sarcastic allusions to Lord Chatham) than our great patriots themselves, to get a place or a pension, or both; and, for aught I know, make the subject of your consultation that appeal to heaven, that has been spoken of. Once establish a dispensing power, and you cannot be sure of either liberty or law for forty minutes."

The drift of Junius is palpable. George Grenville is spoken of as a great and honest minister, while, with regard to Lord Temple himself, a marked silence is preserved, with what must look like an apprehensive consciousness to many readers. Except in the commencement, where he is merely alluded to, and not named, there appears a studied show of avoidance, with respect to so prominent a man, such as he himself would (as the generality would conclude) be led into, were he the writer of the letters. The matter has thus struck all who have advocated that inadequate nobleman. Again, that letter of December 15, 1768, addressed to George Grenville, just before the name "Junius" began to make itself famous, was a wonderful confirmation of the belief that identified the anonymous writer with the Grenvilles. We need not multiply demonstrations of this kind. They are well known, and have long sent inquirers after the mask to Stowe. Sir James Mackintosh, in the *Edinburgh Review* for June, 1826, bids them be sure to look in that direction. Like all the rest, he walked innocently straight after a thing which "doubles to mislead the hound"—moves deliberately zig-zag. Many persons entertain an idea that Lord Chatham was on good terms with the Grenvilles, his brothers-in-law. But it has been shown that at this time they were at feud;* and we can, therefore, clearly perceive how a show of supporting

* A few weeks before the publication of the first letter, the ill-feeling between the Grenvilles and Chatham was aggravated by the refusal of the latter to make George Grenville First Lord of the Treasury.

George Grenville just then, and being a Grenvillite, would most admirably second the desire of Lord Chatham to keep himself free from suspicion.

But, of course, he would not confine himself to one system of *ambages* and feints. His object would be to distract inquiry by other demonstrations. And we, accordingly, see that he desires to look like Edmund Burke, a man whose great ability, quickness of feeling, and tone of principle, together with a certain audacity of speech, would lead many to suspect him. In the *Public Advertiser*, under date of October 22d, appeared Junius's melo-dramatic account of a "Grand Council" of ministers on the affairs of Ireland.* A day or two after, another writer (we think we do know that sharp Roman hand!) gives, in the same paper, what he calls a real account of what passed, at the same time charging Burke with being the author of the satire. In his account, he introduces the latter into a pretended dialogue, under the name of "Brazen," and makes him talk in the most bombastic and ridiculous style of a political partisan, till he is fairly turned out of the room. With the letter signed "Y. Z."† Junius sends for publication to the *Public Advertiser* a speech recently spoken by Burke in his place, against the ministry, the king's speech, *etc.*, but not published regularly by Mr. Burke till 1772. Burke's advocates have greatly relied on this fact, and proved, with critical success, that Burke, desiring to remain forever unknown as Junius, would send one of his speeches to be

* Miscellaneous Letter vii., Oct. 22, 1767.

† Ibid. ix., Dec. 5, 1767.

printed through the recognized channel of that writer. In March, 1768, Junius writes sharply against his own letter of March 4th (Mnemon's), signing himself "Anti Van Teague"*—the opponent of that Irishman! Then Junius comes out again as "Anti-Stuart,"† in retort against "Anti Van Teague." Again, in that letter already alluded to, signed "Y. Z.," where he speaks of "a party of us," Junius shows his design; and also in his letter to Woodfall, where he says "there are people about me whom I would wish not to contradict, and who would rather see Junius in the papers ever so improperly, than not at all."‡ Every one was aware of the fact that Edmund Burke's house was full of his relations and namesakes—William Burke, and his brother Richard, being public writers as well as himself; and it was believed by their opponents that they were always concocting vituperation against every one and every thing opposed to the Rockinghams. That family was, in fact, called "a nest of adders," as we see from a passage in Burke's Correspondence,§ lately published. In another place, "Modestus" (who is also Junius), writing to contradict Junius for some of his assertions in the Gansel case, tries to make the public think Junius an Irishman, concluding thus: "I recommend it to you to tie up that over-drove animal, John Bull,‖ who seems indeed to be stimulated

* Miscellaneous Letter, xv., Mar. 11, 1768.

† In a subsequent chapter we shall speak more at length of this dividing and going to buffets with himself, practiced by Junius.

‡ Private letter, No. viii., Sept. 10, 1769.

§ "Burke's Correspondence," edited by Earl Fitzwilliam and Gen. Bourke.

‖ Miscellaneous Letter lxvii., Nov. 28, 1769. This is, probably, in to madness, that he may no longer profane a respectable name, but own that which he received from his godfathers and godmothers—Sir Patrick O'Bully."

These instances, and others that might be particularized, show the dexterous efforts of the mask to send inquirers in the direction of the only man of that day who approached the intellectual, or, rather, the rhetorical, standard of Lord Chatham.

Having, in his commencement, made the feints we have set forth, and provided for all future collateral guards of his secret, Junius felt himself at liberty to pursue with boldness his cherished object—the annihilation of the ministry, which had been forced on him, and which was, up to October, 1768, calling on him for help, abusing him, deserting to the enemy, and declaring that his sickness was nothing but a sham. Shut up from the world for about two years, during which he only showed himself in public on fitful occasions, he sternly continued, in the midst of questions, calls, and exhortations, from the king and his colleagues, to elaborate his fierce letters against the government, the court party, and all persons and things connected with their policy. The perplexity he left behind was a grim comfort to his solitude; and while the king's horses were wearing themselves out with galloping between the old brick palace and Hayes, we can conceive how the bitter-hearted hermit would bring to mind the king's cunning solicitude to have just such a piebald ministry, and, with a smile of savage pleasantry, murmur to himself, from a

allusion to a letter signed "John Bull," written on the side of Junius, against Gen. Gansel.

favorite author: "*Vous l'avez voulu, vous l'avez voulu, George Dandin; vouz l'avez voulu!*"

Lord Campbell, in his "Lives of the Chancellors," alluding to the political blunders and confusions of this period, says, that the inept and mischievous Lord Northington, one of Chatham's colleagues in that shipwrecked ministry, should have been fairly thrown overboard, and then the vessel might have a chance of righting.* The terrible old earl seems to have been of his lordship's opinion—only that he went a little further, and did his best to throw them all overboard.

* "Lives of the Chancellors," vol. v., p. 267.

CHAPTER V.

LORD CHATHAM'S UNDENIABLE LITERARY ABILITY, AND THE REMARKABLE VERSATILITY OF HIS INTELLECTUAL POWERS.

William Pitt, the Cicero and Roscius of his age.
LORD ALBEMARLE.

His eloquence was of every kind; his invective was terrible.
LORD CHESTERFIELD.

To show the identity of Chatham and Junius, it may be necessary to dwell upon the fact, that the great minister was an accomplished literary man, master of many expressions, ranging from grave to gay, from lively to severe, and thus meet the objections of those who speak from certain acquired notions, and without investigating the matter for themselves. One great dissuasive of the belief we hold, is the idea the world has entertained of that venerable historic personage, who talks with such loftiness, and falls with such dignity upon the stage—an idea at variance with the truculent activity and bitterness of the letters. Another is the impression, pretty generally made, that the earl was no letter-writer. Lord Mahon, who labors hard in his history of England, to avert suspicion from his ancestor, tries, in some passages, to throw discredit upon the earl's letter-writing abilities. In one place he quotes, for the purpose, from a letter written by Burke to the Marquis of Rockingham, in 1769, and referring to the probable object of Chatham's late visit at the king's levee: perhaps "to talk some significant, pompous, explanatory, ambiguous matter, in the true Chathamic style."* Commenting on this, Lord Mahon says: "These words, it must be allowed, describe with considerable aptness, though not without exaggeration, as even now we may trace them, Lord Chatham's epistolary faults."† Burke is speaking of the earl's way of *talking;* but Lord Mahon is ever mindful of the letter-writing deficiencies. It is curious, however, to observe that he does not quote Burke correctly; he omits part of a sentence, and that part an expression which sets the character of Chatham in its true light. Burke says, "if the latter went to court without being sent for, it was only humbly to lay a reprimand at the feet of his most gracious master, and to talk some significant, pompous, explanatory, ambiguous matter, in the true Chathamic style." Burke's antithetical expression gives a vivid idea of the grim earl; and Burke knew him well. But that idea would not at all suit Lord Mahon, who seems always anxious to show his venerable relative behaving like a fool, a crazy-brain, or, best of all, a driveling sycophant. He quotes from the "Grenville Papers," with great unction, the incredible story of Chatham bursting into tears in presence of the king, unable to bear his majesty's kindness! He also quotes, of course, the saying of Wilkes, that Lord Chatham was the best orator, and the

* "Burke's Correspondence," vol. i., p. 173.

† "Lord Mahon's History of England," vol. v., p. 369.

worst letter-writer of his age, and gives his own belief that the earl "was careless in literary composition, inexact, loose, and repetitionary." This opinion, indeed, has been long entertained. It is adopted by Heron (the man who left his book at sixes and sevens, in such a curious way), and the later critics seem to fall in with it very easily. A glance, however, at the oratorical and literary side of Lord Chatham's character will tend to weaken these preoccupations and fallacies. The great statesman had no half faculties; he was a man of many faculties, and whatever he did, he did well; except in those cases where, as we shall hereafter try to show, he wrote and acted purposely in an odd, feeble manner; and truly in this, also, he may be said to have done well; that is, successfully, and according to the intent. Lord Mahon has been showing the sham "faults" of his relative's literature and life. We shall show the genuine faults; for, no doubt, the angry, ambitious man had a good many.

The earliest notices of William Pitt represent him as a miracle of mental activity. His education was a good one; he was skilled in composition, loved Milton, Spenser, and the Georgian dramatists, was familiar with French literature, and wrote verses with much elegance. Witness his lines to David Garrick, the "vagabond" of another sort of missive. Horace Walpole has given us glimpses of Pitt, that show he was no mere political orator; but a many-sided mind, an intrepid censor, a Pericles in high figurative eloquence, a lively satirist, full of wit, sarcasm, and a terrible invective—a gladiator, in fine, unrivaled in the use of a brilliant and varied armory. Writing to the Hon. H. S.

Conway, on 15th November, 1755, he gives him that spirited account, already quoted, of Pitt's general assault at the Cockpit, on the continental policy of England, his usual *cheval de bataille.* Writing on the 16th to Richard Bentley, he says: "Pitt surpassed himself; and then I need not tell you he surpassed Cicero and Demosthenes. What figure would they, with their formal, labored cabinet orations, make *vis-à-vis* his manly and dashing eloquence, at one o'clock in the morning, after sitting in that heat for eleven hours? He spoke above an hour and a half, with scarce a bad sentence. The most admirable part was a comparison he drew of the two parts of the new administration to the conflux of the Rhone and the Saone—the latter a gentle, feeble, languid stream, languid but not deep; the other, a boisterous and overbearing torrent; but they meet at last, and long may they continue united, to the comfort of each other, and the glory, honor, and happiness of this nation."* The peculiar irony of this sentence, describing the union of

* "Walpole's Correspondence," vol. i., p. 309. It is curious that Walpole did not recollect the lines of Lord Roscommon which contain the imagery made use of by the orator, and which, it is very probable, the latter quoted, in the words of the poet, as follows:

"Thus have I seen a rapid, headlong tide,
With foaming waves the passive Saone divide,
Whose lazy waters without motion lay,
While he with eager force urged his impetuous way."

It is likely Walpole did not hear the speech, but took its points on the report of some of his friends who either forgot, or did not recognize the poetical quotation of the speaker. Lord Byron, whose style of writing and turn of thought, in prose, show how familiar he was with Walpole's letters, has taken this image of the rivers, used by the two other lords, to express his idea of Madame de Stael's conversation with, we believe, Counsellor Curran—the lady being, of course, the Rhone.

the energetic Fox with the easy mediocrity of Newcastle, at a time when he himself was so pointedly excluded from office, will remind the reader of the conclusion of Anti-Sejanus's letter: "May that union, honorable as it is, subsist forever; may they continue to smell at one thistle, and not be separated even in death!"* Again, on 17th December, 1755, Walpole, writing to the same correspondent, says: "In short, I never heard so much wit, except in a speech with which Pitt concluded the debate of the day, on the Treaties. His antagonists endeavored to disarm him; but as fast as they deprived him of one weapon, he finds a better. I never suspected him of such a universal armory. I knew he had a Gorgon's head, composed of bayonets and pistols; but little thought he could tickle to death with a feather. On the first debate of these famous Treaties, last Wednesday, Hume Campbell, whom the Duke of Newcastle had retained as the most abusive counsel he could find, against Pitt (and hereafter, perhaps, against Fox), attacked the former for his eternal invectives. Oh, since the last Philippic of Billingsgate memory, you never heard such an invective as Pitt returned. Campbell was annihilated. * * * Some day or other, perhaps, you will see some of the glitttering splinters that I have gathered. I have written under his print these lines, which are not only full as just as the original, but have not the tautology of "loftiness" and "majesty."

"Three orators, in three distant ages born,
Greece, Italy, and England did adorn.

* Miscellaneous Letter iii. Anti-Sejanus, June 24, 1767.

The first, in loftiness of thought, surpassed,
The next, in language, and, in both, the last.
The force of nature could no further go,
To make the last, she joined the other two."*

The reader may possibly be led to suspect the motive of those, well-informed on everything else concerning Lord Chatham, who still persist in saying a man of such force and versatility of mind could not write very nearly as well as he spoke. Lord Charlemont, and others, have recorded their admiration of Pitt's amazing vigor of intellect. "Heavens, what a fellow is this Pitt!" exclaims the former, after some of the oratorical displays of 1766; and he goes on to say that, whereas he already had Pitt's bust, nothing less than his statue could satisfy him now. It is a pity, Walpole and the rest do not give some of the "glittering splinters"—some specimens of what they so describe. But we can find enough to supply the omission. There is enough in Lord Chatham's printed speeches and letters to show he appreciated the amenities and facilities of literature and style, and how admirably he could employ them. We do not mean to lay any stress on his letters to his nephew, Thomas Pitt; but we cannot conceive how any one who reads them could say Lord Chatham was not able to write good letters. There is much scholarly elegance, and the tone of the old academe in them, and, though couched in the didactic style, which becomes them, they exhibit as much easy vivacity as good sense and refinement. Looking over Thackeray's collection of his speeches, we find these sprinkled with quotations, Latin and English, full of apt-

* "Walpole's Correspondence," vol. i., p. 312.

5

ness, native idiom, and wit. Like all greatest men, he was not afraid of compromising his dignity by stooping to the commonplace and playful. He knew how to raise such things to the level of the occasion, and give them a significant grace by adopting them; he knew, in fact, that a vernacular idiom is the best and truest vehicle of eloquence or poetry. During a debate, in 1763, on the Cider tax, which he opposed, George Grenville, nettled by the opposition to his measure, grew angry, and asked, where else, then, was he to lay the necessary impost; when Pitt, whose purposes went beyond cider to the displacement of all incapables, merely smiled, and sneered, and walked out of the house, humming, in his own inimitable way, the words of the song: "Gentle shepherd, tell me where?" sure of the laughter which followed. He had his ends of verse, and sayings of philosophers, for all occasions. But what respectable orator would wind up an appeal on the grave subject of reconciliation between England and America with the lines of the farce:

> "Be to her faults a little blind;
> Be to her virtues very kind!"

During the debate in the House of Lords, on the subject of the House of Commons, which he had denounced as venal and corrupt, he would exclaim:

> "Fie on't, O fie, 'tis an unweeded garden,
> That grows to seed; things rank and gross in nature
> Possess it merely."

Lord Chatham could compose very respectable verse, and was partial to dramatists and dramatic readings. The "Chatham Correspondence" tells us how he used to encourage his children to act little plays; and it is very probable he wrote and adapted them, on occasion.* He was intimate with Garrick, and, no doubt, a great admirer of a histrionic genius in many recognized respects so congenial with his own—for Lord Chatham was called the Roscius of his age by those who knew him best. In his sixty-fourth year, he wrote the following lines, and sent them through Lord Lyttelton to the great actor. Garrick is at Mount Edgecombe, near Plymouth, and he is invited, seemingly, to the ex-minister's farm:

Leave, Garrick, the rich landscape, proudly gay,
Docks, forts, and navies brightening all the bay,
To my plain roof repair, primæval seat;
Yet there no wonders your quick eye can greet,
Save you should deem it wonderful to find
Ambition cured, and an unpassioned mind;
A statesman without power and without gall,
Hating no courtiers, happier than them all;
Bowed to no yoke, nor crouching for applause,
Votary alone of freedom and the laws.
Herds, flocks, and smiling Ceres deck the plain,
And interspersed, a heart enlivening train
Of sportive children frolic o'er the green;
Meantime pure love looks on and consecrates the scene.
Come, then, immortal spirit of the stage,
Great nature's proxy, glass of every age;
Come, taste the simple life of patriarchs old,
Who, rich in rural peace, ne'er thought of pomp or gold.†

* In "Madame D'Arblay's Memoirs," we are informed how a dear old friend of hers, Mr. Crisp, sent his play of Virginia to Mr. Pitt, in 1754, in order to receive the correction or the criticism of his acknowledged fine taste. This great man, who did not know how to write a letter (according to Lord Mahon), seems to have been regarded as one of the Mæcenases of his time—the arbiter of literary elegance. Thomson, who addresses him in the Seasons, knew what he was.

† See Lord Mahon's "History of England, vol. iv., p. 197. These Arcadian verses were written more for posterity than for David Garrick.

Some months previously, on 10th of November, 1771, Junius had written his fierce note to Garrick, calling him a vagabond, and bidding him keep to his pantomimes, at his peril. If Garrick had been suggesting that Lord Chatham had a hand in the dreaded letters—and this is very likely, here was a rather staggering piece of poetry! After this, he had nothing to do, of course, but to take back everything he may have been whispering about the inexplicable earl.*

A variety of literary levities and quotations shows Lord Chatham's familiarity with the poets and dramatists—shows how he, who was Roscius as well as Cicero, could relish a little farce, too. Writing to the absent countess on 18th April, 1772, he gives a ludicrous description of the household: "George, Jack Groom, Podge, the helper Tilly—all in tribulation and brimstone. Podge sustains the courage of all by his *bons mots*. Being condemned by Mr. Saunders, he only asked the doctor if one might eat with his distemper. The answer being in the affirmative, Podge thanked the doctor, and said he did not care, then, for a little scratching. The pestiferous are all stuffed together into a room, and communication cut off. Podge again, hearing the order for close confinement, says, why don't my lord shut us up in the great coop, and have our victuals put through on forks, as they feed the birds."† Again, on January 18, 1775, his lordship, writing to the same, says: "For God's sake, sweet

* It is only in a fragmentary and indirect way we are likely to come at the true idea of Lord Chatham's literary accomplishments. In the "Table Talk" of the poet Rogers, lately published, we have him stating he always understood the orations of Pericles, in Smith's Thucydides, were translated by the great English orator.

† "Chatham Correspondence," vol. iv., p. 215.

life, don't disquiet yourself about the impudent and ridiculous lie of the hour. The plot does lie very deep. It is only a spiteful device of fear—court fear, and faction fear. If gout does not put in a veto—which I trust in heaven it will not—I will be in the House of Lords on Friday, then and there to make motions relative to America. Be of good cheer, noble love!

> Yes, I am proud, I must be proud, to see
> Men, not afraid of God, afraid of me.*

This seems to show that Junius had not gone to foreign parts, but was in England still. In another letter, of January 25, 1775, writing to Lord Shelburne, and alluding to the papers laid before parliament on the subject of America, he says: "What a correspondence! It calls to my mind what some Pope—Alexander VI., Pius, or Leo—said to a son of his, afraid to undertake governing—that is, confounding the nation—*Nescis mi fili, quam parva sapientia hic noster mundus regitur.*† What a dialogue between a secretary of state and a general, in such a crisis! Could these bundles reach the shades below, the remarks of Ximenes and Cortez on them would be amusing. * * * Where it is to end, I do not conjecture; in perdition, I fear. The three regiments are trifling, and the dragoons put me in mind of *le régiment de cavalerie sur les galères de Malte*, in a scene of

* "Chatham Correspondence," vol. iv., p. 371.

† This is popularly known as the saying of the Chancellor Oxenstiern, but Lord Chatham's quotation coincides with that of Selden, as we see in his "Table Talk." It is difficult, perhaps impossible, to find the origin of sayings like the above, based, as they are, on truths of nature and society that impress themselves generally on the minds of men.

Molière."* These extracts will tend to give a true idea of Lord Chatham. That passage about the servants shows his sense of the odd and the laughable, and his power of describing them—something resembling the happy way of Rev. Sydney Smith—while the other shows the impulsive nature of the man, at his age, addressing his old wife as if she was a sweetheart in her prime, and then shaking his head with such a terrible Junian menace, in that couplet. Those paragraphs from the letter to Lord Shelburne are in the truest style of Junius. Such genuine expressions of the earl's mind lead us easily to recognize him, in the sarcastic and farcical style of the Miscellaneous Letters, in which he delineates the "Grand Council of Ireland," calls the oratorical manner of the Duke of Grafton a rigmarole, a riddlemeree, and three blue beans in a bladder; terms Tommy Bradshaw a cream-colored parasite, and Chamier a wonderful Girgashite—a "tight, active little fellow, that would wrangle for an eighth, if in Jerusalem;" and, as "Veteran," laughs with a jocose ferocity at Lord Barrington. Any objection against Lord Chatham's age is met by the fact that at no time of his life was he more full of energy and spirit than in 1770; never did he more gallantly flutter the Volsces in Corioli. That ludicrous epistle about Podge was written two or three years after the date of the Junian levities.

The assumption, therefore, that Lord Chatham could not write good letters, is an utter fallacy. The fact is, that no epistolary writer of his age was equal to him in that line;

* "Chatham Correspondence," vol. iv., p. 386.

and few, who have read what he has left, as corrected speeches or letters, can be so ignorant as not to conceive how Walpole and Chesterfield would sink, and did sink, very far below him. We believe English literature has suffered a great loss, in the lost letters of the elder Pitt, the noblest, most alert, and best-armed intellect of his time. The correspondence put forth by his descendants in 1838, is a comparatively poor collection, containing as much of other people's writing as of his, and giving, doubtless, the mildest of his manuscript. Seeing what he was and what we have, as his recognized remains, we are strongly led to the conclusion that a great amount of his correspondence was destroyed by himself or others. When his son, William Pitt, in company of some of his literary friends, was once wishing, above all things, for one of Bolingbroke's unreported speeches, perhaps he was unaware that his father's letters were better worth wishing for?

Not that Wilkes and the rest have not had a show of reason for their opinion of the earl's letter-writing. Some of his correspondence is, no doubt, what people have said of it—heavy and inexact. But this, we repeat, resulted from the elaborate design of the man, who was, probably, during the greater part of his career, an anonymous political writer; for it would be ridiculous to suppose he only began in 1767. In his common correspondence — at least in that portion which has been printed by his descendants—he sometimes seems careless and lumbering to a degree: one would suppose it was the Duke of Newcastle, and not William Pitt. But our knowledge of the latter, and of his genuine manner, flashing ever and anon from such remains of him as we have, leads the close observer to see that the writer is dissimulating. Some of his letters are so extravagantly clumsy and slavish, that they betray him, and the dullest is scarcely deceived. It was the same with the personal demeanor of Lord Chatham, respecting the king and the court. He used to bend so obsequiously at the levee—especially about the beginning of the Junian controversy—that, as Chase Price used to say, you could see, from behind, the tip of his hooked nose between his legs! There were few who did not suspect all this extravagance in the manner of such a terribly bold, irrespective man; and it was, certainly, the perfection of hypocrisy. Of the same character was the style of his lumbering letters to the king, in which the grammar as well as the writer seems *kootooing* at the feet of one whom he disrespected—as the world knows. Lord Mahon, who seems but too happy to quote anything respecting the poor-spirited subserviency, as well as the shocking syntax of Lord Chatham, does not think those airs of deference too trifling to speak about in his History of England. Alluding to a letter from Pitt to Bishop Warburton, who had been getting up an address in his diocese (terming that hated peace of 1762 an adequate peace), he says: "The reply of Pitt is couched in his usual epistolary style of humility, bordering on obsequiousness, which affords such a strange contrast to the proud and lofty tenor of his life. He first declares he should be guilty of temerity were he to presume to exercise his own judgment in such a case. But he then proceeds to lay, as the bishop afterwards confessed, his finger on the weak parts of this transaction:—'I will only venture to observe, my lord, that the Cathedral of Gloucester, which certainly does not stand alone in true duty and wise zeal towards his majesty, has nevertheless the fate not to be imitated by any other episcopal see in the kingdom, in this unaccustomed effusion of fervent gratitude on the peace.' "* The slow, stern irony of the letter exhibits a remarkable evidence of design, and reveals a gleam of the Junian sarcasm which also flashes from that heavy, round-about missive to the Duke of Newcastle, already quoted. Lord Mahon says the earl was "unduly pompous in the language and humble in the tone" of his gratitude to the king for making him a peer; and Lord Brougham has also recorded his unfavorable opinion of that strange humility. "It is painful," he says, with reference to the letters to the king, "to add, what truth extorts, that this is really not the sentiment and the language with which a patriot leaves his sovereign's councils, for a broad difference of honest opinion, and after being personally ill-used by that monarch's favorites; but the tone of feeling and even the style of diction, in which a condemned felon, having sued for mercy, returns thanks when his life has been spared. The pain of defacing any portion of so noble a portrait as Lord Chatham's, must not prevent me from making the traits of a somewhat vulgar and sordid kind, which are to be found on a closer inspection of the original."†

We believe there is "a closer inspection of the original" which his lordship does not seem or pretend to be aware

† "Lord Mahon's History of England," vol. v., p. 64.

* "Statesmen of the Times of George III." First Series, p. 47.

of. Why did that haughtiest and most intrepid of men, who almost called George the Second a coward; who, about 1762, called George the Third the falsest hypocrite in Europe (as Wilkes intimates in a letter to Junius, whom he believed to be, if not the earl, some one working under his eye), and who, in 1770, declared aloud that the king had deceived him—why did that gladiatorial genius write in such a curiously slavish style? This is not the natural blemish of such a portrait, but a strangely unaccountable daub or blot on the picture, setting every one wondering how it ever came there. That it was the result of a deep-laid purpose, is very evident. The theory of these pages gives it an easy explanation. No doubt, in all these dull, obsequious letters to his majesty, there is conveyed a vast amount of sarcasm and irony, peculiar to Pitt's nature—such as he employed in an interview with George III., in 1765, when he called himself, knowing he was looked up to by the nation, "a little knife;" and such as palpably looks out from the affected pleonasm of his letters to the Bishop of Gloucester, to Lord Hardwicke, and to the Duke of Newcastle. Along with this, it is, in all likelihood, the truth that, long before the opening of the Junian series, Pitt was in the habit of writing strong public letters, anonymously, especially during the controversy in 1762 and 1763, on the subject of the peace.* For a long series of years he, doubtless, found it necessary to counteract suspicion by a show of loyal duty, and by the other devices

* In a succeeding chapter we shall point to Junius in his usual attitude, standing at a distance of ten years from his recognized chronology.

of a slow and ineffective style. An examination of the old files of the London newspapers might throw great light on this question.

We have thus tried to show Chatham as he was—a man of great mental grasp and dexterity, the master of many literary modes, and very different from that cold, crotchety, ceremonial character, which many represent him to have been. We have also observed what seems the undeniable trace of simulation in his correspondence. The style of it, in some places, so creeping and so full of subserviency, has caused general surprise; it shocks all one's notions of such a man. The biographers, here, stand puzzled in presence of their subject. And not in this respect alone. There are portions of the last decade of his life which they declare past coming at, in any way—shadows, clouds, and darkness rest upon them. The truth is, that the grim earl has, in his own way, been almost as great a riddle as Junius. The investigator would do well to carry this curious similarity along with him. It is one of the parallels. We are now about to consider a few of these.

CHAPTER VI.

A CONSIDERATION OF PARALLEL PASSAGES, IN WHICH THE POLITICAL SENTIMENTS OF JUNIUS AND LORD CHATHAM ARE SHOWN TO BE COINCIDENT.

Fore Gad, they are both in a tale!

DOGBERRY.

The worthy chairman arraigns the hand; I impeach the head. He impeaches the scholar: I the master.

LORD CONINGSBY.

IN the year 1770, Lord Chatham, coming once more into the political arena, like a giant refreshed with wine, delivered two great speeches in the House of Lords, sweeping, with that scope of mind which belonged to the genius of the man, the whole controversial field of politics and statesmanship—a theme on which his mind had brooded long and angrily—and in those speeches (reported by Mr. Philip Francis, a young clerk of the War-Office, and not published till 1791, over twenty years after) are found many passages which curiously show that the great earl and Junius thought and expressed themselves alike regarding the highest questions of national policy. The inference drawn from this similarity by Taylor—as great a tyrant in theory as Procrustes was in practice—and by others, following him, is, that the reporter was Junius! Without any more notes of admiration, we shall trace a few of these parallels, and show how easily and naturally they fall into their places in the regular march to our conclusion—a conclusion very different from Mr. Taylor's.

The first of these Chathamic speeches took place on the 9th of January, and the other on the 22d of the same month, in 1770.

Here follow the parallels. On the first of these days,

Lord Chatham* said he was satisfied there was a power, in some degree arbitrary, with which the constitution intrusted the crown, to be made use of, under the correction of the legislature, and at the hazard of the minister. That on this principle he had himself advised a measure which he knew was not strictly legal, but he recommended it as a measure of necessity, to save a starving people from famine, and had submitted to the judgment of his country.

Junius (writing on the old subject two years later—a subject, by the way, which seems more interesting to him than to anybody else):—That parliament may review the acts of a minister is unquestionable. But there is a wide

* In these pages, wherever it is necessary to quote the letters, we have indicated them by their dates and numbers, rather than by the pages of any edition—seeing that all readers would not have the same. In the passages quoted, writers italicize the close resemblances. But that habit of putting sentences in italics is a bad one. It cherishes a laziness of attention in the reader's mind, and should be condemned along with the system of *claqueurs* in a theatre. The reader here will please italicize for himself.

difference between saying that the crown has a legal power, and that ministers may act at their peril. Instead of asserting that the proclamation was legal, he (Lord Camden) should have said, "My Lords, I knew the proclamation was illegal; but I advised it because it was indispensably necessary to save the kingdom from famine, and I submit myself to the justice and mercy of my country."* Junius has a purpose of mystification in referring to that stale old story. Camden never denied that the act was strictly out of the course of law. He said it was a sort of forty days' tyranny, as we have seen.

CHATHAM:—He owned his natural partiality for America, and was inclined to make allowances even for those excesses. They ought to be treated with tenderness; for, in his sense, they were ebullitions of liberty which broke out upon the skin, and were a sign, if not of perfect health, at least, of a vigorous constitution, and must not be driven in too suddenly, lest they should strike to the heart.

JUNIUS (subsequently to the speech):—No man regards an eruption upon the surface, when the noble parts are invaded, and he feels a mortification approaching his heart. * * * I shall only say, give me a healthy, vigorous constitution, and I shall hardly consult a looking-glass to discover a blemish on my skin.†

We may observe here, that this favorite figure might have been suggested to Lord Chatham, by the large warts that, as we see in his portrait, marked his own face, and his nose. Lord Chatham, like Pericles, Bacon, Kossuth, and

* Letter lx., Oct. 15, 1771.

† Private letter to Wilkes, Sept. 18, 1771.

all vigorous and vivid thinkers, loved to give his meaning in metaphorical shapes. Nothing, we think, more unconsciously shows the identity of the orator and writer in this argument. Good figures are excellent things, and nobody ever strikes out a felicity of the sort without reproducing it, on more than one occasion.

CHATHAM:—The Americans had purchased their liberty at a dear rate, since they had quitted their native country, and gone in search of freedom to a desert.

JUNIUS (near a month before the speech):—They (the Americans) left their native land, in search of freedom, and found it in a desert.*

CHATHAM:—The privileges of the House of Peers, however transcendent, however appropriated to them, stood, in fact, upon the broad bottom of the people. The rights of the greatest and meanest subjects now stand upon the same foundation, the security of law common to all.

JUNIUS (two months subsequently):—However distinguished by rank, or property, in the rights of freedom we are all equal. As we are Englishmen, the least considerable man amongst us has an interest equal to that of the proudest nobleman, in the laws and constitution of this country.†

CHATHAM:—This writer (Robertson), in his life of Charles V., a great, ambitious, wicked man, informs us that the peers of Castile were so far reduced and cajoled by him, as to join him in overturning that part of the Cortes which represented the people.

* Letter xxxv., Oct. 19, 1769.
† Letter xxxvii., Mar. 19, 1770.

JUNIUS (near two years subsequently):—I am persuaded you will not leave it to the choice of seven hundred persons notoriously corrupted by the crown, whether seven millions of their equals shall become freemen or slaves. Without insisting on the extravagant concession made to Henry VIII., there are instances in the history of other countries of a formal deliberate surrender of the public liberty into the hands of the sovereign.*

CHATHAM:—He (Charles V.) made use of the people, whom he had enslaved, to enslave others, and employed the strength of the Castilians to destroy the rights of their free neighbors of Arragon.†

JUNIUS (a year later):—We are the slaves of the House of Commons, and, through them, we are the slaves of the king and his ministers.‡

CHATHAM:—The man, who has lost his own freedom, becomes from that moment an instrument in the hands of an ambitious prince, to destroy the freedom of others.

JUNIUS (two months later):—We can never be really in danger, till the forms of parliament are made use of to destroy our civil and political liberties—till parliament betrays its trust, by contributing to establish new principles

* Dedication of the Letters.

† We may observe as a matter of literary curiosity, that Lord Chatham seems to have got his Junian motto from one of the speeches of Harley, Earl of Oxford, who said (1711), speaking of the States of Castile: *Sunt magni nominis umbræ.* The critics have traced the motto to Lucan's Pharsalia; but it is very probable Pitt did not find it there any more than the Edinburgh Reviewers found their epigraph in Publius Syrus. The most learned people don't always quote their Greek and Latin from the original.

‡ Miscellaneous Letter xcv. Signed "A Whig," April 9, 1771.

of government, and employing the very weapons committed to it by the collective body, to stab the constitution.*

Chatham :—I speak it boldly, it were better for them to perish in a glorious contention for their rights, than to purchase a slavish tranquillity, at the expense of a single iota of the constitution.

Junius (subsequently):—I confess, sir, I should be contented to renounce the forms of the constitution once more, if there were no other way to obtain substantial justice for the people.†

Junius repeatedly expresses these sentiments, so full of the spirit of Lord Chatham.

Chatham (with reference to the conduct of the House of Commons in the expulsion of Wilkes) :—My lord, there is one plain maxim to which I have invariably adhered through life. That in every question in which my liberty or my property were concerned, I should consult and be determined by the dictates of common sense.

Junius (on the same subject, six months previously):—It is a point of fact, on which every Englishman will determine for himself. As to lawyers, their profession is supported by the indiscriminate defense of right and wrong, and I confess, I have not that opinion of their knowledge or integrity, to think it necessary that they should decide for me on a plain constitutional question.‡

Chatham :—I confess I am apt to distrust the refinements

* Letter xxxv, March19 1770. † Letter xliv., April 22, 1771.
‡ Letter xiv., June 22, 1769.

of learning. But Providence has taken better care of our happiness, and gives us in the simplicity of common sense a rule for our direction.

JUNIUS (subsequently):—This proposition is singular enough, and turns upon a refinement very distant from the simplicity of common sense. (Again—addressing Lord Mansfield, on his charge to the jury in Almon's case.) Now, my lord, without pretending to reconcile the distinctions of Westminster Hall with the simple information of common sense, etc.* (And again, in a letter to Woodfall.) The Latin word *simplex* conveys to me an amiable character, and never denotes folly. With a sound heart be assured you are better gifted than if you were cursed with the abilities of a Mansfield.†

CHATHAM:—My lords, I must beg the indulgence of the House. Neither will my health permit me, nor do I pretend to be qualified to follow that learned Lord (Mansfield) through the whole of his argument. No man is better acquainted with his abilities and learning, nor has a greater respect for them than I have.

JUNIUS (subsequently, addressing Mansfield):—When I acknowledge your abilities, you may believe I am sincere. I feel for human nature, when I see a man so gifted as you are, descend to such vile practice.‡ (Again.) Let it be remembered, that Junius never pretends to be a better lawyer than Lord Mansfield. On the contrary, he takes every opportunity to acknowledge the learning and abilities of that wicked judge.§

* Letter xli., Nov. 14, 1770. † Private Letter, No. xliv., Nov. 27, 1771.
‡ Letter xli., Nov. xliv, 1770.
§ Miscellaneous Letter cvi. Signed "Anti-Belial," Feb. 6, 1772.

Chatham:—My lord, I affirm they (the Commons) have betrayed their constituency, and violated the constitution. Under pretense of declaring the law, they have made a law, and united in the same persons the offices of legislator and of judge.

Junius:—The crime, like the punishment, was in their own bosom. They were *ex post facto* legislators; they were parties; they were judges; and, instead of a court of final judicature, acted as a sort of criminal jurisdiction in the first instance. The absolute power of the crown, by the assistance of the handmaid, corruption, puts on the disguise of privilege. The cabal advances on us, as an army once did upon a tower. It displayed before it a multitude of nuns, and overawed the resistance of the besieged by the venerable appearance.*

This figurative sentence is very characteristic. The sentiments of the above are repeated in other parts of the Junian correspondence.

Chatham:—My lords, I am a plain man, and have been brought up in a religious reverence for the original simplicity of the laws of England.

Junius:—Is this the law of parliament, or is it not? I am a plain man, sir, and cannot follow you through the phlegmatic forms of an oration. (Again, writing to Sir William Draper):—Suffer me, then, for I am a plain, unlettered man, to continue that style of interrogation which suits my capacity.†

* Miscellaneous Letter xcii. Signed "An Englishman," etc., March 25, 1771.

† Letter vii., March 3, 1769.

CHATHAM:—The noble lord assures us that he knows not in what code the law of parliament is to be found; that the House of Commons, when they act as judges, have no law to direct them but their own wisdom: that their decision is law, and, if they determine wrong, the subject has no appeal but to heaven. What, then, my lords, are all the generous efforts of our ancestors—are all their glorious contentions, by which they meant to secure to themselves and transmit to their posterity a known law, reduced to this conclusion, that, instead of the arbitrary power to the king, we must submit to the arbitrary power of the House of Commons? Tyranny, my lords, is detestable in every shape; but in none so formidable as when it is assumed and exercised by a number of tyrants. But, my lords, we have Magna Charta, we have the statute book, we have the Bill of Rights.

JUNIUS (over a year subsequently):—The House of Commons judge of their own privileges without appeal. * * * Surely, sir, this doctrine is not to be found in Magna Charta. If it be admitted without limitation, I affirm there is neither law nor liberty in this kingdom. We are the slaves of the House of Commons, and through them the slaves of the king and his ministers.* * * * The power of the legislature is limited. If this doctrine be not true, we must admit that kings, lords, and commons have no rule to direct their resolutions but their own will and pleasure.†

CHATHAM:—What security would the people have for

* Miscellaneous Letter xcv. Signed " A Whig," April 9, 1771.

† Dedication of the Letters.

their rights, if once they admitted that a court of judicature may determine every question that came before it, not by any known positive law, but by the vague, indeterminate, arbitrary rule of what the noble Lord (Mansfield) is pleased to call the wisdom of the court?

JUNIUS (some months subsequently, addressing Mansfield on the subject of judicial decisions):—Instead of those certain positive rules, by which the judgment of a court of law should be determined, you have fondly introduced your own unsettled notions of equity and substantial justice. The Court of King's Bench becomes a court of equity, and the judge, instead of consulting strictly the law of the land, refers only to the wisdom of the court, and the purity of his own conscience.*

CHATHAM (alluding to the expulsion of Mr. Walpole, in a preceding reign):—Incapacity was, indeed, declared, but his crimes are stated as the ground of the resolution, and his opponent was declared to be not duly elected, even after his incapacity was established.

JUNIUS (some months previously):—Now, sir, to my understanding, no proposition can be more evident than that the House of Commons, by this very vote, themselves understood, and meant to declare, that Mr. Walpole's incapacity arose from the crimes he had committed, not from the punishment of the House annexed to them. They did not infer from Mr. Walpole's incapacity that his opponent was duly elected; on the contrary, they declared Mr. Taylor not duly elected, and the election itself void.†

* Letter xli., Nov. 14, 1770.

† Letter xx., Aug. 8, 1769.

CHATHAM:—That it violates the spirit of the constitution, will, I think, be disputed by no man who has heard this day's debate.

JUNIUS:—He not only betrays his master, but violates the spirit of the English constitution. * * * To what extent a king of England may be protected by the form, when he violates the spirit of the constitution, deserves to be considered.*

This mode of expression occurs repeatedly in the letters.

CHATHAM:—Let us not, then, degenerate from the glorious example of our ancestors. Those iron barons (for so I may call them, when compared with the silken barons of modern days) were the guardians of the people.

JUNIUS (subsequently):—I should be glad to mortify those contemptible creatures who call themselves noblemen.†

He also speaks of the bloody Barrington as a silken, fawning courtier.

CHATHAM:—My lords, this is not merely the cold opinion of my understanding, but the glowing expression of what I feel—it is my heart that speaks.

JUNIUS (subsequently):—The formality of a well-repeated lesson is widely distant from the animated expression of the heart. * * * Forgive this passionate language. I am unable to correct it; the subject comes home to us all; it is the language of my heart.‡

* Preface to the Letters.

† Private Letter to Wilkes, Sept. 7, 1771. A critic points to this as a proof that Junius could not have been a nobleman—a shrewd criticism!

‡ Letter lviii., Sept. 30, 1771.

CHATHAM:—In his (Wilkes's) person, though he were the worst of men, I contend for the safety and security of the best; and, God forbid, my lords, that there should be a power in this country of measuring the civil rights of the subject by his moral character.

JUNIUS (some months previously):—Let Mr. Wilkes's character be what it may, this at least is certain, that, circumstanced as he is with regard to the public, even his vices plead for him. The people of England have too much discernment to suffer your grace to take advantage of the failings of a private character to establish a precedent.*

CHATHAM:—Be it so; there is one ambition at least which I will ever acknowledge, which I will not renounce but with my life. It is the ambition of delivering to my posterity those rights of freedom which I have received from my ancestors.

JUNIUS (previously):—We owe it to our ancestors, to preserve entire those rights which they have delivered to our care. We owe it to our posterity not to suffer their dearest inheritance to be destroyed.†

CHATHAM:—His majesty will then determine whether he will yield to the united petitions of the people of England, or maintain the House of Commons in the exercise of a legislative power, which heretofore abolished the House of Lords and overturned the monarchy.

JUNIUS (previously; in his famous letter to the King):—By depriving a subject of his birth-right, they (the Commons) have attributed to their own vote an authority equal to an

* Letter ix., April 10, 1769.

† Letter xx., August 8, 1769.

act of the whole legislature, and though, perhaps, not with the same motives, have strictly followed the example of the Long Parliament, which first declared the regal office useless, and soon after, with as little ceremony, dissolved the lords. The same pretended power which robs an English subject of his birth-right, may rob an English king of his crown.*

CHATHAM:—I should be sorry to trust to their (the Commons') future moderation; unlimited power is apt to corrupt the minds of those who possess it—and this I know, my lords, that when law ends, tyranny begins.

JUNIUS (to the King):—When once they (the Commons) have departed from the great constitutional line, who will answer for their future moderation? Your majesty may learn, hereafter, how nearly the slave and tyrant are allied.†

We now come to the vehement speech of the 22d of January, on the motion of Lord Rockingham, for a day to consider the affairs of the nation.

CHATHAM:—Rather than the nation should surrender its birth-right to a despotic minister, I hope, my lords, old as I am, I shall see the question brought to issue, and fairly tried between the people and the government.

JUNIUS (subsequently, on the same subject):—The time is come when the body of the English people must assert their own cause; conscious of their strength and animated by a sense of their duty, they will not surrender their birth-right to ministers, parliaments or kings.‡

* Letter xxxv., Dec. 19, 1769. † Ibid.

‡ Letter xxxvii., March 19, 1770.

CHATHAM :—I have been bred up in those principles, and know that when the liberty of the subject is invaded and all redress is denied him, resistance is justified. If I had a doubt upon the matter, I should follow the example set us by the most Reverend Bench, with whom I believe it is a maxim, when any doubt in point of faith arises, to appeal at once to the source and evidence of our religion—I mean the Holy Bible. The constitution has its political bible, by which, if it be fairly consulted, every political question may, and ought to be, determined. Magna Charta, the Bill of Rights, and the petition of Rights, form that code which I call the Bible of the English Constitution.

JUNIUS (subsequently):—The civil constitution, that legal liberty, that general creed, which every Englishman professes, may still be supported, though Wilkes, and Horne, and Townsend, and Sawbridge should obstinately refuse to communicate, and even if the fathers of the church, Saville, Richmond, Camden, Rockingham, and Chatham, should disagree in the ceremonies of the political worship, and even in the interpretation of twenty texts in Magna Charta.*

This last is one of those lights which reveal the writer most incontestibly.

CHATHAM (on the subject of Corsica):—By suffering our natural enemies to oppress the powers less able to make resistance, we have permitted them to increase their strength, and found ourselves at last obliged to run every

* Letter lix., Oct. 5, 1771.

hazard in making that cause our own, in which we were not wise enough to take a part, while the expense and danger might have been supported by others. With respect to Corsica, I shall only say, that France has obtained a more useful and important acquisition in one pacific campaign (the Duke of Bedford's Treaty of Paris) than in any of her belligerent campaigns; at least, while I had the honor of administering the war against her.

JUNIUS (previously) :—If, instead of disowning Lord Shelburne, the British court had interposed with dignity and firmness, you know, my lord, that Corsica would never have been invaded. The French saw the weakness of a distracted ministry, and were justified in treating you with contempt. Either we suffer the French to make an acquisition, the importance of which you probably have no conception of,* or we oppose them by an underhand management, which only disgraces us in the eyes of Europe. From our secret, indiscreet assistance, a transition to some more open decisive measures becomes unavoidable, till, at last, we find ourselves principals in the war, and obliged to hazard everything for an object, which might have originally been obtained without expense or danger.†

CHATHAM :—I see that even where their (ministers') measures were well chosen, they are incapable of carrying them through without some unhappy mixture of weakness or imprudence. They are incapable of doing entirely right.

* Certainly neither Grafton nor any of the politicians of that day, including Lord Chatham himself, could truly estimate the importance of that acquisition to France. Napoleon Bonaparte had been born a French subject about nine months previously, in the island.

† Letter xii., May 3), 1769.

JUNIUS:—It is not that you (Duke of Grafton) do wrong by design; but that you should never do right, by mistake.*

CHATHAM:—My lords, I revere the just prerogative of the crown, and would contend for it as warmly as for the rights of the people. They are linked together and mutually support each other. I would not touch a feather of the prerogative. The expression, perhaps, is light, but since I have made use of it, let me add that the entire command and power of directing the local army is the royal prerogative, as the master feather in the eagle's wing. And if I were permitted to carry the allusion a little further, I would say they have disarmed the imperial bird—*Ministrum fulminis alitem;* the army is the thunder of the crown.

JUNIUS (a year after):—The king's honor is that of the people, their real interest and honor are the same; private credit is wealth, public honor is security. The feather that adorns the royal bird, supports his flight. Strip him of his plumage and you fix him to the earth.†

This is another strong flash of identity. Mark how the war-minister, in both places, contends for the free thunder of the crown. No mere demagogue like Wilkes would stand up for the king's prerogative in that way.

CHATHAM:—Whoever understands the theory of the English constitution and will compare it with the fact, must see how widely they differ.

JUNIUS (subsequently):—Certainly, nothing can be less

* Letter xii., May 30, 1769.

† Letter xlii., Jan. 30, 1771.

reconcilable to the theory, than the present practice of the constitution.*

CHATHAM:—Will any man affirm that, as the House of Commons is now formed, that relation is in any degree preserved. My lords, it is not preserved; it is destroyed. Let us be cautious, however, how we have recourse to violent expedients. The boroughs of the country have been called the rotten parts of the constitution. But, in my judgment, these boroughs, corrupt as they are, must be considered as the natural infirmities of the constitution. The limb is mortified, but the amputation might be death.

JUNIUS (subsequently):—That the people are unequally represented, is unquestionable. But let us take care what we attempt. As to cutting away the rotten boroughs, I am as much offended as any man at seeing so many of them under the direct influence of the crown; yet I own I have both doubts and apprehensions in regard to the remedy you (Wilkes) propose. * * * I am startled at the idea of so extensive an amputation. When you propose to cut away the rotten parts, can you tell what parts are perfectly sound—at what point the mortification ends?†

CHATHAM:—The infusion of health, which I now allude to, would be to permit every county to elect one member more, in addition to the present representation.

JUNIUS:—Lord Chatham's project, for instance, of increasing the number of knights of shires, appears to me admirable.‡

* Private Letter to Wilkes, No. 66, Sept. 7, 1771.

† Ibid. ‡ Ibid.

Junius also expresses his approval of the idea conveyed in the same speech, of infusing a portion of new health into the constitution to enable it to bear its infirmities.

Such, briefly stated, are a few of the parallels to be gathered from a comparison of the speeches of Lord Chatham and the Letters. Some of them seem to be merely verbal. But a person's identity is often marked by trivial modes of speech, and they have at least the significance of a man's accent. But the greater part are calculated to carry conviction, especially the metaphoric portions, so eminently distinctive of the mind of the Earl of Chatham. The reader who has not been already familiar with the subject, will be surprised to know that it is from these parallels Mr. Taylor mainly concludes that young Francis, the reporter, was Junius. He sees nobody but Francis in the business. He does not even recognize the earl so much as to try and push him out of the way. He thinks him nothing to the purpose. The complacency of his logic is extraordinary, and yet this same logic is followed by Lords Campbell and Mahon, by the editors of the "Chatham Correspondence," and by all the rest of the Franciscans.

Mr. Taylor was a most infelicitous theorist. He began by saying, on some crude assumption, that Junius was Dr. Francis, father of Sir Philip. He then amended his theory and advocated the son; and lastly, in the most unlucky way, he adds a final chapter to his book, which infallibly leads the reader into the terribly suggestive presence of that bewildering earl, where we see Francis wearing the proportions of a secretary, active and imitative, and doing his best to guard an important secret. This theory is helplessly managed, indeed. The more we follow it, the more do we tend to what Mr. Taylor would call the wrong man—to the very issue against which one of his followers, in particular (Mr. Bohn's editor), is brought up, with great damage to his hypothesis. Not an argument is set forth for the "good juvenal," that is not found encrusted and embossed, as it were, upon the statesmanship, the eloquence, and the general policy of the veteran Whig chief.

It will be observed that, in several of the preceding parallels, Junius first expressed the sentiments and figures discoverable in Lord Chatham's speeches. On the 9th and 22d of January, 1770, the earl made allusions to the Americans who left their native land to find liberty in a desert—found in the letter of the preceding 19th of December; to the dictates of common sense on any constitutional question—answering to the spirit of the letter of June 22d; to the want of precedent for the expulsion of Wilkes—resembling a passage in the aforesaid letter of December 19th; to Wilkes's character as no justification of persecution—anticipated on the 10th of April; to the transmission of the rights of election to posterity—first dwelt on, on July 8th, and August 8th; to the tyranny of the Long Parliament, and the danger of the monarch—a sentiment found in the above-mentioned letter of 19th December; to the fact that where law ends, tyranny begins—paralleled in the same letter; to the easy acquisition of Corsica by France—repeated from May 30th, of the year in which the foregoing dates also occurred—1769.

These facts must, of course, upset any hypothesis, that the young man transplanted into his letters the opinions and felicities of the harangues which he reported. The alternative would seem an embarrassing one, but the coryphœus of the Franciscans, Mr. Taylor, does not appear embarrassed. He meets the facts with an easy unapprehensiveness which excites admiration, saying, merely, and only with reference to the first of them that comes in his way: "In this instance, the speech copies the letters. To suppose that Lord Chatham and Junius reciprocally borrowed from each other, is to encounter a greater difficulty for the sake of avoiding a less. But the resemblance is not surprising if we imagine that Junius was the reporter; and, as we proceed, it will appear that no other solution can be given for this mutual application of each other's sentiments and language." Such is his mode of grappling with the difficulty! As he proceeds, he is not a whit more explanatory, or less helpless. Nothing of what he promises appears from him. He does not show how "no other solution can be given." With this slurring-over and sliding-out, he goes on with his book, which, certainly, from beginning to end, exhibits no more satisfactory demonstration of evidence than you find in the foregoing quotation. "The resemblance is not surprising," he says, "if we imagine," etc. Then he rambles on, leaving the reader trying to make something out of that broken-backed syllogism. To bridge the way to what seems his conclusion, he should have argued that Francis put forcible opinions and phrases into the mouth of the orator, which the latter never uttered. But he does not state this, being probably ashamed to pronounce anything so preposterous; and so, leaving the inference hanging loosely, he proceeds with his slip-shod ratiocination, huddling his no-proofs and general assumptions together, like one who wishes to hide, even from himself, the want of any clear, firm tissue of evidence in what he is setting forth. He is always pushing his head with a purblind fatality against Lord Chatham, drawing it back again, but still making his way after the young reporter; always, be it repeated, followed close behind by Lords Campbell and Mahon, Mr. Macaulay, Bohn's editor, and all the rest of them.

Along with the foregoing parallels, Mr. Taylor has given certain other resemblances between the Junian letters and the letters and speeches of Francis. But they are, for the most part, ridiculous, being made up of exclamations, adjurations, quotations, expletives, and so forth. No doubt a great many of them, such as "I vow to God," and "pray, sir," are sufficiently like the modes of Junius to be observable; and, in a subsequent chapter, we shall endeavor to show how they were meant to subserve one of the most cherished pretensions of Sir Philip's life; and how, with not less force than the evidences drawn from Lord Chatham's speeches, already quoted, they tend to discredit the hypothesis Mr. Taylor brings them forward to support.

Sir Philip's claims are countenanced by certain accidents of time and place, which his advocates make the most of, and which are too closely entwined with the truth of this mystery ever to be disassociated from it. But a few plain considerations will suffice to put him aside—have sufficed, on other pages. He was the creature, secretary, reporter, and amanuensis of Pitt. "How warmly I was attached to his person," says Francis, in 1787, "and how I have been grateful to his memory, those who know me know." Again, in 1791, he declares Lord Chatham's was a name he could never recollect without admiration and reverence. To suppose that such a youngster of twenty-seven should, as "Poplicola," "Anti-Sejanus," and so forth, call that venerable man a black-hearted villain who should be hanged on a gibbet, is ridiculously absurd; and the absurdity is made more intense by the fact that this War-Office clerk continues to communicate through Calcraft (as we see from the "Chatham Correspondence," or, rather, to say the truth, as we are left to infer; for we see nothing), with the man he is stabbing, and, as the earl's reporter, goes dutifully to the lords, to report, "with great exactness," the speeches of that apostate and lunatic—speeches which the amazing juvenile furthermore powders and peppers with his own high felicities of diction and of thought!

Again, you ask who is he that fulmines against the king, lords, and commons of England, with the censorial thunder of a mind so evidently conscious of an adroit veteran strength, so evidently on the level of them all? A young man, they tell you, of twenty-seven—a smart little Girgashite in the War-Office, doing duty as a clerk. At the age of thirty-two, this clerk is supposed to have achieved the lordly celebrity of Junius, after which it is allowed that like Toots, in the story, he suddenly ceased to blow; and when he began to have ripe years and statesmanship, left off having any Junian brains. His advocates are obliged to employ this curious logic, seeing that the ability to write the letters is a test which Francis cannot stand for an instant. There is no need to waste words in maintenance of this. Mr. Bohn's editor admits—is obliged to admit—enough for our purpose. With the strongest desire to make the most of Sir Philip's meagre pretensions, he settles the Franciscan claim, on that point, in the following sentence, the antithesis of which is likely to make the reader smile: "With the fire of a Chatham in his bosom, to electrify the senate, with the acumen, knowledge of human nature, and mastery of language of a Hume, a Robertson, or a Gibbon, to adorn and invigorate history, Sir Philip was destined to leave, as his avowed productions, only a pile of well-nigh forgotten speeches, protests, pamphlets, manuscript notes on book-margins, and fugitive verses."* Well, what of that? The editor still argues that he was a man of precocious gifts. He blew suddenly and strongly into the magisterial eloquence of Junius, from the age of twenty-seven to thirty-two; and then lost stamina, exhausted, naturally, by such a powerful efflorescence! "Admitting, by way of illustration," he says, "the inferiority of the later writings of Francis to those of Junius, I reply, that Francis was certainly a person of precocious gifts." Alas! what a falling off is here—the genius which could win gold medals at college, and then write those immortal Junian letters which shook the War-Office and fulmined over England, from Middlesex to Louis Bourbon's throne, subsiding, at last, into still-born pamphlets, mouthy speeches, forgotten letters, love verses, and marginal notes!

So ran the famous Roman Way,
So ended in a mire.

* "Bohn's edition of Woodfall's Junius," vol. ii.

CHAPTER VII.

POLITICAL BATTLES OF 1770 AND 1771, IN WHICH JUNIUS AND LORD CHATHAM ARE ON THE SAME SIDE, AND USE THE SAME WAR-CRIES.

> C'est Mirabeau, tonnant contre la Cour.
>
> BERANGER.

> I boarded the king's ship; now on the beak,
> Now in the waist, the deck, in every cabin
> I flamed amazement!
>
> SHAKESPEARE.

THE antecedents of Lord Chatham's life show how naturally and consistently he converts himself into Junius; and the circumstances of that Junian interval confirm the identity in the most emphatic manner. All the foes of Junius were the foes of Lord Chatham; every blow the Mask struck was in Chatham's battle. Of course we pass by the curious feints (proved to be such by the subsequent behavior of Junius) by which the venerable Whig earl and his *fidus Achates*, Lord Camden, are first denounced for vague, venial matters, and, in the end, glorified. Looking at the history of the time, we can understand how Lord Chatham would entertain the sentiments expressed by Junius concerning the king, Lord Bute, the dukes of Grafton and Bedford, Lords Mansfield, Barrington, Hillsborough, Northington, etc. With respect to tnese, the secret writer could not compromise his true opinions without marring his purpose in writing at all, and throughout his hostility against them, there is no faltering, nor any shadow of turning. They are struck and scowled upon, to the end, with a show of hatred, in which no insincerity is ever detected.

We have already shown, what history shows, in a manner not to be mistaken, that Lord Bute was one of the most insidious opponents of Lord Chatham, and that, in concert with the Princess of Wales, and in aid of the king, he did all in his power to pull the earl down from his place of chief minister, and take it himself.

The Duke of Grafton deeply stung Lord Chatham; at first professing great devotion to him, and then joining the Rockinghams in the Lutestring administration. When the latter began to totter, his grace left it, saying no one could save the country, but Lord Chatham, under whom he said he would serve in any capacity, even with a spade and mattock. Under the premiership of the earl, he began, in that strange absence of the chief, to cherish independent ideas, and, at last, supported by the king, and some of the hated Bedfords, aspired to the first place. Almon, who understood the intrigues of that day pretty well, says that if Grafton had remained faithful to Lord Chatham, and scorned an alliance with the Bedfords, and king's friends, the great Whig alliance of the Chathams, Rockinghams, and so forth, would succeed in winning upon power, and having everything their own way. The defection of Grafton, and then his premiership, rankled in the heart of Lord Chatham, who thus saw himself baffled and supplanted by the man he had first brought into notice. The fact was, his grace was too high and haughty to be one of the instruments which the great earl wished to use; and it is easy to conceive how Lord Chatham's dislike of Grafton would be more bitter than even his enmity against Lord Mansfield. In his speech of March 2d, 1770, Chatham said of his grace: "As for the noble duke, there was, in his conduct, from the time of my being taken ill, a gradual deviation from everything that had been settled and solemnly agreed upon by his grace, both as to measures and men, till, at last, there were not left two planks together of the ship which had been originally launched." Walpole mentions the fact that Grafton was in the habit of attacking his irascible old patron, who (this is significant) bore the attacks with a show of contemptuous indifference, like that with which Mansfield affected to regard Chatham's attacks on himself. Junius was, at that time, girding at the duke, and, in this manner, compensating the silence of the earl.

The Duke of Bedford was a rival chief, who, cordially seconding the policy of Lord Bute, and the king's party, made the peace of 1762—a peace which flung contempt upon Pitt's expensive and glorious war ministry. "Belleisle, Goree, Guadaloupe, St. Lucie, Martinique, the Fishery and the Havana," exclaims the angry Mask, with a fierce irony, in keeping with the rest of his assaults, "are glorious monuments of your Grace's talents for negotiation."* All these places had been acquired by Pitt's victories, and signed away "with a stroke of the pen." Again, in the first

* Letter xxiii., Sept. 19, 1769.

distress of his falling ministry, Lord Chatham was advised to put his pride under his feet, and ask the assistance of the Bedfords. But the duke's terms were too haughty, and the rivals parted in anger. The "Bedford Correspondence" lately published, shows that "the Bloomsbury gang" were in the habit of agreeing among themselves, that the gouty earl was *non compos.* Mr. Rigby, writing to the Duke of Bedford on the 14th of May, 1770, speaks of a motion in the House of Lords for the dissolution of parliament, as "the mad motion of the mad Earl of Chatham."* Chatham's dislike of Bedford was a cordial as it was intelligible.

As regards Mansfield, Pitt's rivalry of him began in boyhood, and they were antagonists to the last syllable of Lord Chatham's parliamentary career. We read how, in the House of Commons, Murray "suffers for an hour," under the taunts of Pitt; how the latter, scowling upon the Chief Justice in his grand tragic way, tells him he is about to speak daggers to him, and then, with a stare, which Kemble could never equal, cries out:—"Judge Felix trembles; he shall hear from me some other day!" When the relatives of Sir William Pynsent wanted to get back the estate left by that baronet to Pitt, the lords commissioners of the Great Seal, influenced by Lord Mansfield's opinion, decided against the right of the legatee. Though the House of Lords reversed the decision, we can fancy how this business would further embitter the old hostility of Pitt against Murray. In the House of Lords, Chatham was the most forward to impugn Mansfield's decisions in the cases

* "The Bedford Correspondence," vol. iii., p. 412.

of Woodfall and Almon, the bailment of Eyre, the expulsion of Wilkes, and other public questions, exhibiting the same spirit manifested by Junius in his letters on these subjects.

For Hillsborough, Barrington and the others—they formed vulnerable parts of a system which Junius was assailing along the whole line; and they were personally inimical to the Earl of Chatham. The offensive dismissal of Pitt's successful general, Sir Jeffrey Amherst, from the governorship of Virginia, procured for him by the great war-minister himself, was mainly effected by the agency of Hillsborough, acting, of course, with Grafton and the rest. Sir Jeffrey was set aside for Lord Bottetourt—the man who had worried the Privy Seal about the Warmly mines, and got the three shabby commissioners appointed to take the earl's place for a time. This treatment of one of his soldiers tormented the latter worse than the gout; and Junius (as "Lucius" in the Miscellaneous Letters) discharged a volley of bitter epistles at Hillsborough's head. The Duke of Grafton called at Hayes, and showed a desire to explain the affair; but the Earl would not see him—left him to hold that diplomatic *tete-à-tete* with the countess, to which we have already alluded, and next day sent back the Seal by Lord Camden, declaring that he could never sufficiently regret the dismissal of General Amherst and Lord Shelburne.* In his speech of 13th of November, 1770, Lord Chatham turned fiercely upon Hillsborough, who had interrupted him, and told him his ideas were mean, frivolous, and

* "Chatham Correspondence," vol. iii., p. 333.

puerile; and "Domitian," some weeks afterwards, took up and completed the castigation of that lord. As for "the bloody Barrington," he was a trimmer, like Grafton, "a silken, fawning courtier." "Veteran"* taunts him with a desertion of Lord Chatham, after he had been adulating and looking up to him. Barrington garbled and new-modeled the system of the War Office, and "Testis" accuses him of declaring there was not a single great officer in the kingdom qualified to command an army.† This was an insult to the late war-minister, who had formed so many good officers, and, at the same time, it threw discouragement on the idea of that Spanish war, to which Chatham was looking forward with so much expectation. The concluding letters of the Miscellaneous series are vehement and sarcastic assaults on Lord Barrington for his venality, for the changes and the tergiversations of his past career, and the blunders he committed while ordering troops to foreign stations—particularly to Gibraltar. Barrington was, in fact, the mismanager of that "thunder of the crown," which Lord Chatham felt he himself had the best right to wield.

We now come to consider the earl's feelings towards the king. The parliamentary history of 1770 and 1771 shows what they were, and we have on record what his majesty, on his side, thought of that overbearing and subtle chieftain. Wilkes, writing to Junius, in 1771, says Lord Chatham told him, ten years before, that the king was a false hypocrite. Now Wilkes well knew that he was either addressing Chatham, or some one in his interest, and that the

* Miscellaneous Letter cvii., Feb. 17, 1772.

† Miscellaneous Letter lxxvii., Nov. 19, 1770.

earl would read his words; so that we believe his statement. In his place in the lords, the Earl of Chatham proved to all men, and to posterity that reads his letters, that his slavish demonstrations of loyalty to the king were as hypocritical as any part of his majesty's conduct could well be. His lordship was then showing himself in his true Junian colors. What the king thought of such a turbulent man we can easily imagine. But we are not left to mere imagination in the matter. We can gather a good deal of the monarch's *arrière-pensée* from some letters in the "Chatham Correspondence," showing that he distrusted and defied the machinations of his impracticable servant. And we have still stronger evidence of it in a letter from George III., to Lord North, respecting the putting of William Pitt on his father's pension-paper for £3,000 a year. This letter appeared in the *Edinburgh Review*, and is quoted by Lord Brougham in his Series of the Statesmen of the Times of George III. The reviewer (his lordship, apparently) answers for its authenticity; and it has the internal evidence of genuineness. It runs thus:—"The making Lord Chatham's family suffer for the conduct of their father is not in the least agreeable to my sentiments. But I should choose to know him totally unable to appear on the public stage, before I agree to any offer of the kind, lest it should be wrongly construed a fear of him; for, indeed, his political conduct, last winter, was so abandoned that he must, in the eyes of the dispassionate, have totally undone the merit of his former conduct. As to any gratitude to be expected from him or his family (the Grenvilles are meant), the whole tenor of their lives has shown them void of that most honorable sentiment. But when decrepitude or death puts an end to him as a trumpet of sedition, I shall make no difficulty in placing the second son's name instead of the father's, and making up the pension of £3,000."* The hearty sincerity of the last sentence—which Dr. Johnson would be disposed to love, though Lord Brougham calls it savagery—might truly and consistently express the angriest feeling of the king against the other "trumpet of sedition" —Junius. We have very little doubt that his majesty—one of the shrewdest of his family—brought both very close together, in his own mind. Another indirect, but scarcely less forcible, evidence of the king's feeling, is furnished by the courtly echo, Lord Bathurst. When, on the death of Chatham, a bill was introduced to reward his family, this lord rose and contended that the deceased had been rewarded enough. "We cannot suppose," he said, "that his majesty will be offended by our exercising our right to reject or amend this bill. Before I conclude, I must use the freedom to declare I see no reason to despond, because the Earl of Chatham is no more. There still remain as firm well-wishers of the country, and men as capable of doing it real service."† These decided sentiments, pronounced at such a moment, show that Bathurst was quite sure of the king's. Such was the general feeling of George III., towards Lord Chatham; and the latter knew it right well, and his animosity against the king finds the truest expression in the anonymous letters of Junius.

We may now, by way of impressing these truths more

* *Edinburgh Review*, vol. lxvii., p. 158.

† "Lord Campbell's Lives of the Chancellors," vol. v., p. 461.

vividly, look to the movement of the characters, survey the identity in action—in historic action—as it appeared in 1770 and 1771.

Of all the open fights in which William Pitt—Great Commoner or peer—was ever engaged, that continuous one of those two years was the sharpest and most momentous. In it, the reader will find expressed, in terms of parallel significance, almost every marked sentiment of patriotism, lofty contempt, and intrepid sedition, to be found in the Junian literature. We cannot particularize them all, and shall content ourselves with tracing the main courses and chief outlines of the resemblance, in a rapid way.

Lord Chatham, in the beginning of 1770, having spurned, with an impatient vigor which had never left him, his piebald ministry of 1768, had entered, once more, into the old Grenvillite alliance, strengthened by the adhesion of the Rockinghams, Richmonds, and their followers. When he flung away his Privy Seal, he flung away his crutch along with it, and stood erect upon his feet, with something of the resolved agility of Sixtus. The great Whig league then prepared to storm the ministerial strong-hold, against which the masked battery of Junius was, all the time, playing vehemently. The single session of 1769 being overpast, the confederates ordered their line, and nowhere, in the history of constitutional party, do we read of a more terrible onslaught than that which ensued. On one side was the king, resolved to keep the door of his closet, and round him the ministry, the court, the House of Commons, and the Court of King's Bench, with their champions.

On the other side rallied the Grenvillites, the Rockinghams, the Richmonds—the soldierly vehemence of Barre, the pomp and proud precipitance of Burke, while, issuing from his strange seclusion, like the hero of old from his sullen station beside the ships, the Achilles of debate, sending his shout before him as he came, "The king's men must be all destroyed as a corps!" took up his position at the head of the assailants, showing himself in high spirits, and in fury—to use the expressive words of the Duke of Portland*—and greatly astonishing the gossips, who had fancied he was a cripple, and crazy, and quite incapable of doing anything—as Junius had been telling them so persistently!

On the first day of the Session, Lord Chatham, in his place, begins the onset:

> ———his fiery charge,
> Makes, for a space, an opening large!

The Earl of Coventry, the Dukes of Beaufort and Manchester, and others, are driven out of the enemy's lines, and the Marquis of Granby, having been previously staggered,† is, on 17th January, fairly captured, and brought off, in spite of the efforts of the king and the Duke of Graf-

* "Memoirs of Rockingham," by the Duke of Albemarle, vol. ii., p. 143.

† Junius, sending to Woodfall the Miscellaneous Letter, No. lv., addressed to Lord Granby, and signed "Your Real Friend," requests an immediate insertion, as the marquis, whom they had been laboring to detach from the ministry, is already staggered (Second private note). Junius well knew he was staggered, for he had chastised him with the valor of his tongue only a week before, at Hayes, as we see in the Chatham Correspondence, vol. iii., p. 356.

ton, who, like a pair of Widringtons, strive to retain him "on their knees!" Then follow the defection and defiance of Lord Camden, sending dismay into the royal ranks, and Lord Shelburne cries aloud: "the Seals are going a begging!" demanding, at the same time, if any man will be so infamous as to accept them. But the king wins over poor Charles Yorke to take them, nevertheless, and in a couple of days the suicide of the remorseful Chancellor gives a character of deadliness to the strife. Lord Chatham's great effort of 22d of January follows; after which the Duke of Grafton turns, and fairly flies from the ministerial ranks. The hopes of the fierce earl are now in full flush, and Junius discharges a terrible missile at his fugitive grace, shouting: "When the members drop off, the main body cannot be insensible to its approaching dissolution!"* Dowdeswell makes a motion in the Commons, condemning that body for the expulsion of Wilkes; and Rockingham makes a similar one next day, in the lords, where Chatham, defending the cause of the expelled member, uses the words of Junius, to the effect that, let the man's character be what it may, the stab to the constitution is the same. The Earl of Marchmont rises, inflamed, to threaten the bringing in of foreign assistance, if the king is to be borne against, in this way, and is called to order. On 2d of March, Chatham thunders again, to declare that ministers allowed the Court of Turin to sell England to France; that he had been duped and deceived by the king, and that there was something behind the throne greater than the

* Letter xxxvi., Feb. 14. 1770.

throne itself! Whereupon, Grafton flings himself before the infuriated chief, crying: "I rise to defend the king; these words come from a distempered mind, brooding over its discontents!" The earl refuses to deny or retract anything, and appears to pass Grafton by, who, however, shall not be passed by, elsewhere.

The grim *strategos* is in all his fortitudes. Now there is a loud cry of "clubs!" and the citizens and sheriffs of London and Westminster, headed by the lord mayor in person, bear themselves into the strife. A Petition and Remonstrance, on the House of Commons business, are presented on 8th of March, at George III., who asks, in disgust, what is the meaning of it, and then rebukes it; whereupon the burghers prepare a second remonstrance. In the civil list debate, of the 14th March, Lord Chatham denounces the corruption and illegal acts of the Commons, declaring that Camden was dismissed for his vote on 9th of January, in favor of the right of election, and his attack is interrupted by cries of "order!" and "to the bar!" Lord Marchmont moves that his words be taken down, while, "with careless gesture, mind unmoved," the earl bids him take them. The lord mayor, on 22d of March, banquets the allies, and waits his majesty's reply to the second remonstrance. Meantime, Junius orders Woodfall to make haste and disperse hand-bills to draw attention to letter Thirty-six. "Now is the crisis," he exclaims; "for God's sake,* let it appear to-morrow!

* The reader, marking the feverish interest of Junius in this vehement contest, must smile at the devices of the two letters in the Chatham Correspondence, and the three in the Grenville Papers, in which that rare masquerader declares frankly that he is alone—writes merely for fun—

Lord Chatham is to go to the hall to support the remonstrance. I have no doubt we shall conquer them at last."* On the 3d April (Letter xxxviii.), Junius fiercely assails the ministers, sustains the city of London against the House of Commons, and tries to intimidate George III.; and, on the 10th, as "Moderatus,"† he argues and taunts in the same style. On May 1st, he again assails the ministry with a bill to reverse the judgment of the Commons, in the case of Wilkes. In spite of his vehemence, the bill is rejected. In three days he is on his legs again, and moving that the advice to the king to reject the city Remonstrance is dishonoring to the monarch, and dangerous to the constitution. He denounces ministers again, and lauds the City of London for its old burgher dignity, and its proud lord mayors, one of whom affixed his mailed hand to the great Charter long before many of the noble families, represented in that house, were founded. That motion is, also, negatived. In a few days, the Duke of Richmond, in the lords, and Burke, in the Commons, make nearly simultaneous motions, respecting the American troubles. But these are, also, negatived. It must be confessed that all these negatives rather compromise the Achillean character of the Whig war. But the unwearied leader persists. On 10th May, he makes a motion for the dissolution of parliament, which Mr. Rigby, of "the Bloomsbury gang," calls a mad motion, and this is,

has no party feeling—has a mere speculative ambition—is a mere abstract idea, living in the shade. The fraud of these five letters is gross, open, palpable, as the absurdity of those who credit them.

* Private Note to Woodfall, No. xxii., March 18, 1770.

† Miscellaneous Letter lxx.

also, negatived. On 23d May, the king rebukes the city remonstrants, and Lord Mayor Beckford makes, somehow, the reply yet read upon his pedestal at Guildhall.

There is a pause in the strife. The Session is now over, and a consequent gap is seen in the private and public letters of Junius. In the private letters there is a *lacune* of near seven months, in the Miscellaneous Series of over three months, while the regular collection shows three letters in about six months. Junius pauses in the somewhat discomfited pause of Lord Chatham, at a time when the king's firmness grew ominous of the fate of those Whig alliances. But the earl is not cast down. On 23d of May, he writes an enthusiastic letter of thanks to Lord Mayor Beckford for that brave codicil speech in the king's presence,* and, on the 28th, says to Calcraft, with an eye to the less vehement Rockinghams and Camdens, and urged, probably, by that recklessness which embitters a sinking hope : "Moderation, moderation, is the burden of the song among the body; for myself I have resolved to be in earnest for the public, and shall be the scarecrow of violence to the gentle warblers of the grove!"† What a ravenous old politician of 63! Junius now writes his Thirty-ninth letter, sustaining the flagging spirits of the City combatants, and still striking at the ministry—that wretched ministry which does not even know when it is beaten. In August,‡ he hurls a missile at the lubber-friend of the king, Lord North. In October, several letters, with the signatures of "A Whig and an Englishman," which Junius expresses some anxiety to dis-

* "Chatham Correspondence," vol. iii., p. 462.

† Ibid., vol. iii., p. 469.

‡ Letter xl., August 22, 1770.

own, appear in the *Public Advertiser*, warmly eulogizing Lord Chatham as the only man whose ministry would be welcomed by the nation in this crisis.

The autumn Session now begins; and

> The war that for a space did fail,
> Now, trebly thundering, swells the gale.

On 12th November, Junius says, of Lord Mansfield: "We have got the rascal on his knees; let us strangle him if it be possible."* The Chief Justice had been charging the jury in the trial of Almon for republishing the famous letter to the king, and had told them they were to decide on the simple fact of printing, not on the law of the case. On the 14th, the Mask discharges one of his fiercest missiles at Mansfield, denouncing him for his un-English law, and taunting him with his early attachment to the Stuarts, and that drinking of the Pretender's health. A few days later, Lord Chatham, in the House of Lords (without a mask), turns round, in the course of his speech, and, looking sternly at Mansfield, affronts him with the Junian taunt, so harped upon to the last: "There are other men, my lords, who, to speak tenderly of them, were not quite so forward in their demonstrations for the reigning family." On 22d of November, on the question of naval impressment, Lord Chatham contends that such a power is part of the common law prerogative of the crown; an argument used some months afterward by Junius, where he says, "I see that right, founded upon a necessity which supersedes all

* Private Letter to Woodfall, No. xxiv.

argument, and is established by usage immemorial."* On the same occasion, when Lord Hillsborough interrupts him, to explain his meaning, the indignant earl tells him his conduct is indecent, and his distinctions mean, frivolous, and puerile. A few weeks after, "Domitian" thus pays his respects to Hillsborough: "The stage was deprived of a promising actor when poor Lord Hillsborough gave his mind to politics. The Princess Dowager saw what part this man was capable of acting, and, with regard to himself, it signified but little whether he represented Prince Volscius at Drury Lane, or Secretary of State at St. James's."† On the 5th of December, Lord Chatham moves, that the expulsion of Wilkes was not conclusive—his case being only cognizable in a court of law; contending that "the right of election is the vital circulation of the body politic: stop it, and we are politically destroyed;" a sentiment previously and somewhat similarly expressed by Junius when discussing the same subject: "It is an eternal truth, in the political as well as the mystical body, that where one member suffers, all the members suffer with it."‡

On a report, that the Duke of Grafton is coming back to the ministry of Lord North, Junius assails his grace bitterly in his letter signed "Domitian," vituperating him for his treachery to Rockingham and Chatham, and scoffing at him as a suppliant to Lord North for office, so impatient to be first Lord of the Admiralty, that the prime minister "can

* Letter lix., October 5, 1771.

† Miscellaneous Letter lxxix., Dec. 8, 1770.

‡ Miscellaneous Letter lxxxvii., January 17, 1771.

hardly keep the fawning creature from under his feet." He also gives a ludicrous imitation of the Duke's oratory, and calls his style "a rigmarole in logic, a *riddlemeree* among schoolboys, and, in vulgar acceptation, three blue beans in a bladder ; the perpetual parturience of a mountain, and the never-failing delivery of a mouse."*

It is in these slight sarcastic sallies that the grim earl is most clearly visible. On Tuesday, December 11th, Chatham is thundering at the gates of the ministry, like the Black Knight at Torquilstone, striking as if "ten men's strength were in his single arm." He makes a speech against Mansfield, one portion of which explains how the Chief Justice traveled out of the record; and, in three days, that portion appears, verbatim, in the letter of Junius, signed "Phalaris," without any mark of quotation. "Phalaris," however, having used it, goes on to say that he affirms, with Lord Chatham, his (Mansfield's) conduct was irregular, extrajudicial, and unprecedented.†

In the next debate, on the naval and military resources and foreign policy of the country, Lord Chatham speaking of the defenseless condition of Gibraltar, Lord Marchmont gets up to move that strangers be turned out. The earl makes repeated efforts to go on and deliver what he has to say, in the midst of the tumult and Marchmont crying out: "Clear the *Hoose!* clear the *Hoose!!*" But the earl is forced to stop, the strangers, reporters, and all, are turned out, and having signed a protest against such a proceeding, Lord Chatham and many of his friends leave the house,

* Miscellaneous Letter lxxii., June 27, 1770.

† Miscellaneous Letter lxxxii., Dec. 17, 1770.

too. This was very awkward, seeing that the earl, for good reasons, never sent his speeches or abstracts of them to be printed, without the ostensible mediation of a reporter. But this syncopated speech was not entirely lost. Its meaning, chiefly relating to Spain and the Falkland Islands, is preserved in the letters of Junius, Nos. 42 and 43, printed a few weeks later, in the letter signed "A member of Parliament,"* and others signed "Vindex."

The Chathamic war on the ministry is now beginning to fail in earnest. George Grenville has just died, Earl Temple is disheartened, Camden and Rockingham are "moderate," and Suffolk and Wedderburne have fallen over to the enemy, while Lord North, entrenched in his majorities, laughs the siege to scorn, slaps his large sides, good-humoredly, admits he is "that thing called a minister, and not such a very bad thing neither,"† and prepares to push a new empire into existence twenty, perhaps fifty, years before it would have come, without his assistance. Lord Chatham is now looking hopefully to a fight with the Spaniards, who are blustering about the Falkland Islands, but who, very provokingly, soon consent to negotiate and give them up, with a reservation something like that hanging over Gibraltar. A reservation! Ah! the honor of England is compromised. The great earl is for war, decidedly; dreams of cutting Spanish throats. A war would require a powerful hand at the helm. All his friends, Calcraft among them, prophesy war, and send him rumors of it. The high-hearted old *Polemarch* snuffs the smoke of armaments, and has

* Miscellaneous Letter lxxxviii., Feb. 13, 1771.

† Butler's "Reminiscences."

plans for making the House of Bourbon tremble once again. All his efforts tend to make a warlike need of a warlike genius. His private correspondence echoes the belligerent sentiments of the Junian letters on the foreign policy of England. He tells Lord Shelburne he does not doubt it will be war.* On 8th December, he writes: "War, I take to be certain, be the ministry what it may at Versailles."† "Domitian," on 24th December, says: "Give me leave, Mr. Woodfall, to ask you a serious question: How long is this country to be governed by a boot and a petticoat, by the infamous tool of a Scotch exile, and her Royal Highness, the Princess Dowager of Wales, by North, Ellis, Barrington, Jenkinson, Hillsborough, Jerry Dyson, and Sandwich? I will answer you with precision. It will last till there is a general insurrection of the English nation, or till the House of Bourbon have collected their strength to strike you to the heart."‡ How plainly the veteran Boanerges speaks in this intrepid language, waiting impatiently for the first cannon-shot which should set all these poor incapable people a-scampering, and clear the ministerial stage for *men* to act upon it!

Speaking in the House of Lords, the earl exclaims: "I know the strength and preparation of the House of Bourbon; I know the impoverished and defenseless condition of this country." On the 16th of January, 1771, Junius writes to Woodfall: "Depend upon the assurance I give you, that every man in administration looks on war as inevitable."§ In expectation of war and the Chatham as-

* "Chatham Correspondence," vol. iv., p. 25. † Ibid., vol. iv., p. 46.
‡ Miscellaneous Letter lxxxiii. § Private Letter to Woodfall, No. xxviii.

cendancy, Sir Edward Hawke deserts the ministry—a cause of great triumph to Junius. Yet the earl now begins to despond, fearing it will be peace, after all. The obstinate firmness of the king and his ministers, and their evident wish to avoid war, cause him a great deal of uneasiness. On the 21st of January, writing to Calcraft, he says: "A very short space must bring all to light, and show if the nation of England is the tamest and vilest in Europe; I grieve to add my fears it may be found so."* On the 23d, he writes: "England, at this day, is no more like old England, or England forty years ago, than the Monsignori of modern Rome are like the Decii, the Gracchi, or the Catos."† The earl had reason to speak in this melancholy strain; for the very day before, the king had announced that the dispute with Spain was settled! But there is one comfort left him, whatever peace may be abroad, there must be war at home.

He now prepares a motion for the 5th of February, concerning that disgraceful huddling-up of the Spanish difficulties, and, on the 31st of January, sends Woodfall three or four paragraph notices for his paper, to the effect that ministers are about to throw open the doors of the House of Lords to strangers, hoping by this means to induce them to do so, or, rather, desiring to bring increased odium on them, by thus exciting expectations which he knew they would disappoint. Anticipating a refusal, he adopts the other mode of placing the whole matter before the public; and, on the 30th of January, appears a highly exasperated letter of Junius, in which he ranges, like an angry lion, over

* "Chatham Correspondence," vol. iv., p. 70.

† Ibid., vol. iv., p. 83.

the field of public affairs. With a sweeping denunciation of the domestic policy of the country, he dashes into that Spanish question, and vituperates the king for his cowardice and dishonor, in making such a contemptible peace, in going about, in fact, with "the mark of a blow upon his face," and telling his army that he was too mean-spirited to show himself at the head of them any more.* When Rebecca tells Ivanhoe that the Black Knight is, alone, battering in the gate of Torquilstone, he raises himself joyfully on his couch, and says he thought there was but one man in England who could perform so bold a deed; and we believe the reader will be inclined to say the same thing respecting this terrible 42d letter. There was but one man in England who could have written it, and George III. knew who that man was, as certainly as he knew the face of William Pitt, Earl of Chatham. That letter brings out the Attorney-general, who sends a note to Woodfall on the subject, menacing a prosecution. But the intrepid Mask writes a note also to the same, bidding him not be afraid, for it will all end in smoke; and so it does. The king refuses to meddle with Woodfall or his writer. So formidable is the hubbub raised by the Earl of Chatham, and by Junius, about the Falkland Islands and that unbearable peace, that Dr. Johnson, by special desire, brings forward his ponderous logic, to defend the king and the ministry. The attempt to smother the matter between the tapestries is a failure; the newspapers overflow with the fierce controversy, and the birds of the air carry the matter.

* Letter xlii., Jan. 30, 1771.

There seems to be one more Whig battle to bring up. If the ministry are not to be conquered, they shall be desperately thrashed. That exclusion of reporters at the will of Parliament is a crying grievance, and Lord Chatham's good friends in the city will try conclusions about it. In March, 1771, several printers give parliamentary reports, and are summoned to attend the House of Commons and answer it. Some refuse, and messengers go to seize them. Wheble, of the *Middlesex Journal*, is taken before the Alderman of Farringdon Without, who, being John Wilkes, lets him go, of course, and binds him to prosecute the messenger. Miller, of the *Evening Post*, is advised, should the messenger come for him, to take the messenger. He does, and brings him before the city magistrates, who send him to prison. The Commons summon Lord Mayor Crosby and Sheriff Oliver, and send them to the Tower. They also summon Wilkes; but he will not go; and they adopt the course recommended by Dogberry, on a somewhat similar occasion, and let him alone. There is much municipal uproar. Chatham says, on the 26th of March: "I hold also as fully that, in a conflict of jurisdiction, the Lord Mayor and city magistrates, acting under an oath of office, cannot be proceeded against criminally by the House."* Junius denounces the proceedings of the Commons on the 8th and 9th April. Under the last date, he says: "The Lord Mayor or Mr. Oliver had nothing to regard but the obligation of their oaths and the execution of their laws." At the close of the same letter he says a dissolution of the existing parliament, "which

* "Chatham Correspondence," vol. iv., p. 129.

had nothing to expect but contempt, detestation, and resistance, could alone restore tranquillity to the people, and to the king the affection of his subjects."* On the 22d of April, Junius follows up these blows, and says the world is weary of the House of Commons, and demands its dissolution. Regarding the principle of resistance against it, he says: "As to the injury we may do to any future and more respectable House of Commons, I own I am not now sanguine enough to expect a more plentiful crop of parliamentary virtues in one year than in another. * * * I think no reasonable man will expect that, as human nature is constituted, the enormous influence of the Crown should cease to prevail over the virtue of individuals. After all, sir, it is immaterial whether a House of Commons shall preserve their virtue for a week, a month, or a year. The influence which makes a septennial parliament dependent on the pleasure of the Crown, has a permanent operation and cannot fail of success." At the close of the letter he says: "I confess I should be contented to renounce the forms of the constitution once more, if there were no other way to obtain substantial justice for the people."†

On May 1st, Lord Chatham, in the Lords, repeats the sentiments of the foregoing: "Not that I imagine this act (of dissolution) sufficient. No! I have no such sanguine expectation. The influence of the Crown is become so enormous that some bulwark must be erected for the defense of the constitution." He also said: "I publicly declare myself a convert to triennial parliaments." This is nearly

* Miscellaneous Letter xcv. Signed "A Whig," April 9, 1771.

† Letter xliv., April 22d, 1771.

the sentiment expressed by Junius in the dedication of his letters, where he says that long parliaments, like the septennial, give undue influence to the crown.

The battle—to carry on this somewhat damaged metaphor—has lost its former vigor, and the hopes of the allied Whigs grow less and less. The prorogation of parliament extinguishes the city conflagration, like a wet blanket; and on the 8th of May, Lord Chatham declares if he were a younger man, he would go to America and live there. But he is too old. And then, there is that treacherous deserter, the Duke of Grafton, actually coming back again to the ministry—nay, he is made Privy Seal on the 12th of June! Junius is at him again, with ferocity unabated: "Though I am not so partial," he exclaims, "to the royal judgment as to affirm that the favor of a king can remove mountains of infamy, it serves to lessen, at least, for, it undoubtedly divides the burden. While I remember how much is due to his sacred character, I cannot, with any decent appearance of propriety, call you the meanest and basest fellow in the kingdom. I protest, my lord, I do not think you so."* How significant is the fact, that all this outrageous abuse of the king should be completely passed over! His majesty bore it, feeling it was useless to contend with the man whom he certainly knew to be Junius. If Junius was an understrapper, Woodfall would have been crushed in one week, or hanged from a lamp-post. In his next letter, the dreaded Mask resumes the assault: "Let me return to your grace; you are the pillow on which I am determined to rest all my resentments."†

* Letter xlix., June 22, 1771. † Letter l., July 9, 1771.

Dissensions now creep into the councils of the city Whigs, Wilkes and Horne go together by the ears, and the cause begins to grow somewhat ridiculous. Junius attacks Horne. The latter retorts, and very nearly knocks off the mask of his antagonist, so that the latter is glad to turn from this episodal skirmish—after making a curiously constrained eulogy of Lord Chatham (already quoted), to mislead public inquiry. Junius gets to his pillow; but not to sleep. His hopes of ministerial change are almost gone; for the king, with a knowledge and insight of things, which we do not rightly appreciate at this distance, refuses to have anything more to do with Lord Chatham. He hates his very name, as cordially as ever did George II. But the spirit of aggressiveness is still strong in the old earl. One stern satisfaction remains—the power of assaulting his enemies, and tormenting the very loftiest of them, in such language as the following: "Low craft and falsehood are all the abilities that are wanting to destroy the wisdom of ages, and to deface all the noblest monuments that human policy has erected. I know such a man. My lord, I know you both (the king and Grafton), and with the blessing of God—for I, too, am religious—the people of England shall know you as well as I do. I am not very sure that greater abilities would not, in effect, be an impediment to a design which seems, at first sight, to require a superior capacity. A better understanding might make him sensible of the wonderful beauty of that system he was endeavoring to corrupt. The danger of the attempt might alarm him. The meanness and intrinsic worthlessness of the object (supposing he could attain to it) would fill him with shame and disgust.

But there are sensations which find no entrance in a barbarous, contracted heart. In some men there is a malignant passion to destroy the works of genius, literature, and freedom. The Vandal and the monk find equal gratification in it."* Before all this towering audacity of abuse, the king sits quiet. He hears it, and the courtiers hear it, with uplifted hands and eyes, and the fingers of the Attorney-general tingle to be clutching; but they all sit still; they all cower under the blows of—whom? Why, Lord Mahon and Mr. Macaulay will tell you—of young Mr. Philip Francis, to be sure!

That memorable warfare is ceasing in all parts of the field. There is a great deal of reluctance and defection among the assaulters; for there is no hope of beating the king's ministry now; and the champion in the mask, animated by those personal motives which alone could have kept alive such an animosity for such a length of time, sees himself almost single-handed in that bitter business of attacking. Towards the close of 1771, he finds Mansfield bailing a man named Eyre who has been purloining paper, and breaks out into an elaborate and wonderful rage. He falls upon the Lord Chief Justice as freshly as if he was but just then beginning. "With the blessing of God," he cries to Wilkes, "I'll pull Mansfield to the ground." In the last letter but one, of his more famous series, "Murray suffers for an hour," once more. Junius there drags him like a victim to the altar of public justice, and calls on Camden to act the *haruspex*, and finish him with a knife. But the

* Letter lvii., Sep. 28, 1771.

ex-Chancellor has no stomach for such bloody business; he is weary of all these barren battles, and feels with the Rockinghams and the rest of the "moderates," that the unprofitable fierceness of Lord Chatham, a man so hated by the king and court, may have the effect of damaging those connected with him, and preventing their chances of place in any future changes of government policy; and so the war is at an end; and the ascendancy of the Whigs is forced to give way to a new order of things—going, in a great measure, to sleep, till roused in 1830, by the fusillades of one of the French revolutions.

Having surveyed the occurrences of this period, which wear such a "battailous aspect," even in the mildest style of narration, we have seen the statesman and the masquer—so to speak—maintaining each other's opinions, using each other's language, and striking each other's enemies—and that in so remarkable a manner, that it is only by an effort we can preserve the distinct idea of each in the hurly-burly. Junius loses, in a great degree, the caution of his earlier demonstrations; he is dreadfully in earnest, and more bent on striking than parrying; so that in the wildness of the mellay, the mask is at times knocked away, and you get a violent glimpse of the flashing eye and the diabolical *rictus*, as the grim earl tomahawks the Mansfields and the Graftons, or affronts the king himself, with more than the loftiness of a king.

Passing on from these troubled waters into the calmer currents of Lord Chatham's life (where our biography shall come to a close), we can also see how, to the very last, he remains true to the words, ways, and opinions of Junius.

Writing the dedication of the letters, when the battle was over in 1772, he employs a favorite mode of expression; and frequently afterwards, as he had, doubtless, done previously. He says: "If, when the opportunity offers, you neglect to do your duty to yourselves and your posterity, to God and your country, I shall have one consolation left in connection with the meanest and basest of men—civil liberty may still last the life of Junius." A short time before his death, the thoughts of Chatham, running in the old channels, are expressed in words pretty similar to the foregoing, in a letter to Dr. Addington: "Where is this ruin to end? Heaven only knows. I hold out hitherto. Perhaps I may last as long as Great Britain."* At another time, in conversation with the Earl of Buchan, on the never-exhausted subject of the national disasters and grievances, he consoles himself by saying, the gout, however, will end him before the end of England comes. In January, 1772, he writes to Calcraft: "With regard to that larger home, our country, that house so fatally divided against itself—little presents itself to view but infatuation and degeneracy. I do not see the smallest good can result to the public from my going up to the meeting of parliament. A headlong, self-willed spirit has sunk the city into nothing."† The city was always the grand ally of Lord Chatham. Writing, for the last time, to Woodfall, in 1773, he says, in the same mood of mind: "In the present state of things, if I were to write again, I must be as silly as any of the horned cattle (Junius loved a pun on occasion) that

* "Chatham Correspondence," vol. iv., p. 484.

† Ibid., vol iv., p. 197.

run mad through the city, or any of your wise aldermen. I meant the cause and the public; both are given up. I feel for the honor of this country, when I see that there are not ten men in it who will unite and stand together on any one question. But it is all alike, vile and contemptible."* There is yet another parallel, which still more remarkably identifies the language of Junius with the feelings of the Earl of Chatham, and also shows the implacable tenacity of the man's mind. In the last letter with his signature, Junius, in *pose plastique*, stands for ever in the attitude of hauling Lord Mansfield forward to be stabbed at the altar.† In the last scene of all, that ended the parliamentary history of the elder William Pitt, the dying man, wrapped in flannels and leaning on his crutch, bent his angry brow, and delivered his last missile in the direction of that abhorred Scotchman. In one part of his speech, as appears from a letter of Sir Matthew Featherstonhaugh to Lord Clive (for the rest of the reports are silent on this significant fact), he ridiculed the fears of invasion, enumerating those formerly threatened—a Spanish invasion, a French invasion, a Dutch invasion. "Many noble lords," he went on, "have read in history, and some noble lords may, perhaps, remember a Scotch invasion"—holding Lord Mansfield, all the time, with his glittering eye! This was the last genuine undeni-

* Private Letter No. lxiii., Jan. 19, 1773.

† In "Rogers' Table Talk" we find a notice of one of the great orator's assaults on his enemy, the Chief Justice. "No," said Foote to Murphy, "we will not leave the gallery; let us wait till he has made the little man (Murray) vanish entirely." It is a pity such onslaughts are merely matters of hearsay and tradition, while the ballyragging of Cicero and Clodius, in the other House of Lords, remains on record.

able flash of Junius. To the last, he turned an angry face on the Lord Chief Justice, mindful of that poetical prize at college, and the rivalry continued through all the stormier scenes of his life.

CHAPTER VIII.

A CONSIDERATION OF THE CURIOUS AND COMPLICATED SYSTEM OF ATTACKS AND DEFENSES ADOPTED BY LORD CHATHAM IN THE MANAGEMENT OF HIS MYSTERY.

> Sometimes I'd divide
> And burn in many places ; on the topmast,
> The yards, the bowsprit, would I flame distinctly,
> Then meet and join.
>
> ARIEL (*in the Tempest*).

> Trinculo, come forth ; I'll pull thee by the lesser legs. If any be Trinculo's legs, these are they.
>
> STEPHANO (*in the Tempest*).

IN this chapter we offer considerations and a course of evidence never yet, that we know, set forth in any Junian investigation. The reader is requested to bewilder himself a little here, plunge somewhat further below the surface for what we seek, though it does not, by any means, need a diver of Delos to come at it. In the foregoing pages we have identified the angry heart of the thwarted politician and the powerful and versatile brain of the educated statesman. We have now to point to the subtlety of the first of strategists. Until that subtlety be shown, Junius is not shown.

Reading over his Miscellaneous Letters, we are apt to feel as Gyblin, the goblin-page of Scott's romance, does over the book of gramarye. No true critic ever doubted they came from the pen which wrote the letter to the king; yet what a coil and a complication they present! Instead of one man, there is the appearance of half-a-dozen, skirmishing in various places—a series of scuffles all over the field. Junius seems to divide and go to buffets with himself, in a manner utterly bewildering to our common conceptions of the duello. Perhaps it is not to be wondered at, that hasty inquirers should turn aside from such an entanglement to the more open tracts of theory, or that people should be so ready to say, of the letters of the Miscellaneous collection that seem in opposition to the Mask, "these are not by Junius." Nevertheless, they are certainly by Junius. They greatly mistake, who try to circumvent a riddle by the ordinary rules of ratiocination.

In these Miscellaneous Letters, which are, as it were, the *tirailleurs* and *voltigeurs* of the more regular battle moving under the sign of Junius, we must be struck with numerous instances of that curious legerdemain, and led to the conviction that a crowd of epistles, not recognized as his, would be found on a critical examination of the journals of his time.

We would direct the reader's attention to a few instances of his cunning generalship. And, first, we shall look at the assaults upon Lord Hillsborough, who, as Secretary of State for the colonies, was the agent in General Amherst's dismissal from the governorship of Virginia—an act designed to punish Lord Chatham for his savage retreat. "L. L."* opens the attack, stating the dismissal of

* Miscellaneous Letter xxx., August 5, 1768.

this meritorious officer, and the fact that, after the conquest of Canada, Pitt had given him the governorship, with an assurance that it should be permanent, and require no residence in Virginia. Lord Hillsborough, conscious of the motive of this dismissal, was not disposed to discuss the matter, and affected to treat anonymous attacks with contempt. But the masked writer was prepared for this. In another letter we can trace his whole scheme. He says to his lordship: "I must tell you plainly, they must and shall be answered; you may affect to take no notice of them, perhaps, and tell us you treat them with the contempt they deserve. But this shall not avail you here.

Num negare audes? Quid taces? Convincam si negas.*

Lord Hillsborough will seem bullied into reply; there are to be answers! Next day, accordingly, we have the letter of "Cleophas," who comes out in defense of his lordship, and gives an explanation of the secret intrigue of Amherst's dismissal, and Bottetourt's appointment. He makes assertions which leave the secretary's case vulnerable, and (lest there should be mistakes in what he asserts) he is made to admit that he only heard these things at second hand. Then "Lucius," in the succeeding letter, falls upon poor "Cleophas:" "You are pleased to assume the character of a person half-informed. We understand the use of this expedient. While you pursue these artifices, it is impossible to know upon what principles you really rest your defense."† But "Cleophas" was not the only writer

* Miscellaneous Letter xxxv., August 2, 1768.
† Ibid. xxxvii.

on Hillsborough's side, to produce the deadly damage of a feeble and absurd defense. "A Considerate Englishman," writing in the *Advertiser*, asserts that the secretary's abilities are brought into employment to correct the blunders of Mr. Pitt's administration. This letter is not included in the Miscellaneous Collection. But there is no doubt of its authorship. "Lucius," in the letter we have quoted, alludes to it, and, pointing to the astounding assertion that Hillsborough was employed to correct Pitt's blunders, says: "Your emissaries, my lord, have rather more zeal than discretion!" The noble secretary must now have begun to wince under the "defense" of his unknown friends, and wonder who they were! A dust of controversy is flying; but he protests he has no hand in it. "Cleophas, Junior" (whose letter is not in Woodfall's Collection), now comes out to help the other "Cleophas," and then "L. L." (Letter xxxviii.) follows, and denounces the Junior, informing the public that Lord Hillsborough is driven to the mean and paltry art of employing nameless defendants to throw out insinuations which he knows to be false; yet, judging from the general run of mankind, flatters himself that at least part of them will be believed. This is the sublime of subtlety. Then follows "Lucius" (Letter xxxix.), who says, mercilessly: "In your lordship's letter, signed 'Cleophas, Junior,' you are pleased to assert," etc. And he concludes thus: "You seem determined to go through the whole family of 'Cleophas.' Be it so. If your pedigree extended from Denbigh to St. Davids, I would not cease to pursue you, from father to son, until I had fairly extirpated the whole race." Then comes "Cleophas" again (Letter xl.), who makes the most plausible and provoking admissions of what tells against the unhappy man he seems to be defending. He says: "It is strange, Lucius, you cannot write one line without abuse!" He calls the conduct of "Lucius" *ungenteel*, and, in a style purposely slip-slop, says: "The scurrilous language you use, even when your arguments are just, prove you unacquainted with the gentlemen and sense of honor;" and ends foolishly with "In justice to him, I must declare that I am not, know not, never saw, nor ever spoke to the Earl of Hillsborough in my life but just as formerly." "Lucius" comes out again, in the next letter, saying: "I foresaw that poor 'Cleophas' would soon be disavowed. It seems the poor gentleman never saw nor spoke to your lordship, but just as formerly. The saving is a good one. After the particulars collected by 'Cleophas,' it looks like trifling with the public to confess that his accounts were collected in a coffee-house, and that he will neither answer for facts, nor be directed by dates." The reader knows that Junius was obliged, in the character of Hillsborough's defender, to make up his defenses from report, and all must admire the cunning with which he could thus convert his own ignorance into a help. "These," he goes on, "are evasions which I scorn to imitate. * * * 'Cleophas,' alias your lordship, says he has ground to believe the government was not given away, etc. * * * You ask if there was any harm in this, or any fault in that. What is that but crying *peccavi*, the very language of misery and despair?" In conclusion, he says to his lordship: "I know the ostensible defense you give to the public (in the letters) differs widely (it did, indeed,) from the real one intrusted privately with your friends. You are sensible that the most distant insinuation of what that defense is, would ruin you at once. But I am a man of honor, and will neither take advantage of your imprudence, nor the difficulty of your situation."

What cunning is in that glance at the secret influence, meaning, of course, that the king was the first mover in the business! Then, out comes another defender of Hillsborough (what a bloodhound pertinacity in all this!), named "Scrutator" (his letter is not in the Collection), who thus ends with a scarcely sheathed sarcasm against the indecent precipitation of the man he seems to defend: "I honor Lord Hillsborough for having his man ready, ready not only for his place, but for the province; ready, not only to kiss hands, but to take his passage. And from the watchful activity his lordship has exerted in every known instance in his arduous employment, I have not the least doubt but that if Lord Bottetourt had refused to go, or, on any pretext, delayed his departure, Lord Hillsborough had still some other man in his eye who would have made ample amends for the deficiencies of both." That defense is demolishing! But "Lucius" comes on again: "Your change of title makes no alteration in the merits of your case. You argued as well, and were full as honest a man, under the character of 'Cleophas' as you are under that of 'Scrutator.'" He then goes on to hit his lordship on the exposed parts of his defense. To "Lucius" there were several replies. "Chrononhotonthologus," discovers a mistake in a date, and "Corrector" follows to sustain "Lucius," and emphasize that gross affront to Sir Jeffrey Amherst.

Neither of these letters is in the Junian Collection. Out comes "Lucius," again,* and winds up the furious argument, by shaming his lordship with a list of the scurrilous epithets flung by Hillsborough, in the course of the debate, against him—"Lucius!"

We believe the curiosities of literary history have never furnished anything to equal all this. We are forced to stand in amazement at such a complication, and confess that the force of cunning could no further go. The steady vindictiveness of it is unexampled; but it is perfectly in keeping with the spirit of the man who says to Lord Mansfield: "Let it be my humble office to collect the scattered sweets (of public reprobation), till their united virtue tortures the sense."† It should also be remembered, in connection with this hubbub, that the public did not care much about the cause of it—that, but for the angry spirit of Junius, not a single letter would probably have been written on the matter. But Hillsborough had insulted Lord Chatham, and had also said he never meant to notice any public attacks. *Hoc fonte derivata clades.* After perusing that hurly-burly, how it strikes us to fancy the whole proceeding from the quiet writing-desk of a single secluded individual!

Another case of cross-purposes occurs in March, 1768, when "Mnemon," "Anti Van Teague" and "Anti Stuart," fight a triangular duel. We get from the man who opposes "Van Teague," the hint that "Mnemon" is an Irishman—that masked writer, who abuses every respectable character! And yet another instance occurs in July, where "Insom-

* Miscellaneous Letter xliii., Sept. 15, 1758.

† Letter li., November 14, 1770.

nis" and "C." quarrel about the Board of Trade. The cunning machinery of these tussles is plainly visible to every reader, seeing the letters, *pro* and *con*, are included by Woodfall. We can see the man arranging his puppet-work. It is natural to conclude that there is more of the machinery out of sight, that is, not discoverable by the letters stamped with Woodfall's *imprimatur*. And this conclusion will, we are sure, be found just. Printed in the notes of Bohn's edition, we find some letters in reply, or in reference, to those in the text, and the former as forcibly prove themselves to be from the pen of Junius as the latter. They are all alike component parts of a design which we see distinctly in every case. In demonstration of what we say, we would point to a remarkable letter in abuse of Lord Chatham, and not included by Woodfall. It is found to throw a new light upon the whole question; and a knowledge of the Hillsborough legerdemain enables us the more truly to comprehend it.

On the 10th of December, 1770, a few weeks after Junius's terrible attack on the Lord Chief Justice, in his 41st Letter, Lord Chatham assailed Lord Mansfield, in the House of Lords, for his mode of charging the jury in Woodfall's trial case. On the 14th, four days after, a letter, signed "Nerva," appeared in the *Public Advertiser*, vituperating Lord Chatham in the bitterest way, for his treatment of the Lord Chief Justice. The reader will remember that Mansfield was a man who always affected calmness and contempt in reply to any attacks of his opponents; and Horace Walpole tells us that, in this same spirit, he used often to listen to Lord Chatham himself. But on this occasion, after the Chief Justice had been dreadfully discomfited in the House, the letter of "Nerva" came out, and everybody read it as an angry and highly-abusive defense of the Earl of Mansfield. As such, it has been read from that day to this. But that letter is, as Carlyle would say, a sham from beginning to end, and was written by Lord Chatham himself—his subtle spirit and science gleaming palpably from every paragraph of it. He will show the world the spectacle of the serene and lofty Mansfield stung into a scolding rage; he will show him writing or dictating a letter full of truculent feeling, strangely contrasting with the dignified equanimity of his usual manner; he will have loose-tongued anger, mawkish complaint, feeble explanation, and feeble style mixed up together, and he will have the world exclaim: "What a defense of himself! Mansfield was completely floored in the Lords on Monday, but he really cuts a more ridiculous figure in this letter." And so "Nerva" wrote, and so all this truly came to pass. The letter to Lord Chatham begins thus: "My lord, I saw, on Monday, in a certain great assembly, the most striking contrast of character that ever was exhibited on any public occasion. On the one hand, decency, propriety, dignity, wisdom, and temper; and on the other, presumption, insolence, absurdity, meanness, folly, ignorance, and rancor. Your lordship sat for one of the pictures, and, I am sorry to say it was not for the best. To speak without metaphor (!), what demon, save the demon of malice, could inspire you with an objection to the fair, the equitable information which Lord Mansfield offered to the House? The proposal itself, the terms in which it was conceived, would have conciliated a barbarian; but your animosity is worse than a barbarian's (!), and betrays the principle from which it springs. In an unprecedented, extrajudicial, captious, and insidious manner, you had taken occasion to censure that great man's opinions in the court of justice where he presides. Though you endeavored to take him by surprise, that you might catch at some unfair advantage from his answer, you were baffled and disappointed. He answered you with the noble simplicity of innocence, and the wisdom that never forsakes the *mens conscia recti*. He fairly stated his opinions and the principles on which they were grounded, and, without recrimination, he threw down his glove to you all, daring you to convict him of an error upon fair and legal argument."

To see the glaring absurdity of this defense, it is only necessary to remember, that never was Lord Mansfield more completely put down and dumfounded, than he was on that occasion, by Lords Chatham and Camden. It is this, in fact, which gives the letter all its deeply-studied point and venom. The behavior of the Lord Chief Justice, on being challenged by Lord Camden, to "fix a day," for discussing the law-points of the charge to the jury (which the ex-Chancellor declared to be illegal), was shuffling, hesitating, and helpless to a degree that astonished the whole house. Under some secret court influence, which dissuaded his previously formed, or expressed intention, he shrunk from the interpellation, and refused either to answer questions or name a day. Horace Walpole says: "The dismay and confusion of Lord Mansfield were obvious to the whole audience, nor did one peer interpose a syllable in his behalf." Lord Campbell, in his "Lives of the Chief Justices," says: "He was so closely pressed on the point, that he would not answer interrogatories by Lords Chatham and Richmond, that the house became desirious the matter should drop, from consideration of the embarrassment of the Chief Justice."* It was on all hands declared and allowed, that Lord Mansfield was never so discomfited.† And, in the opinion of the public, the letter of "Nerva" was an outburst of his spiteful humiliation. Dire, indeed, they concluded, must have been the defeat which could sting him or his friends into the use of such language. "Nerva" goes on to defend Mansfield, in an argument cunningly feeble and fallacious; and then flies out in this way: "All the world knows you are ignorant of every science. This country severely smarts for your ignorance in politics and finance. Your ignorance of the law may not, perhaps, produce such fatal consequences; but it was such on the occasion I speak of, that your dependent (Camden), the man who has sold himself to you, body and soul, who trembles at his tyrant's frown, durst not say a word in defense of your position, nor even by a distinctive endeavor to shade the glare of your absurdity. I know you are not ashamed of the grossest ignorance and absurdity; but I would ask you one question. When the great man, whom you had treated so injuriously, rose up to explain, and, with the most amiable

* "Campbell's Lives of the Chief Justices" (Life of Lord Mansfield).

† Lord Mansfield did not show himself graced with "the power of words," and was apparently more "known" than "honored at the House of Lords," on that occasion. Pope's couplet has all the air of a covert sarcasm. One of the authors of Martinus Scriblerus could only write in such a sinking style, prepensely. The line, "Plain truth, dear Murray, needs no flowers of speech,' seems written in the same vein.

moderation and intuitive perspicuity (Mansfield was, as all the world knows, stammering at the time, and not knowing rightly how to explain himself),* pointed out your mistake and rectified your blunder, had you no feelings of remorse for your injustice towards him? Did you not see *how lovely virtue was, and mourn your loss?* (The italics are "Nerva's," and, at that bit of sarcastic snobbery, we can see the grim *rictus* of the writer ridging his countenance from ear to ear.) Did not the demon of faction and malice (a favorite expression of the Chief Justice) retire dejected from your heart, and leave you in the momentary possession, at least, of better angels?" We need not quote the entire letter. But it ends in a paroxysm of rage: "You, my lord, have imposed long enough on the world. You are a memorable exception to the general rule of humanity; for years and exercise have not endowed you with experience or wisdom, and you possess, together with the cold heart of age, the hot brain of rash and intemperate youth. Already hath your furious prodigality brought this nation to the brink of ruin. Retire from the stage, and try, in retirement, to repent of the evils you have brought on your country." Such was the letter of "Nerva," completing, in face of the country at large, the humiliation that had fallen upon the Lord Chief Justice, before the Tapestries. That Lord Mansfield, who never condescended to appeal to the public at any time, should do so with reference to a defeat, which he would rather have buried in forgetfulness, and do so

* Horace Walpole says, the Lord Chief Justice tried to mollify Lord Camden on this occasion, by complimenting him in the most abject manner.

in such a foolish way, too, is a thought which must instantly suggest the true character of Nerva's truculent epistle.

In reply to "Nerva," "Phalaris" comes out, saying calmly: "As far as assertion goes, no man argues better than your correspondent 'Nerva.' If we are contented to take his word for it, Lord Chatham is a hair-brained desperate old fellow (the very style of a man talking disparagingly of himself), and Lord Mansfield is the quintessence of wisdom, integrity, moderation, and firmness. I wonder he did not assure us this worthy judge never drank the Pretender's health on his knees."* Thus, with the old Chathamic taunt, does Junius wind up his double discomfiture of the Lord Chief Justice.

In this Miscellaneous Series, we repeat, the evidences of this legerdemain are found in many places. There is a bewildering jumble of epistles,† in which Y. Y. declares that "Junius and his journeyman have engrossed the whole alphabet," and a similar one appears towards the close of that collection,‡ where Lord Mansfield, doubtless, to his own astonishment and vexation, finds himself squabbling turbulently in the streets by means of his apparent partisans, and his bailment of Eyre is discussed in a tempest of writers; those on his side maltreating Junius with the most abusive asperity, and calling him (we recognize that voice) "an Irishman, a liar, and a Jesuit!" In the letter signed "Augur,"§ the writer speaks of "Poetikastos," "Silurus,"

* Miscellaneous Letter lxxxii., Dec. 17, 1770. † Ibid. liv., et seq.
‡ Ibid. ci., et seq. § Ibid. lx., Sept. 8, 1769.

and "Pericles," as dirty and foolish writers for administration. "Silurus," on his side, says he knows Junius, a man sprung from the lowest dregs of the people—an assertion which, of course, sent a hundred critics, who had been looking for the Mask in an upper direction, down altogether the other way. Without having read all the letters of these names, we are as confident as Leverrier was about his planet, that they are from the same unequaled Briarean hand. There is also a "Monody," on the supposed death of Junius, signed "Poetikastos," and attributed to Sir John Macpherson. This poem says that Junius was bribed by ministers, "he fell 'neath arrows tipt with ministerial gold," implying that he was a poor mercenary hack. We think we know the pen of "Poetikastos," also. Again, there is, in the *Public Advertiser*, a fierce, recognized letter, signed "Zeno," who vituperates Junius as "the Jesuit of St. Omer's." This, together with the forcible feeble style of the abuse, leaves no doubt about "Zeno." In December, 1771, "Anti-Junius," "Scœvola," (called by Junius, in a private letter to Woodfall, "the wretchedest of dirty fools,") and "One of the Three" (all unrecognized), make, along with "Cambriensis" and "Juniper" (recognized),* a violent close mellay over the Duke of Cumberland's marriage and that horrible business of Lord Irnham. None but Junius would dare stir up such matters. Again, during the strife of 1770, just at the crisis when Lord Chatham was preparing a grand assault on the government, several letters, signed "A Whig and an Englishman," appeared in the *Public Advertiser*, speaking

* Miscellaneous Letters cii. and civ., Nov. 13 and Dec. 4, 1771.

very much in favor of the restoration of Lord Chatham to office. With reference to these, Junius thinks it necessary to write thus, to Woodfall: "By your affected silence, you encourage an opinion that I am the author of the 'Whig,' though you very well know the contrary. I neither admire the writer nor his idol."* This solicitude betrays the writer. Junius, in a curious, gratuitous way, pretends to think Woodfall was allowing people to think Junius wrote the "Whig." The truth was, the honest printer was not dreaming of being affected in the matter. But he put in a paragraph, to say those 'Whigs' did not come from Junius. *Credite posteri!*

Having made these statements, which any man possessing the London journals of the Junian time may greatly improve for himself, we now come to another of those political sham battles, which will, perhaps, be still more interesting to the reader. We had an opportunity of introducing this in a former chapter, where we expressed a suspicion that Junius had written many things before 1767, but could not venture to do so, without having premised the peculiar strategy just indicated—a strategy for which no other dissertation seems to have prepared the inquirer. Having marked the undoubted hand of Junius in "Nerva," we are prepared to show as clearly, at least, as we show anything in these pages, that Lord Chatham wrote two very remarkable letters, which were published in London, in 1760.

In 1841, Mr. N. W. Simons, of the British Museum, dis-

*Private Letter, No. xxiii., Oct. 19, 1770.

covered several marks of Junius in one of those two letters viz:—the letter to an Honorable Brigadier-general. Mr. Simons' convictions were correctly produced, by a comparison of passages discoverable in the letter of 1760, to the brigadier (subsequently Lord Townsend), with some in a couple of the Junian letters, in which that nobleman is satirized. He truly saw the footsteps of Junius; he wondered at the talons in the dust, seven or eight years off from the usual haunt of that literary lion. But as he could not show the face, he obtained less credit than his discovery merited. Mr. Britton subsequently took this last as a basis, and made a Geryon-Junius too monstrous for general recognition. The knowledge drawn from the peculiar case of "Nerva" enables us to reach a conclusion here which Mr. Simons did not suspect. He could see the mask of Junius in the letter to a Brigadier-general. We can see the man himself in the "Refutation," published in reply to that letter, and printed along with it, by Mr. Simons, who was not aware of the amount of subtle evidence wrapt up in his pamphlet. We shall explain these two documents.

Brigadier-general George Townsend (along with two other brigadiers—Murray and Monckton) went with Wolfe to the conquest of Canada, in 1759. Wolfe was killed on the Heights of Abraham, and Monckton wounded, and the capitulation was managed by Townsend. Townsend's first letter home said nothing in praise of Wolfe; while, in a letter to the Speaker of the House of Commons, he almost claimed the honor of the success for himself; and he was also highly lauded by Lord Buckingham on the occasion.

The Brigadier-general was a self-willed, eccentric man of quality, who, previous to his departure on the Canada expedition, had shown himself indisposed to bow very low to the great minister, Pitt. We must remember that Wolfe was Pitt's officer—his own choice, his obedient and devoted hero, his heaven-born general and thunder-bolt of war, so to speak. He was a young man, of a forward, impulsive nature, in whom the eagle eye of the Secretary saw the spirit of a paladin. Before the expedition sailed, Pitt and Temple got him to themselves at a dinner-table one day, and we can fancy how the look and talk of the great war-minister would fire the young man's blood. Warmed by the glow of Pitt's thought—and very possibly by his Bordeaux wine along with it—the red-headed hero, before he left their presence, touched, or half-drew his sword, and, with the enthusiasm which could make him quote poetry as he drifted on his path to battle, pledged to them his sword and his life in the cause of England.* Pitt gloried in him. The men of quality did not understand Wolfe's character; they said he was mad—very like the minister himself in that respect. "Is he mad, eh?" said

* See Lord Mahon's "History of England" (vol. iv., p. 228) for the story, somewhat unworthily told, on the authority of Lord Temple. The enthusiastic movement of a fine-souled youth, who loved poetry and glory, is not truly described as "gasconading with a drawn sword about the room;" and the assertion that Pitt was so astonished and hurt at the sight, as to lift up his eyes and regret he should ever have intrusted the fortune of the war into such hands, is not to be credited. It seems as silly a piece of gossip as "Jerningham, Jerningham, bring me my garters!" No doubt, the wine was in Wolfe's head; no doubt his voice was more rapid than ordinary; but when he touched his sword, the war minister's prophetic eye saw Canada British. This is the true version of the story —begging Lord Mahon's pardon.

George II. on one occasion; "then I wish to heaven he would bite some of my other generals."*

Along with the news of Wolfe's glorious conquest and death came those dispatches from Townsend, who had opposed his commander's plan of attack, and had done little or nothing in the achievement, but who now did not hesitate to slur over the merits of the dead general. Less things could set Pitt's blood in a flame at any time. After the fall of Quebec, Townsend had left the army and returned home; and at the same time the French were mustering their strength to retake the city. Then in 1760 appeared the letter to "An Honorable Brigadier-General." It is full of the aggressive spirit of Junius. The sarcastic phraseology, the haughty taunts of cowardice, and so forth, are not to be mistaken—though, of course, the truculent passion of his later period of disappointment is wanting. In holding Townsend up to contempt and ridicule, the writer aggravates the punishment by coupling him with his friend and favorite, Lord George Sackville, then the most unpopular man in the kingdom, being considered a coward. The juxtaposition was calculated to be very galling. The letter began thus, with a generalizing flourish, such as Junius mostly affects, as a preliminary of his assaults: "In my religious doubts, I apply to the divinity of Whitfield; in my theatrical difficulties, I consult the canonical criticisms of a certain Right Reverend (Warburton, Shakespeare's com-

* Pitt was mad, it seems; so were Wolfe, Burke, Byron, Grattan. To listen to the critics and common masses of society, one would suppose men got most of their lights of the world and demi-gods of fame out of Bedlam.

mentator, made bishop by Pitt himself); and in my polite misadventures, the physician of Ludgate Hill (one Dr. Rock) is my *celer atque fidelis,* secret and speedy. To whom, therefore, shall I appeal in my military doubts, but to the man whom fortune, that never-erring judge of merit, in one short campaign made a *soldier* (in the *errata* he says this should be printed *colonel*) a general and commander-in-chief?" The letter ends in this way: "Ask his lordship (Lord George Sackville) why did not the cavalry charge at Minden. He cannot answer; but he does not blush. Ask *you* why you are not at your post, or why you receive the pay of two regiments for nothing. I know you cannot answer, and I believe you will not blush." That style, we should think, is not to be mistaken. None but Pitt could have written the opening paragraph.

The letter contains many passages, sentences, and peculiarities resembling others in the Junian letters. Mr. Simons has collected them with much acuteness and industry, but we need only notice a few. Brigadier Townsend (afterwards Lord-Lieutenant of Ireland) had a talent for painting, particularly in the grotesque line, and for drawing caricatures. The masked writer makes it the subject of many sarcastic hits. In the letter of 1760, we have:

"As you appear to have made the hero of Minden* your

* History wrongs Lord George in calling him a coward. He was no more a coward than Admiral Byng, and was, like him, sacrificed to the English war-system, as ineffective, after the long Walpolean peace, as it was found later, in the times of Nelson, Moore, and Wellesley, and, more recently, in our own, when the bluff Sir Charles Napier, an original war-genius, saw his employers flinging over upon him the odium of their own

model of all military virtue, I would encourage you to imitate his great example, by making a sort of natural resemblance between you—a resemblance far stronger than any in your own collection of portraits—though his royal highness himself (the Duke of Cumberland, whom Townsend disliked), your great *chief d'œuvre*, be there." Eight years later, Junius taunts in the same way:

"His Excellency, the Lord-Lieutenant of Ireland, is said to have a singular turn for portrait-painting, which he willingly employs in the service of his friends. He performs *gratis*, and seldom gives them the trouble to sit for their pictures. * * * Amidst all the license of your wit, my lord, I must entreat you to remember there is one character too sacred even for the pencil of a peer (he hints that Townsend caricatures the king), though your lordship has formerly done business in the family."* (That is, for the Duke of Cumberland.) The taunting use of the word *caricatura* occurs repeatedly in the letter of 1760, as well as later, in the letters of Junius.

Again, the writer of the former says, referring to Quebec: "You were at a safe and honorable distance from the scene of action when you were told you commanded." This quoted expression is in Townsend's dispatch; and we shall see how Junius never forgets it. In the Grand Council of the affairs of Ireland, reported by Junius with his usual comic

shuffling policy, and felt, perhaps, in his heart what Nelson used to say more openly, that government ministers are among the greatest scoundrels that ever lived! Instead of being shot on his quarter-deck, Sir Charles was delivered over to the jocose executioner, *Punch*.

* Miscellaneous Letter v., September 16, 1767.

sarcasm, Lord Townsend, the viceroy, is introduced, with the rest of the nick-named ministers, as Sulky *Bout de ville*, and made to say: "I was quiet enough at Raneham, when I was told I was Lord-Lieutenant of Ireland. For a man to be told that he commanded a kingdom, or an army, when he dreams of no such matter, forms a situation too difficult for a head like mine. My lords, I speak from experience upon another occasion; indeed, I found the business done to my hand by a person who shall be nameless."* (This refers to Wolfe.)

In the letter of 1760, the writer taunts Townsend for his partiality to the Scottish regiments; and, harping on an expression in the dispatches of how the highlanders "took to their broadswords," he says: "The court which his lordship (Lord George Sackville) and you have paid to the highlanders has been, truly, of some use to both. We are told, in a letter from Quebec, that the highlanders took to their broadswords—no doubt a very military phrase—and drove part into the town," etc. Junius, in a scene already quoted, makes Sulky say: "I believe I had best follow my Lord Bute's advice, to carry over with me a battalion of gallant disinterested highlanders, who, if there be any disturbance, may take to their broadswords. Where plunder's to be had, they'll do anything. I have seen it tried with astonishing success, and sure never man was in such a taking as I was (Junius, as we have said, loves a pun at times). * * * However, I shall at least have the satisfaction of drawing their portraits. I believe the best thing

* Miscellaneous Letter vii., Oct. 22, 1767.

I can do, will be to consult my Lord George Sackville. His character is known and respected in Ireland, as well as here, and I know he loves to be stationed in the rear as well as myself."*

We believe there is no need of any more evidence to show that the writer of the letter to the Brigadier-general was Junius. Mr. Simons presents many more such passages. But we quit them, to offer evidence more original and more curiously corroborative. It is in the "Refutation" of this letter, published a little after, that we detect the finest Junian artifice, and see the inside, as it were, of his subtle machinery.

This "Refutation" is in the very spirit of Nerva's letter. The object is to damnify Townsend still further by the show of a mean, vulgar, sputtering, and contemptible defense—a defense far more discomfiting to the Brigadier-general than the direct blows of the assailant. Such is the unparalleled strategy of Junius! In the first place the motto of this reply is a mocking and an equivocal one: "Urit enim fulgore suo." The writer sets out with saying that the man who could begin to talk of Whitfield, the right reverend, a quack doctor, and so forth, in that ridiculous manner, must be out of his senses. Such a slip-slop attempt at sarcasm, of course, only proves, ostensibly, the stupidity of him who makes it, and the object is to give in this reply the style of the Brigadier himself as much as possible. In answer to the taunt, that Townsend was colonel, general, and commander-in-chief in one campaign, the "Refuter" (to

* Miscellaneous Letter vii., Oct. 22, 1767.

coin a word) asks if his assailant has never read of that great Roman, who, "from reading and private application alone," showed in the field the qualities of a consummate general!

To the assertion that Townsend hung back, he replies, that the brigadier did right in not wantonly "exposing the troops under his care to any further fatigue and unnecessary effusion of blood, which might have been productive of dangerous consequences; for, let it be remembered, that Bougainville was coming up" (!). At the assertion that Townsend protested against Wolfe's plan of attack, "Refuter" lifts up his hands: "In a most infamous light the author of such a gross calumny ought to be held!" And he thus goes on: "That he did protest against the attack proposed by General Wolfe, is not denied (!); but what was the object thereof, and where was it to be made? Why, not immediately against Quebec, but to attack the French in their intrenchments. To have attempted forcing the French in their intrenchments, must have been productive of a horrid slaughter, at least—that people ever having been formidable in such situations" (!).

The reader is now beginning to see the nature of that Refutation. The hardest and most galling things in the attack are copied into it, so that, under cover of a vindication, they would be sure of going where the letter itself would not. In another place, the defender admits that Townsend must have acted from "quite another motive than the mere soldier of fortune (the vulgar slip-slop of this syntax—reminding the reader of "Cleophas," etc.—is in keeping with all the rest), who wants to rise in the world and make his way by the profession of arms, which was not at all his case. He, therefore, could have been actuated by no other spirit than patriotic heroism. It was her truly glorious inspiring to his truly British soul (fancy the sardonic smile of the defender as he put these parts of speech together!) that made him voluntarily—he not being liable to any command—fly from pomp, wealth, and domestic happiness, to encounter toils, perils, and death, under new aspects, in a remote and barbarous world. If General Townsend is blamable for anything, it is for having done too much, more than the public, by his then situation at going abroad, had a right to expect from him, and for which his family might with reason rebuke him. Therefore, all persons opposed to, and revilers of, such natural desert as his, whether the public consider him as the promoter of the long wished-for militia, or the glorious reducer of Quebec (!), are to be branded with equal contempt—though hitched in the cell of a prison, or a more elevated lodge." How the wretched Brigadier-general must have writhed when he read this exquisitively ridiculous defense! The reader perceives the art with which the attack on Townsend is attributed to some jail-bird or lofty garretteer.

"Refuter" goes on, worse confounding the cause of Townsend at every paragraph, to defend Lord George Sackville, in the manner of a warm friend (Townsend was the intimate friend of Lord George), and flouts Prince Ferdinand—the commander at Minden, and, next to Wolfe, the popular hero of the day. This part of the vindication seems amazingly absurd and reckless. In one part, we read:—"The superiority of genius, talents, education, and knowledge, with which Lord George Sackville is so uncommonly endowed, made the German leader shrink into a diffidence of himself!" With what a shout of laughter that must have been read throughout England! The two unfortunate soldiers of quality must have trembled with horror at the preposterousness of such a defense. Regarding the imputation on Lord George's courage, "Refuter" seems to be puzzled what to say; but he says that Turenne himself was always in a tremor in the beginning of his battles, and that it is very presumptuous to pretend to judge from any man's countenance what his feelings are—unless a person was a most extraordinary physiognomist" (!). He goes on to sneer at Prince Ferdinand as a confused sort of a man, who was "absolutely ignorant he had gained the victory; in which, however, Lord George had some share, inasmuch as the battery of his contrivance greatly annoyed the enemy." At this distance, we cannot pretend to estimate the great amusement and amazement with which all this was received in its day.

Then follow more silly malevolence against Prince Ferdinand, and some very clumsy, vulgar banter about caricatures, quite in the style of Sulky. Justifying the hasty retreat of Townsend from Quebec, he says: "His friends, his family, his country, the British constitution sighed, wished for, nay, demanded his return, in order to see him at the head of a national militia, of which he was the great promoter. What a glorious example it is, to see the reducer of Quebec march at the head of a regiment of militia!" Here you can almost hear the laughter of the secret writer.

In answer to the question, "Why do you receive the pay of two regiments for nothing?" the champion brazens it out, as if it were a personal matter, gratuitously insulting Lord Blakeney, as well as Prince Ferdinand: — "If true, the taking of Quebec deserves a great deal more. General Blakeney was made a Knight of the Bath and a peer with a pension of one thousand pounds per annum, for giving up Minorca. Prince Ferdinand has two thousand five hundred per annum on the Irish Establishment, etc.; I should be glad to learn for what. What was General Townsend's promotion on his return? What has he received?" There is no need of dwelling any further on the palpable design of this most subtle performance, so farcical in its irony and sarcasm, from beginning to end.

In connection with Lord Townsend, there is one more instance of this sham-fighting, which we may add to the rest. Junius, with the signature of "Moderator," on 12th October, 1767, speaks of his lordship's conduct at Quebec, and gives currency to some taunts flung at him by a certain writer called "No Ghost." This "No Ghost" and "Philo-Veritas" are fighting *pro* and *con*, about the courage or cowardice of the Brigadier-general at Quebec, and elsewhere, till his character is quite covered with the dirt they are flinging. "No Ghost" and "Philo-Veritas" (unrecognized) and "Moderator" (recognized),* are one and the same; and this is another of those wonderful little mellays that you meet with in passing over the field of this Miscellaneous Collection. It is one man pulling so many wires.

* Miscellaneous Letter vi., Oct. 12, 1767.

All this presents Junius in a new light, enlarges his surroundings, and makes the reader desirous of looking further, both before 1767, and after 1773. An opportunity of examining the old London journals would enable him to do so, and thus arrive at a truer idea of this most restless, double-minded, and formidable newspaper-writer that ever lived. We are convinced that, taking the true direction, he would be enabled to find in the course of Pitt's career, from his going into parliament to the Junian dates—a space of thirty years—another volume of his writings, as large, perhaps, as Woodfall's book. We cannot, for a moment, contemplate such a terrible cornet of horse, such an assaulter of kings and wielder of democracies, with a versatility of eloquence which struck his age with admiration, and which cannot be shuffled entirely out of sight in ours, and not fancy him as "attacking" with his pen as with his tongue, from the very first. We cannot fancy him neglecting to grasp the most effective weapon in the war of such a pamphleteering time. Posterity has been too much in the habit of looking on him as a sort of *grand homme manqué*, seeing a great portion of his energetic life obliterated, as it were, and the rest under a curious cloud of confusion. The suggestion of these pages—and, we are very confident, the true one—would probably lead to some restorations of his biography, or, at any rate, make him less of a riddle than he is, in many eyes. It is too much, we repeat, the custom of inquirers to stay groping at the shadow's heels, disputing with one another about dates, coincidences, catchwords, and so forth, looking at what he pleases to show them, and believing what he pleases to tell them. Some of them, with a commended sagacity, confine themselves to the inclosure of the regular series; others, with greater daring, explore the Miscellaneous; but still with a kind of uncertainty, as if they were not exactly working *selon les règles.* As for this idea of Junius bespattering himself as "Nerva," they may possibly reject it as too violent—not even give it the welcome of a stranger. And, certainly, if it is to be Francis, or Temple, or Macleane, they do right to reject it. In such a case, Junius was not the writer of "Nerva's" letter, nor of the "Refutation" of 1760.

CHAPTER IX.

CONTEMPORARY EVIDENCES; SHOWING THAT THE ACUTEST JUDGES OF THAT PERIOD CONSIDERED JUNIUS TO BE LORD CHATHAM.

Well, well, we know, or we could an if we would: or if we list to speak!

HAMLET.

Chacun parle a son gre de ce grand cardinal
Mais, pour moi, je n'en dirai rien;
Il m'a fait trop de bien pour en dire du mal,
Il m'a fait trop de mal pour en dire du bien.

CORNEILLE.

THE foregoing pages contain all we meant to indicate—leaving out minor considerations. If our demonstration is true, enough has been written; if not, we have said too much. Still, having gathered the materials of this theory, we find it hard to throw them away. Besides—in consequence of indiscreet compression—our matter threatens to look disparagingly thin between the covers, when all is done; and everybody know that a certain portliness, not to say, corpulence, of a book carries its own general trade recommendation along with it. Making use of those materials, then, we shall go on, to trace the limbs and outward flourishes of our subject.

It is interesting to consider what the cotemporaries of Junius thought of his identity. And we shall find in the expressions of those most familiar with the political arena of the time, and most capable of knowing the various actors on it, a strong suspicion—an apparent consciousness of the truth—very little short of a direct statement of belief. Many of the foremost men of that day could see that strange and malcontent Lord Chatham, behind the mask of Junius; but so terrible was the nature of the secret with regard to that nobleman and his family, and so guarded was it by a circumvallation of shows and seemings, that no one cared or dared to speak of it freely. There was no direct proof to be had, and respect, fear, or prudence, kept people silent. But a great amount of indirect evidence shows that it was either known or suspected. John Horne Tooke seems to have been convinced that Junius was Lord Chatham; he very nearly pulled off the mask in that epistolary contest on the subject of the city differences. He struck the shield with the point of the lance. "The darkness," he says, "in which Junius thinks himself shrouded, has not concealed him, nor his artifice of only attacking, under that signature, those he would pull down (whilst he recommends by other means those he would have promoted), disguise from me whose partisan he is." The parenthesis points to those letters eulogizing Lord Chatham, signed, "A Whig and an Englishman," to which we have already alluded, and which Junius was so anxious to disavow.

Horne goes on: "When Lord Chatham can forgive the awkward situation in which, for the sake of the public, he was designedly placed by the thanks to him from the city, and when Wilkes's name ceases to be necessary to Lord Rockingham, to keep up a clamor against the ministry, then, and not until then, may those he now abuses expect the approbation of Junius. Mr. Wilkes is supported and assisted in all his attempts as long as he continues to be 'a thorn in the king's side.' This is the very extremity of faction, and the last degree of political wickedness. Because Lord Chatham has been ill-treated by the king, and treacherously betrayed by the Duke of Grafton, the latter is to be the pillow on which Junius will rest his resentments, and the public are to oppose measures of government from mere motives of personal enmity to the sovereign." This told dangerously against the Mask—seeing that Chatham's anger against the king and the Duke of Grafton was well known. A little further on, Horne says, that Junius, with all his partiality for Wilkes, never, any more than Lord Chatham, contributed a farthing to Wilkes's expenses. He ends this harping on the earl, by declaring that the principles of Junius—who, he knows, is looking ambitiously to a change of ministers—will suit no form of government. "They are not to be tolerated under any constitution. Personal enmity is a motive fit only for the devil."* This motive was that attributed by the court party, and a great portion of the public, to the fierce parliamentary onslaughts of Lord Chatham. These thrusts at his identity must have greatly discomposed Junius. Horne, in effect, identifies him with Lord Chatham. What shall he write now? If he show consciousness he is lost, for the eyes of the public are on him. To show any leaning to the earl, would only confirm the suspicions suggested by Horne. So the critics would suppose. But Junius thinks more cunningly. He comes

* Letter liii., July 31, 1771.

out with an air of boldness, and writes that eulogy on Lord Chatham which we have already quoted. The public curiosity was thus ably met and imposed on. In a letter written about a fortnight after that of Junius (the 54th), Horne says: "I am as well satisfied with your panegyric as Lord Chatham can be"*—a sentence affecting us with something of the same dubiety which touches the readers of the passage it refers to. Short as it is, it has an equivocation suggestive of what we believe were the secret beliefs of Mr. Horne. The latter certainly told truth when he laid down his knife and fork at the dinner-table and said, with such sternness: "I do, sir."

Edmund Burke would not, perhaps, have taken his oath that Lord Chatham was Junius, or dictated the letters; but we are persuaded he firmly and potently believed it. Let us mark how this clear-seeing politician, so familiar with the *penetralia* of the Whig party, regards the Mask. He speaks remarkably of Junius in his place in parliament, and he speaks with emphasis, on more than one occasion, of the conduct and character of Lord Chatham; and while his honorary mention of the former proves he did not think the letters came from any mere clerk or secretary, the peculiar manner and similarity of style in which he introduces both the one and the other, show the degree in which the subjects were identified in his mind. In 1768, at a time when Lord Chatham kept himself shut up in the country, and re-

* It is to be remarked as highly significant, that both Wilkes and Mr. Butler, the writer of the "Reminiscences," thought there was something ironical in the language of that passage, and Robert Heron could find nothing in it but a burlesque meaning. No wonder that a thing so full of constraint and hypocrisy should puzzle the critics.

fused to come out for a million of prayers, Burke, alluding to the perplexity of the ministers, speaks thus of the Lord Privy Seal: "But, perhaps, this house is not the place where our reasons can be of any avail; the great person, who is to determine this question, may be a being far above our view—one so immeasurably high, that the greatest abilities (looking to Mr. Townsend), or the most amiable disposition (to Mr. Conway), may not gain access to him—a being before whom thrones, dominations, princedoms, virtues, powers (waving his hand all the time over the Treasury Bench, behind which he stood), all veil their faces with their wings. But though our arguments may not reach him, our prayers may." Burke then apostrophized the great Minister above, who governs all, to have mercy on the work of his hands; to have mercy on the public credit, of which he has made so free and large a use: "Doom not to perdition that vast public debt—a mass of seventy millions—which thou hast employed in rearing a pedestal for thine own statue!" Here he was called to order by Mr. Hervey, who probably thought the orator was verging too closely on the profane, and checked in mid-volley, greatly to the regret of many in the House, who thought they were getting something more interesting than the usual dinner-signal.

We shall now see how he speaks of Junius, in the same figuratively-imaginative way, as of one in whom also the assembly he addressed would be largely interested. The following language, spoken in such a place, was meant for none but some lofty and magisterial agency: "How comes this Junius to have broke through the cobwebs of the law, and to range uncontrolled, unpunished, through the land?

The myrmidons of the Court have been, and are still, pursuing him in vain. They will not spend their time upon me or upon you, when the mighty boar of the forest, which has broke through all their toils, is before them. But what will all their efforts avail? No sooner has he wounded one, than he strikes down another dead at his feet. For my own part, when I saw his attack upon the king, I own my blood ran cold. I thought he had ventured too far, and that there was an end of his triumphs. Not that he had not asserted many bold truths, by which a wise prince might profit. It was the rancor and venom with which I was struck. But while I expected from this daring flight his final ruin and fall, behold him rising still higher, and coming down, souse, upon both houses of parliament! Yes, he made you his quarry, and you still bleed from the effects of his talons. You crouched, and still crouch, beneath his rage. Nor has he dreaded the terrors of your brow, sir (Sir Fletcher Norton, the Speaker); for he has attacked even you; and I believe you have no reason to triumph in the encounter. Not content with carrying away our royal eagle in his pounces, and dashing him against a rock, he has laid you prostrate; and king, lords, and commons, thus become but the sport of his fury. Were he a member of this House, what might not be expected from his knowledge, his firmness, and his integrity? He would be known by his contempt of all danger, his penetration, and his vigor. Bad ministers could conceal nothing from his sagacity; nor could promises nor threats induce him to conceal anything from the public."* All this, surely, makes the idea of a clerk-

* Debate on the Address, November 27, 1770.

Junius, or secretary-Junius, utterly ridiculous. That Burke looks up to some great and distinguished man, is visible in such language; and he knew who Junius was as well as any man in England.

The speeches we have quoted proceeded from impressions similarly made on the mind of the orator. On a former occasion, he produced the same soaring and pouncing fancy by which he had understood and depicted Junius: "The style of Lord Chatham's politics," he says, "is to keep hovering in the air over all parties, and souse down where the prey may prove best." To this we may add that Burke admitted to Sir Joshua Reynolds, he thought he knew who Junius was, and that he always avoided the subject of the identity.*

We now come to consider how John Wilkes regards the man in the paper mask. This little squinting scoffer, who seems to venerate nothing in the world, looks reverently to his veiled correspondent—he almost worships him. Replying to Junius, he says: "I do not mean to indulge the impertinent curiosity of finding out the most important secret of our time—the author of Junius. I will not attempt, with profane hands, to tear the veil of the sanctuary. I am disposed, with the inhabitants of Attica, to erect an altar to the unknown god of our political idolatry, and will be content to worship him in clouds and darkness."†

* Writing to Charles Townsend, in 1771, Burke seems to express his consciousness of the mode in which Junius managed his secret, the better to baffle inquiry. He says he himself is incapable of treating the character of his friends, and even his own character, with levity, in order to be able to attack that of others with less suspicion.

† Private Letter No. lxix., September 12, 1771.

Again: "I did not go to Woodfall to pry into a secret I had no right to know; the letter itself bore the stamp of Jove." Wilkes tells Junius that he is thinking of making an onslaught on the House of Lords concerning their usurped powers,* and insidiously asks his opinion, strongly suspecting he would not be very favorable to such a proceeding. Junius, in reply, says: "Do now as you think proper. I have no resentment but against the common enemy, and will assist you in any way that you will suffer yourself to be assisted. When you have satisfied your understanding that there may be reasons why Junius should attack the king, the minister, the Court of King's Bench, and the House of Commons, in the way that I have done, and yet should desert or betray the man who attacks the House of Lords, I would still appeal to your heart."† This unconsenting, round-about sort of reply was enough, it seems, for Wilkes, whose proposal was a significant feint, and he let the matter drop. He always agreed with Dr. Mason, that Junius was a man of high rank. He never dreamed he was an understrapper of any sort.

Let us now come to Woodfall. This man, receiving all the letters of Junius, privy to his system of feints and cross-purposes, and likeliest to make the shrewdest guess at the identity of one who was certainly wealthy, and carried such an undeniable tone of command with him, shows himself all deference to the will of his correspondent. His language, in addressing him, is that of a man looking up. He buys a franchise, and begs the shadow of a name will

* Private Letter No. lxxx., November 6, 1771.

† Ibid. No. lxxxi., November 9, 1771.

deign to instruct him how to vote. Woodfall was not the man to address any clever clerk or amanuensis, such as Francis, Lloyd, Boyd, or Macleane, in that manner. He knew the world about him too well, and well knew that none but a man of the most powerful rank could have protected him against the consequences of publishing the letters.

Dr. Johnson will furnish us with one more evidence of the impression made upon the best-informed cotemporaries of Junius by that writer. The dogmatical doctor, who had received a pension from George III., was brought forward during the tempest of the still-vexed Falklands, to show his science against that terrible assailant of the ministry.* He wrote a defense of them, which they were very proud of, and in this "Thoughts on the late Transactions respecting the Falkland Islands," he denounces both Lord Chatham and Junius, leaving a strong impression that he identified them, in chief opposition to the policy of the government. In one part of the pamphlet he alludes thus to Lord Chatham, whom he does not name: "This, surely, is sufficient answer to the feudal gabble of the man who is every day lessening that splendor of character which once illuminated the kingdom, then dazzled, and afterwards inflamed it, and for whom it will be happy if the nation, at last, dismiss him to nameless obscurity, with that equipoise of praise and blame which Corneille allows to Richelieu, a

* There was some talk of bringing the doctor into parliament; but Lord North objected, saying the philosopher was something of an elephant, and would be just as likely to trample down his friends as his enemies in any of the mellays of the House of Commons.

man who, I think, had much of his merit and many of his faults." The doctor speaks of Junius in a rather elaborate passage in another part of the pamphlet. He says: "It cannot be said, as of Ulysses, that he scatters ambiguous expressions among the vulgar; for he cries havoc without reserve, and endeavors to let slip the dogs of foreign and civil war, ignorant whither they are going, and careless what may be their prey. * * * Junius knows his own meaning, and can, therefore, tell it. He is an enemy to the ministry—he sees them hourly growing stronger. He knows that a war, at once unjust and unsuccessful, would have certainly displaced them, and is, therefore, in his zeal for the country, angry that war was not unjustly made, and unsuccessfully conducted."* This is the undoubted portrait of Lord Chatham in 1771.

It seems strange that Dr. Johnson should think it a happiness for the earl, that he should be dismissed to obscurity for opposing the ministry. But if we suppose the doctor knew him to be implicated in something less dignified and

* "Johnson's Works," vol. viii., London, 1806. It is to be remarked, that the doctor does not write very savagely against the Mask. He is gravely severe, and no more. We can fancy good reasons for this. Frederick, Prince of Wales, in whose household Pitt spent some of his earlier years, was a great patron of literary men, among them Dr. Johnson, whose "Rambler" he greatly admired. It is not very improbable that the doctor found Pitt, on occasion, a welcome go-between—especially as the rising statesman then enjoyed as great a reputation for literature as for political eloquence, and wished to maintain it. If Johnson believed he was called upon to denounce a mere clerk, secretary, or other person of that sort, we should have something in his own squelching and truculent style, very different from those measured terms of blame in which he has expressed himself. Corneille's sentiments regarding Richelieu are apparently those of Johnson towards Lord Chatham—a man who was very likely to have laid the doctor under obligation.

more factious, we can account for that *disrespectful* style of language applied to so great and venerable a man. No doubt Dr. Johnson could make as close a guess at the identity as any one in London. But we believe it would have been a very desperate proceeding, even in "Mun" himself, to question him about it, in any of those grand ursine moods of his, at the Club.

We have to mention another instance, in which Lord Chatham is brought into close connection with Junius.* Beckford, the admirer and adherent of that great man, on being asked if his lordship was not Junius, said: "No, for, if so, they would all have known it," that is, Chatham's friends—Beckford among them. But that self-sufficient reason is of course inconclusive. Beckford, very likely, knew the truth. He told the inquirer that Dr. Wilmot, a great Whig, and a great friend of Lord Chatham, was the man. Wilmot, he said, knew all about the court, and was the clergyman who married George III. to Hannah Lightfoot, and William Pitt and a lady named Taylor were the only others present at the ceremony. This last is a curious piece of gossip. But it is to be observed, how Beckford, to ward off suspicion from Chatham, is obliged to say that Junius was his lordship's close friend. Then, undoubtedly, Chatham must have known all about the business. So that, having got into the adyta, led by this intimate of the great minister, we find the latter a portion of the secret, as it were. But, there is no Junian theory extant, in which we do not jostle the grim earl, more or less closely. Whatever

* *New Monthly Magazine*, vol. ii., p. 276.

point of view be adopted, the inquirer is always sure to see him, frowning beside or above the theme, just as Vesuvius—to quote from one of Victor Hugo's fine odes—still forms the severe background of all the soft vistas which the traveler finds round the Bay of Naples.

In addition to the foregoing, we may observe that, up and down in our literature, we meet with a great many passages concerning Lord Chatham or Junius, which have the effect of sustaining, in some degree, the conclusions of these pages. We have noticed some of these passages in the Memoirs of Lady Hester Stanhope, whose character was so wonderfully like that of her grandfather. Her very tones resembled his so much, that William Pitt used to say: "Good God, if I were to shut my eyes, I could almost think it was my father." She had all the earl's pride, eccentricity, voluble sarcasm and general waywardness—a more powerful, though less elegant specimen of womanhood than Mrs. Pitt, her grand-aunt, who was such a distinguished woman in her day. Dr. M., who writes the Memoirs, allows himself, in an apparently unconscious manner, to express a foregone conclusion—such as he must have gathered from the conversation of her ladyship, where he considers—"Whether Lord Chatham might not have been the author of Junius's Letters." He says this in a passing way, as if led to it by some natural course of thought, and as if the world would not consider the idea rather a violent one. As we have said, he knew Lady Hester well, and heard her conversations, and these must have had their effect on him. At one time, she said to him: "My grandfather was perfectly capable and likely to write and do things which no human being would dream came from his hands." This would be a better epigraph of our book, than Pope's verses. It contains a very remarkable admission; and when we consider that Lady Hester was on bad terms with her family, and would say things to displease and spite them, which she would otherwise keep secret, her words are among the most significant, bearing on this curious question. She goes on to say that Lord Chatham employed many spies and secret writers, and talks of one who, in the dress of a sailor, gave him much information on American and West India events. Speaking of her relatives, who had just published the Chatham Correspondence, she says: "They are totally ignorant of the politics of my grandfather's age, and of the style of language used at that period; and absolutely ignorant (mark how curiously close she comes again) of his secret reasons and intentions, and the real or apparent footing he was upon with many people, friends and foes. *I* know all that from my mother, who was his secretary, and, as Coutts used to say, the cleverest man of her time in politics and business," etc. It is Hester,* Lord Chatham's daughter, who is here spoken of as such a clever assistant of the earl.

* We are not sure this name is set down correctly—not having a Debrett. It may be a wrong one. And we may as well observe, here, that in these pages two or three other names or dates may be involved in the same uncertainty. But any slips will be surely found out. We leave them, however, to those who know how to deal with them—the *feræ literaturæ*, whose natural prey they are. We mean simply to approach and point to the true Junius—very careless what little obstacles the foot may stumble over in so doing. The pretense of being precisely right at all sides of any human argument, is, perhaps, a ridiculous one after all—generally speaking—and peculiar to an age merely critical.

Sir Nicholas Wraxall, in his Memoirs, also alludes to our subject, and in such a way as shows he thought Junius a man in very high position—one who may possibly have accepted a pension and a peerage from some of the persons he vituperated in his letters. Sir Nicholas was a man remarkably well informed in all the political gossipries and personal histories of his time, and very well enabled to make a shrewd guess at the real Junius. It must be admitted that, in his allusions, he comes wonderfully close to the facts of Lord Chatham's biography. At all events, it is plain he does not look to any of the understrappers or War Office clerks, so insisted on by the acute critics of a later generation.

There is another curious passage bearing upon this question somewhat, and occurring in Mr. Landor's Imaginary Conversations. The two lords, Chatham and Chesterfield, talk about Plato, and the latter seeing a Bible in the hands of his friend, kisses it, saying: "I kissed it preparatorily to swearing on it, as your lordship's power and credit are from this time forward at my mercy, that I never will divulge, so help me God, the knowledge I possess of your reading Greek and philosophy." This is rather a curious close of the colloquy, and seems to imply, on Mr. Landor's part, a feeling that this doing a thing in secret, and having his friends swearing solemnly never to divulge their knowledge of it, was perfectly in character and consistent with the idea of Lord Chatham. Our notion of this seeming may be right or wrong; but if Mr. Landor really meant *miching malheco*, we find his meaning countenanced remarkably by the statements of Lady Hester Stanhope.

CHAPTER X.

LORD CHATHAM'S SPEECHES, AND REPORTERS—AFFECTATIONS AND INADEQUACY OF SIR PHILIP FRANCIS, LORD CHATHAM'S AMANUENSIS AND SECRETARY.

> With purpose to be dressed in an opinion
> Of wisdom, gravity, profound conceit,
> As who should say, I am Sir Oracle.
>
> MERCHANT OF VENICE.

> Rien ne te sert d'être farine.
>
> LAFONTAINE'S CAT.

IN the present chapter, we shall offer a few observations on the subject of Sir Philip Francis, showing his subservient connection with the Junian mystery.

The general opinion that Lord Chatham was an ineffectual, careless writer—the antipodes of such a man as Junius—is a fallacy. We have shown enough to prove that he was among the most elegant and forcible of British writers. Some of his letters, of which we have certainly got the least spirited and characteristic, exhibit the terse and decisive style of the masked writer, while the reported speeches of the great orator echo the Junian cadences in a hundred places, though, doubtless, less close and polished than these last. But, you are told, that the thoughts and cadences of the speeches were those of the young man's manner; that the orator's mind, passing through the reporter, took a Franciscan hue. This fallacy is met by the fact that the speeches reported by Boyd are as full of the peculiar spirit and character of Lord Chatham as those reported by Francis. Indeed, we believe it was impossible it should be otherwise, for, according to all appearance, he corrected and polished his speeches, or rather the reports of them, before sending them to the press. This, at least, was the case with his most important speeches, which have the clear unsuperfluous style of his letters. There is no reporter's "gummy flesh" about any of them, no periphrases; they are spare, muscular and *ad rem.* Some of them begin with an abruptness which discredits the idea of mere reporting. The reader who peruses the speeches of January 19, 1775, and November 18, 1777, first published in 1779—the year after Chatham's death—will find in them the tone and manner of those of 1770, reported by Francis, and none of that peculiar style of strong writing affected by Mr. Boyd.

The greatest difficulty in the way of the Franciscans exists in connection with these speeches of 1770. The number of the parallel passages is very damaging to the pretensions of Sir Philip. Nothing but a desperate resource remains to his advocates. It is necessary to say the young clerk had greater powers than Lord Chatham; and some of them say it. They say the youth powdered the harangues of the noble veteran with his own flowers of thought and language, fancies, figures and felicities; nay, that he did for the orator what the latter could not do so well for himself—write some of his speeches. Lest this should be taken for a scurvy jest, we quote from Bohn's edition of the Letters: "It is not improbable that Sir Philip Francis composed those speeches for Lord Chatham; he certainly composed many of his lordship's speeches."* This conclusion is drawn from the fact that, on the margin of a copy of "Belsham's History of England," Francis once wrote: "I wrote this speech for Lord Mansfield, as well as all those of Lord Chatham, on the Middlesex election." This, to be sure, is an excellent Franciscan argument; but some minds, we confess, would be rather staggered to think Junius wrote a speech for Lord Mansfield! *C'est un peu trop fort.* It is too violent a piece of testimony. But the editor calls another witness in support of his theory, whose evidence is of a still more awkward character. This witness brings forward Lord Chatham, and gives him a position in this argument, from which, we believe, he will not be obliged to recede. She says (for it is Lady Francis who speaks) that the earl was the ally—the powerful ally of Junius. Not Junius himself, but still "a piece of him!" Her opinion is quoted from her very inconsequent letter, inserted by Lord Campbell in his "Lives of the Lord Chancellors." She states that, after the young man had assailed the general policy of the government in the first letter (that is, of the regular series, for her ladyship skips and slurs over the Miscellaneous Letters, as things of no account), a new and powerful ally came to his assistance; and, by this ally, she subsequently says, she means the Earl of Chatham. Then the little demiourgos wrote and wrote, in that vigorous, dreaded

* "Bohn's edition of Junius," vol. i., p. 62.

style; and the sometime Cornet of Horse, who could smite the house of Bourbon with one hand, and wield in the other the democracy of England, exerted himself, assisted by Lords Camden and Temple, Mr. Grenville and Mr. Calcraft, in gathering for the able juvenile the materials of those wide-sweeping assaults on the highest estates and men of the realm, and helping him, with unwearied care and precaution, to protect his clerkly mystery from the world, and from the latest posterity!

Such are the most recent Franciscan views. But we can appreciate the grain of wheat contained in all this bushel of chaff. The strong necessity of truth produces from Lady Francis the admission so damaging to the belief to which she is still attached, that Lord Chatham had a hand in the letters. He certainly had, and a head, too.

Lady Francis sees the necessity of arguing that Sir Philip was a precocious genius, quickly flowering and quickly falling off. She says at seventeen he was Latin secretary to Lord Chatham: "then to an embassy; then to General Bligh; then clerk in the War Office, where he thought himself ill-treated (mark that!). He was at the Court of France in Louis XVI.'s time, when the Jesuits were driven away for offending Madame Pompadour. And yet people say that, at twenty-nine years old to thirty-two, he was too young, *etc.*"* This is not void of a certain lady-like force of reasoning, which all must recognize, and it has the merit of having produced, or strengthened, Lord Campbell's convictions. There is another consideration which inevitably em-

* "Lord Campbell's Lives of the Chancellors," vol. vi., p. 344.

barrasses the Franciscans. Their Junius has all the appearance of being silenced by a bribe. When Junius ceased to vituperate, young Francis was sent, from a clerkship and £500 a year, to an Indian Satrapy and £10,000 a year. Some of his advocates, with a sense of what is really due to the idea of Junius, make an attempt to parry that imputation. They say Francis could not have been bribed, seeing the dreaded letters had ceased to come out, for over a year, when Philip Francis received that princely place and salary. No, the king and Lord North *might* have done this to bribe him, but he was not bribed! If it was a bribe (it is argued) the two occurrences would have taken place together, say within the compass of a week, at least. As regards the splendid nature of the promotion, it is also asserted that young Francis had claims on government (never mind that business of the letters!), and ten thousand a year was not such an inordinate sum in such a case. Lord Campbell does not reason in this way; he thinks, with "Poetikastos," that Junius touched ministerial gold and fell. In his "Lives of the Chief Justices," he says: "At last the great boar of the forest, who had gored the king and almost all his court, and seemed to be more formidable than any blatant beast, was conquered, not by the spear of a knight-errant, but by a little provender held out to him, and he was sent to whet his tusks in a foreign land."* His lordship tries to throw ridicule upon the metaphor of Edmund Burke—a man who often saw Junius face to face—and entertains, apparently, but a scurvy opinion of one

* "Lord Campbell's Chief Justices," vol. ii., p. 492.

accepted by even the flying-stationers as a British classic. We appeal from Lord Campbell's court—and we believe many of his brother Franciscans will do the same—to that of Apollo—or Mercury, a close-contriving god, also a patron of letters. That lawyer-like verdict cannot stand; and the opinion of Lord Byron seems a very sound one:

> The lawyer and the critic but behold
> The baser sides of literature and life.

Turning from such logic and criticism as the foregoing, we pursue the inferences that rise, easily and naturally, from the theory of these pages. We do not pretend to explain every movement and artifice of the negotiation which sent Mr. Philip Francis to Calcutta with ten thousand a year, on the earnest and significant interference of the Earl of Chatham. They are little to our purpose. But it is admitted, and especially by Lady Francis, that Lord Chatham was the man who principally negotiated this business with Lord North—a man who would be very glad to seize any opportunity of propitiating the atrocious mind of that stern old chief. It is not difficult to understand how the deep and subtle genius which had hitherto so successfully guarded his secret, would now plan a coincidence which should, as it were, crown the whole system of strategy, and have the best chance of making the mystery immortal. The ministry were, no doubt, informed that if the dismissed and discontented Mr. Francis were provided for, they would be likely to hear no more of Junius. Then probably followed some negotiations, ending in an appointment of Francis which would best suit the purposes of Lord Chatham—one that would take the young man out of the country. All this implies that the king, his prime minister, and one or two others, were let into the secret, and told that Junius was Francis. This is the belief of some of the Franciscans; and they must, therefore, suppose that Philip Francis would confide his mystery to half a dozen people of the court, yet never once, in the course of his life, give the slightest hint of it to Lady Francis, who would have given her little finger for the information, but who, as we know, was never favored with it. This, however, is one of the slightest of the Franciscan obstacles. The truth is, that both the king and Lord North knew why the real Junius would give over, and they consented to give him the opportunity of doing so, on the terms he desired.

The part played by Francis in the Junian mystery cannot be traced with any certainty. He was the secretary, amanuensis, and reporter of the earl; and we receive from Lord Mahon and others intimations that he was the secret agent and correspondent of the great man. This, certainly, is the truth. We have, therefore, these two men brought together in close and secret intimacy; and the mystery lay between them. The Franciscans know and allow this. The earl had head enough for his purpose, and hands enough also; but not legs. Such a man as Francis was necessary to him—one whom he had distinguished by his patronage and bound to him by the closest ties of obligation. It may be impossible to explain exactly the agency of the young clerk in this secret business; it is, beyond a doubt, impossible to fancy how it could get on without him. And when it is admitted—as it must be—that he must, in any case, have some knowledge of it, we think it may be justifiably concluded that he was the secret and trusted agent of the Earl of Chatham in the management of his mystery. When the time came in which this strife of letters was to have an end, the partner of so perilous a secret was to have such a reward as would keep the seal of honorable silence forever on his lips. The earl would not shrink from negotiating in a dignified way with Lord North, knowing that his own connection with this anonymous literature was too strongly suspected to be successfully ignored, and feeling content to effect such a master-stroke of private policy at the expense of seeming to have been merely the encourager of such a terrible writer. Francis took his Indian employment and £10,000 a year; and yet Junius was not bribed. The understanding that the young man should have a place, did not imply a bribe, in that paltry "provender" sense of such a thing. Junius had already resolved not to write any more, and only wished to procure a reward for his satellite, in the usual way of effecting such things, and so send him off out of harm's way. In this, Junius was certainly not so much accepting a bribe, as playing off his last trick in his own astute style.

Francis took his place and income without dishonor. He had done his patron many and critical services, and enjoyed his reward. Thenceforward it was his duty to be grateful, and to do everything in his power to protect the secret of his best friend; and he did so, as we know, to the end of his life. And this leads us to consider his way of doing it, and those demonstrations that showed him so desirous to attract to himself the suspicion of the world.

In his paper on his Regency, published in 1811, he greatly affects the Junian style. He chooses for his motto part of one of the speeches delivered by Lord Chatham in January, 1770: "There is one ambition which I will renounce but with my life. It is the ambition of delivering to my posterity those rights of freedom which I have received from my ancestors." He then commences: "After the noble speaker of these words, no one has so good a right to make use of them as I have." Now, the sentiment is found in one of the letters of Junius; and he evidently wishes the reader to conclude that he, Francis, who reported the old earl, and who says he has a right to the words, must have used them as Junius. As a mere reporter, he could hardly suppose he had a right in the matter. Elsewhere, he says that Lord Chatham made a certain assertion, "or—it is recorded for him;" thus hinting that there was once a reporter who could put into the orator's mouth words which he might not have said, and thereby leading people to conclude that the resemblance between the speeches and the letters was produced in the same way. No one, who peruses the writings and speeches of Francis with attention, can fail to see a number of indirect meanings, imitations, and so forth, all tending to remind us of *Nominis Umbra.* The consciousness of Junius seems never to leave him, at any time; all his life, he appears to us an imitator; whether looking up to the great earl, with the awe of a clerk or amanuensis, never permitted to sit down in presence of the chief, or guarding the secret of the departed before the observant eyes of men.

In one of his speeches in the House of Commons, in

1792, on the subject of foreign affairs and the negotiations of 1761 with Mons. Bussy, he says: "Was it on the ground of *status quo?* No, I affirm with knowledge, that he (Lord Chatham) would have rejected it with scorn. The principle of that negotiation was an *uti possidetis.* We were to keep all our conquests, unless the contracting parties should agree upon exchanges for their mutual convenience. I attended the conferences (he was a clerk of twenty-one at the time). The documents are in print. But I have other evidence, if possible, more in point and drawn from the same authority. The anecdote I allude to, is of a public nature, and must appear in the records of the Secretary of State's office. When the Court of Spain interposed and endeavored to seduce us to terms advantageous to France, what was the answer of Lord Chatham to the Spanish Ambassador? I am sure of the substance—I could almost answer for the words," etc. In another place, Mr. Francis said he "penned the answer of Lord Chatham, as he did many of his dictating." Mr. Taylor italicizes this declaration, supposing it proves something; but it proves only that the speaker was once a very clever young amanuensis, and that he was subsequently disposed to mystify his hearers, and lead them to think that he was *pars magna* of those old Chathamic affairs which were also among the subjects of Junius. There is another instance of affectation on his part, which we find alluded to in the *Edinburgh Review,* for October, 1839. In 1817, Mr. Brougham, in his place in parliament, said some very harsh things of Mr. Wilkes and his general character. Next day Mr. Francis accosted the speaker at the Club, and, with a great show of temper, began to expostulate with him about his observations of the day before on Wilkes; and then went on to justify the latter, and denounce the principles of Lord Mansfield. This is significantly noted by the Franciscans as something highly noteworthy.

But the most remarkable of these affectations—and there are a great many more of them—may be seen in a couple of his letters written to Edmund Burke, and printed in the lately published correspondence of that statesman. Before the coming out of Burke's "Reflections on the French Revolution," admirable, in spite of the disparagement of Lord Brougham, and the school of Whig reformers, Francis, who has been favored with a sight of the revises, writes to Burke in the most decided way, to try and persuade him to stop the publication. To stop the publication! He puts on his Junian airs, and affects the high trenchant and overbearing style of superiority, declaring that really this pamphlet affair is unworthy of such a man as Burke. He is bluff and earnest. He calls that passage about the Queen of France, a pure foppery. "Pray, sir," he says (and mark the stately severity of Francis, playing Junius), "pray, sir, how long have you felt so desperately disposed to admire the ladies of Germany? Is it nothing but outside? Have they no moral minds? Or are you such a determined champion of beauty, as to draw your sword in defence of any jade upon earth, provided she be handsome? Look back, I beseech you, and deliberate a little before you determine that this is an office that perfectly becomes you. If I stop here, it is not for want of a multitude of objections. The mischief you are going to do yourself, is, to my apprehension, palpable. It is visible. It will be audible. I snuff it in the wind. I taste it already. I feel it is in every sense; and so will you hereafter, when, I vow to God, a most elegant phrase! it will be no sort of consolation to me, that I did everything in my power to prevent it." In another place he says: "Once for all, I wish you would let me teach you to write English. To me, who am to read everything you write, it would be a great comfort; to you, no sort of disparagement. I wish you were at the devil for giving me all this trouble."* What does the reader think of all this—of *nothing but outside*, and *moral minds*, and *any jade upon earth*, and *once for all*, and *I vow to God*, and *let me teach you to write English*, and *I wish you were at the devil*, with the spasmodic little sentences and the gesticular curtness, as of a man in presence of some fierce wrong or imminent peril? Francis, doubtless, thought it perfectly Junian, and we have seen it called "the highest style of Junius." But the melancholy reader will declare that never, in any polite walk of literature, has he met with so much vulgar arrogance, conceit, clumsy affectation and general impertinence, brought so offensively together, in such a limited space. Even at this cool distance, they are offensive. The passionate and poetic Burke received this farrago with wonderful calmness—at least, he answered it with such; but he certainly felt, for the critic, the haughty contemptuousness which became him. It is young Richard Burke who first replies, of course to express those sentiments of rejection and superiority which could not proceed

* "Burke's Correspondence," edited by Lord Fitzwilliam and General Bourke, vol. iii., pp. 128, 132.

with such propriety from his father. In the course of his well-written letter, the young man says: "Do I not know my father at this time of day? I tell you, his folly is wiser than the wisdom of the common herd of able men." The spirit of the whole reply lies in the meaning of the last sentence, and Richard could have devised no more telling retort. The glowing and chivalrous tone of Burke's philosophy would be ill understood by mere men of the world like Francis, whose estimate of things was made by a much lower standard of human sentiment. Burke never allowed that the poetries and loftier feelings of our nature should be sneered down, or made subservient to the practical arguments and solid considerations of society. Writing, himself, to Francis, he sustains his pamphlet and the philosophy of it, and says, with a candid and reasoning fervor, so characteristic of the man: "You find it perfectly ridiculous and unfit for me, in particular, to take those things as my ingredients of commiseration. Pray, why is it absurd in me to think that the chivalrous spirit which dictated veneration for women of condition and of beauty, without any consideration whatever of enjoying them, was the source of those manners which have been the pride and ornament of Europe for so many ages? And am I not to lament that I have lived to see those manners extinguished, in so shocking a manner, by means of speculations of finance and the false science of a sordid and degenerate philosophy? I tell you again, that the recollection of the manner in which I saw the Queen of France, in 1774, and the contrast between that brilliancy, and splendor, and beauty, with the prostrate homage of a nation to her, and the abominable scene of

1789, which I was describing, did draw tears from me, and wetted my paper. Those tears came again to my eyes as often as I looked at that description, and may again. You do not believe this fact, nor that those are my real feelings; but that the whole is affected, or, as you express it, a downright foppery. My friend, I tell you it is the truth, and that it is true, and will be true, when you and I are no more. It will exist as long as men with their natural feelings shall exist."*

Burke, with all his weakness, is infinitely manlier than his small, hard antagonist, made still smaller by a pretension which it is not improbable his correspondent saw through. Francis had all the mannerism, without one iota of the spirit or judgment of Junius. In the words of Burke himself, he had all the nodosities of the oak without its strength, all the contortions of the Sybil without her inspiration—words at first applied to some imitator of Dr. Johnson, but which the orator would often recall in connection with Mr. Francis. We do not need Dr. Parr to assure us that the general lexis of the writings of Francis has no resemblance to the lexis of Junius. Francis was always the mere imitator and servitor, protecting his patron's secret to the end; always contriving to deny his own authorship, in a manner that only served to confirm the public suspicions of it. His short letter of seeming denial to the editor of the *Monthly Magazine*, on the publication of Taylor's pamphlet, is an instance of this. Perhaps, after all, we should not be so hard on him for these affectations. Much

* "Burke's Correspondence," vol. iii., p. 139.

of the duty and obligation of his life was, doubtless, implied by them; and they may be charitably interpreted as his tributes of gratitude to the memory of his dead benefactor.

10

CHAPTER XI.

SOME FURTHER CONSIDERATIONS LYING ROUND THE MAIN TRACK OF THE ARGUMENT.

These are complements, these are humours.
MOTH (*Love's Labor Lost*).

My lady's a Catayan; we are politicians; Malvolio's a Peg-a-Ramsay, and three merry men be we!
SIR TOBY BELCH.

HAVING thus, like Allan McAulay, in the Legend of Montrose, pushed the follower from the upper place into his fitting position below his chieftain, we shall proceed with a few more of those minor considerations, without which, perhaps, the reader may not think the subject properly rounded off.

Junius says: "I am the sole depository of my secret;" and he is believed by a great number. But this was, of course, said to lead inquirers astray. The identity of the secret writer could not be concealed from the reporter of Lord Chatham's speeches; and, therefore, it is certain that Francis was the confidant and agent of a mystery which stood in need of some such medium. Of the exact nature of his coöperation we must be ignorant, as yet. But it may be believed he was employed in conveying manuscripts, and sometimes copying them. As a bringer of reports and general intelligence, he was probably of little use. Lord Chatham had means of knowing the most important or most curious occurrences of politics and high life, far beyond those of any clerk in the War Office. It is enough for our purpose to show—what has been suggested and admitted by Lord Mahon and others—that young Philip Francis was the confidential agent of the Earl of Chatham at that Junian period. We may conclude with certainty that he was not the earl's only aid in the management of such a wonderful business.

If the letters could have been written without the knowledge of Lady Chatham, we believe his lordship could have contrived to dispense with her participation. But concealment from her was an utter impossibility; and, therefore, we are convinced she was his best auxiliary. She was always, as the world knows, the earl's amanuensis, and conducted his correspondence whenever he was ill with the gout, or wished to be thought so. Lady Chatham, sister of Richard Earl Temple and George Grenville, was a woman of strong understanding, fine taste, and literary accomplishments; one capable of comprehending and sympathizing with such a genius as her husband's. It is impossible to suppose she would not be the frequent, it may be too much to say the constant, copier of his letters—especially those signed Junius. In this business she would naturally employ a partially disguised manner, but such as must still leave to her handwriting that feminine character which seems to have struck all those who saw the manuscript of Junius. It is highly significant, that when Mr.

Wilkes and Mr. Butler, author of the "Reminiscences," examined one of the private letters, the former perceived in it a strong likeness to the handwriting on a card of invitation he had once received from the old Countess Temple, mother of Lady Chatham. In this business of writing cards, it is natural to suppose the old lady may have employed her daughters. This, of course, has little in it. But certainly one grand element of such a mystery would be the intimate coöperation of a wife, and especially if she were a highly educated woman of abilities and skilled in the work of an amanuensis, such as Lady Chatham confessedly was. Mr. Thackeray says of her, that "she possessed a very powerful understanding, combined with great feminine delicacy. The ease and spirit with which her ladyship wrote, rendered her letters very delightful to her friends, and enabled her to assist Lord Chatham, during his attendance in parliament or his attacks of the gout, in answering many correspondents." We have already seen enough to show that, during the Junian interval, her ladyship was a participator in the concealments which enveloped the unaccountable Earl.

The Junian manuscripts were not all in the same hand. We can very well conceive how many of them would be in the earl's own hand disguised. His autographs that we have seen are wonderfully loose and sprawling, reminding one of the style of his letters to the Duke of Newcastle and the king, and those bows at the levee, which used to set all the world smiling and staring. It is not to be supposed that such a consummate actor and mimic as William Pitt would neglect that strategy of handwriting. As to the show of crippled fingers, made during his retirement, in getting the power of attorney for her ladyship, it is as fallacious as the pretense of insanity. This device of the attorney, adopted at such a time, is an evidence of design, as we have said. In everything respecting the man who wrote those remarkable letters, you must be prepared to meet with shows and simulations. Whatever the critics may think, Junius was no simpleton, but a match for Machiavelli in cunning. Lord Chatham would not be Junius, if he could not mould his handwriting to another style as easily and dexterously as we have shown he could mould his mind. Such considerations as these, and others which will suggest themselves to the inquirer, must, of course, depend on the general assertion of these pages for their complete validity. They do not pretend to support any theory; they are content to follow it.

It has been argued, and it may appear to some readers of the letters, that Junius and Lord Chatham entertained different opinions on the American Stamp Act, and American affairs in general. It is not inconsistent with the aim of Junius—such as we can gather it, from a perusal of his literature—to compromise his real opinions on subjects lying comparatively aside from his main course, in order to insure his secret. And if Junius and Chatham were at issue on this question, we should hold it as but a slight argument against our position. There is, however, no distinct difference at all, or none that cannot be easily explained. The truth was, that Lord Chatham held very modified opinions on that most bewildering theme; and those of Junius are just as modified.

In the first place, we must consider the necessity of

disguise—that which compelled Junius, on setting out, to abuse the only two men he ever eulogized subsequently. Lord Chatham had opposed the Grenvillite Stamp Act; but more for the danger and impracticability of it; more because it was proposed by an incompetent minister, than on principle. He had, or asserted he had, from the beginning, made a distinction between external and internal taxation of the colonies. But he always stood up for the sovereignty of England over these, and her power to make laws for them. We can easily believe that, if he had been minister, with a heavy war-drain on the treasury, he would have tried to get money from the Americans either by way of local tribute or custom-house impost, which last his luckless colleagues actually decreed in 1768. In this case the colonists would grumble just as surely as they did in the other, and Mr. Pitt would as certainly try to bring them to order. Junius makes a show of blaming Lord Chatham for encouraging the American resistance—the Grenvillite argument—and yet he complains that, after the Stamp Act, in spite of experience, "a new mode of taxing the colonies is invented, and a question revived, which ought to have been buried in oblivion."* He also says, the right to tax the colonists should never be exercised, but never be given up—a right merely speculative.

These sentiments, as the reader sees, are loose and broad enough to cover, with ease, many more differences than we discover between Chatham and Junius, in this matter. Junius taunts the king that the colonists justly complain of an

* Letter i., 21st January, 1769

act of oppression, and says they first went to seek liberty in a desert. Looking to the earl, on the other hand, we do not find him so much on the American side, after all. He had the prejudice of an Englishman as well as the aggressive spirit of an ambitious man in opposition. In 1767, writing to Lord Shelburne, he says: "A spirit of infatuation has taken possession of New York. * * * Their disobedience to the Mutiny Act will leave no room for any one to say a word in their defense."* Again: "The advices from America afford unpleasing views. New York† has drunk deepest of the baleful cup of infatuation; but none seem to be quite sober and in full possession of reason. It is a literal truth to say that the Stamp Act, of most unhappy memory, has frightened these irritable and umbrageous people out of their senses."‡ Again, Mr. Johnson, in his letter to Governor Trumbull (see "Sparks' Works of Franklin"), thus reports part of Lord Chatham's speech of March 2, 1770: "I love the Americans because they love liberty. But I must own I find fault with them in many things. * * * But (I wish every sensible American, both here and in that

* "Chatham Correspondence," vol. iii., p. 188.

† However infatuated the New Yorkers may have seemed in the matter of their liberties, they could admire the character of Pitt, and feel grateful to him for the expressions of his sympathy with them and their cause—expressions which came naturally from one in such truculent opposition, and which, it may also be said, were natural to the moods of so great and bold a man. They erected in Wall street a statue of him, which was mutilated during the occupation of the city by the English troops. The latter knocked off the head and hand, it is said, and the figure was removed after the peace. It may somewhat interest the reading folk of New York, to think that for several years the city held the effigies of Junius in its most public place.

‡ "Chatham Correspondence," vol. iii., p. 193.

country, could hear what I say), if they carry their notions of liberty too far, as I fear they do, if they will not be subject to the laws of the country, especially if they would disengage themselves from the laws of trade and navigation, of which I see too many symptoms, as much of an American as I am, they have not a more determined opposer than they will find in me. They must be subordinate, and, if you don't make laws for them, let me tell you, my lords, they will make laws for you." Again, in a speech of 25th of May, 1774, he speaks of the "guilty tumults" of the Bostonians.

All these things show that Junius and Lord Chatham are not at marked variance on the American subject, as too many suppose. The earl shows the colonists as frowning a face as Junius; and Junius justifies the complaints of the Americans against the ministry.

Lord Chatham, we repeat, was not opposed to the taxing of the Americans, if they would permit it. But the resistance of the colonists proved that George Grenville committed a blunder which Chatham never would have fallen into, and which he could denounce with the happiest force of reasoning. It is very probable—indeed, convincing to some minds—that one motive of Lord Chatham's obstinate retreat, in 1767 and 1768, was a desire to shun the perils of that American question, deprived, as he was, of the aid of any ministry on which he could rely. The Rockinghams, in fact, feeling the hopelessness of their endeavors to bring about an adjustment of the same question, were at that time thinking of retiring, in a body, from Parliament. Lord Chatham was, doubtless, afraid of being forced to act inconsistently with the opinions expressed against George Grenville. His opposition antecedents embarrassed him, as they have embarrassed many another man. That American discussion was a business in which men's minds were very much at sea. Mindless of the laws of nature and geography, ministers were hoping to reconcile contrary principles, to recóncile a complete sovereignty over a society of men with a maimed and half-surrendered right to make laws for it; trying to draw, what Lord Campbell not incorrectly calls, "a flimsy and fallacious distinction" between a power to regulate commerce externally, and the power to impose taxes internally—and this at a time when some farmers, irritated by all that bewildering logic, were preparing those rifle-shots which, fired from the hedges and gable ends, brought down the whole pile of argumentation—the deep philosophy of statesmen and of kings tumbling to pieces, as many fine-spun theories had tumbled before. There can scarcely be a doubt that, if Lord Chatham had been at the head of the ministry, he would have proceeded to quiet the Americans with a high hand, and, exerting all the force of his popularity and his military statesmanship, have stopped, for, perhaps, fifty years, the march of the colonies to independence.* If it were not to consider too curiously, we might try to imagine the effect of Lord Chatham's armaments in America, just as Livy (Book ix.) sets forth the consequences of the invasion of Italy by Alexander the Great. At all events, Chatham died in protest against the diminution of the "ancient and

* Sir George Saville used to say: "The colonists are above our hands, and Grenville's Act only brought on a crisis, twenty, or, perhaps, fifty years sooner than otherwise would be the case."

noble monarchy" of England; and, everything considered and compared, it will be found that, on a subject so calculated to divide and bewilder the minds of most men, for every instance in which he seems to differ from Junius, another can be found in which he seems as plainly to differ from himself.

Turning our consideration to the War Office, we find that the ridicule of Chamier and Bradshaw, and the doings of Change Alley, have been considered below the attention of a great man like Lord Chatham, but quite suitable to the idea of Francis. In the first place, in any scheme of hostility against the ministry, the assaulter would naturally strike at such an important department as the War Office, and any contempt flung upon the subordinates would be sure to react upon those who appointed them. Again, it will be remembered that no department could be better known, to the sometime Paymaster of the Forces and the great war-minister, than that. Lord Chatham knew the War Office—the armory of the thunder of the crown—as well as his own house. As regards the comicalities against Chamier and the rest, the reader is already aware of his admirable powers of ridicule. There is nothing low or mean in these sarcastic attacks. Still, while he laughs, you see his eye is upon his enemies of the highest rank; and mark how he reaches questions of the greatest national import through the persons of these subordinates. It must also be remembered that he has meditated that final arrangement with Francis, and that he would do everything in his power to attach suspicion to the young clerk, by giving his attacks a tone of the War Office. Again, there is nothing that more indicates the feeling of Lord Chatham than those objurgations of Change Alley. Ministerial stock-jobbing, particularly among his political foes, offended his somewhat lofty ideas of statesmanship, and thwarted his prospects of power. On 13th November, 1770, he said, in the House of Lords, winging a missile into the centre of his opponents: "There is a set of men, my lords, in the city of London, who are known to live in riot and luxury upon the plunder of the community which stands most in need of and best deserves the care and protection of the Legislature. To me, my lords, whether they be miserable jobbers of Change Alley, or the lofty Asiatic plunderers of Leadenhall street, they are equally detestable. I care but little whether a man walks on foot, or is drawn by six or eight horses, if his luxury be supported by the plunder of the country, I despise and detest him." On 25th January, 1771, he writes, at a time when he was waiting to hear the first shot fired in a Spanish war: "How it will turn out, I do not yet see sufficiently, but I suspect the weight of the Alley is prevalent."* The jobbers and gamblers in the funds had speculated on the chances of peace, and were, therefore, clamorous against war. The sentiment of Junius, where he exclaims, "The army, indeed, has come to a fine pass, with a gambling broker (Bradshaw) at the head of it,"† is emphatically that of Lord Chatham; and all these War Office vituperations as truly indicate the pen of the earl as any other passages of this anonymous correspondence.

There is another curious consideration, which must not

* "Chatham Correspondence," vol. iv., p. 88.

† Miscellaneous Letter cx. Signed "Veteran," March 23, 1772

be passed over; that is, the secret writer's knowledge of what was passing at court and in aristocratic life. In this respect, the true statement of the identity puts easily aside many of those difficulties existing at first sight, under the supposition that Junius was some threadbare hireling, like Macleane, and with the idea that the further from the court in opinion, the further in person and opportunity. The friends and intimates of Junius and his family were either no strangers to the king's houses, or familiar with those who frequented them; and Junius himself was a great courtier in his time, and always well received whenever he was pleased "to veil the terrors of his beak and the lightnings of his eye." The apprenticeship, in fact, of his stormy political life, was passed in a court — the rebellious little court of Frederick, Prince of Wales — in which he was Groom of the Bed Chamber, while his sister, Mrs. Anne Pitt, was Lady of the Wardrobe or Privy Purse to the Princess of Wales. And it is to this sister that we are more particularly disposed to refer that otherwise unaccountable intelligence of court matters and incidents to be found in the Junian correspondence.* This lady was as remarkable in her day as her brother, he and she resembling one another, as Horace Walpole says, like two drops of fire. She was a bold, beautiful woman (if she had been but brown, she would have merited the happy epithets applied by Evelyn to that other celebrated woman, Lucy Walters, mother of the Duke of Monmouth); voluble and versatile, and fortunate in being mentioned with admiration

* This suggestion is due to Dr. Benjamin Waterhouse.

by the most celebrated men of her age—Bolingbroke, Walpole, Chesterfield, and Burke. The former used to call her "Divinity Pitt," as he called her aspiring brother "Sublimity Pitt." She could exercise all the intellectual fascinations of those sparkling French ladies who were wont to be the centres of literary and political society in the city of Paris, and was, in fact, accustomed to take up her residence in that capital, where she held her *ruelles* and reunions in the style of the Mirepoix, du Haussets, Epinays, Du Barrys, and so forth. Lord Chesterfield, in one of his letters to his son, reminds him that it will make him fashionable and be for his advantage to call on Mrs. Pitt, one of the givers of the highest Parisian tone. And it appears to be beyond a doubt, that this able woman was in the habit of procuring secret political intelligence for her powerful and ambitious brother, who is often, in his taunting speeches against the incapable ministries, found hinting at the knowledge of foreign matters which they do not seem to have been aware of. Mrs. Pitt was as much at home in France as in England, and, on the other hand, her London parties were as well attended and highly spoken of as those of Paris. Remembering this system of intelligence between the brother and sister, and considering that the latter was, during the Junian period, either Privy Purse to the Princess Dowager of Wales, or intimately familiar with the doings of the royal households, we can the more easily understand how the secret information of Junius could reach him—especially that relating to the court: how the king takes cordials when his mind is agitated by any of his turbulent Whig chieftains, and lives for a week on potatoes; how his majesty is callous as a stock-fish to anything but the imputation of cowardice, which so sets the humors afloat that he will not eat meat for a week; how the Duke of Bedford scolded the king in his closet, and left him in convulsions; how Garrick told Billy Ramus, the page, that Junius would write no more (a piece of news that came with remarkable celerity to the ear of Junius); and how the Princess Dowager, whom Woodfall had thoughtlessly pronounced to be recovering, was still obliged to suckle toads from morning till night for a cancer in the breast. The rest of this information might have reached him by means of any common court-gossip; but the last could only come through a woman.

The suspicion that Lord Chatham received much of his secret intelligence from his sister, is involuntarily strengthened by the fact that Lord Mahon, in his "History of England," says, with the appearance of embracing an opportunity, or making one, that Pitt and his sister were at variance—were not on good terms. The latter, we are told, used to sneer at her brother, and say he knew nothing but Spenser.* This saying would be as little honorable to her judgment, as to her sentiments as a sister. It was hardly worth while to repeat such a thing in a grave history at all, unless it was meant to produce the impression that Mrs. Pitt, Privy Purse to the Princess Dowager, could not, of course, be on communicating terms with her formidable brother in those Junian days. As we have already said, we

* "No matter how that was said," Burke used to observe; "but whoever relishes and reads Spenser as he ought to be read, will have a strong hold of the English language."

cannot help our suspicions of Lord Mahon's history in these Chathamic respects. They may be very groundless, indeed, seeing that in a question like this—particularly since the business of our Eighth chapter—and in dealing with so many shams, pretenses, cunning dodges, and general delusions, it may be only natural that we should look for snares at every hand's turn, and come to suspect a little too much, like Deilus or Croaker in the comedy. We must, however, go on to say that we do not entirely credit this variance, between Mrs. Ann Pitt and her brother. In a letter from that lady to Lady Suffolk, in July, 1757, she says: "My brother continues as he began—as soon as the king put him in the place he is in—by giving me the strongest and tenderest proofs of his affection. He has always seemed to guess and understand all I felt of every kind, and has carried his delicacy so far, as never to put me in mind of what I felt more strongly than any other part of my misfortune—which was to think how very disagreeable and embarrassing it must be to him to have me in France." She also speaks of the kindness of her sister-in-law, Lady Hester Pitt. As regards that last quoted sentence, we are inclined to think her stay in France was the very reverse of embarrassing to the Secretary of State, then gathering his intelligence and preparing his plans for the splendid war of the *Quadrennium.* Before the time of "our correspondents," such a head and hand as Mrs. Pitt's would be the most effectual means of obtaining secret information concerning the designs of the house of Bourbon; and she certainly served her brother in that way. Of course we have none of her letters addressed to him; but the politico-gossiping style of some of Mr. Stanley's letters from France to the Secretary, gives an idea of what hers must have been. In one of the Envoy's letters to Mr. Pitt, of 9th of June, 1761, we find passages which show that the great minister paid attention to the lesser as well as the larger diplomacies, and arrived at his results with *rouleaux* as well as thunder-bolts. Stanley sends several requests, which he says it will be for his majesty's interests to comply with, and so make his own commission popular. He says, in one letter, that Mr. Bougainville's request is backed by persons of high rank, and mentions Madame Dexars as a friend of Mrs. Pitt.* This shows the lady's connection with the secret service of her brother's ministry.

The following proves that, in England as well as France, she was in the habit of participating in his views and triumphs of statesmanship. It is addressed by Mrs. Pitt to Lady Suffolk, in August, 1758: "I am not quite so well as I was on the taking of Louisburg. As I felt a most hearty joy on that occasion, I hope you will approve, and even applaud, my having given some demonstrations of it. As my brother has a great many friends at the Bath (she writes from Bristol), I employed one to ask Mr. Mayor if he would approve of my indulging myself in doing what I could to add to the people's rejoicing for the success of his majesty's arms. He sent me word he would take it as a compliment. So I ordered a bonfire, so placed, as, to be sure, no bonfire

* In one place, Mr. Stanley mentions that the King, Louis XV., whenever he goes a-hunting (this was after the affair of Damien), is apt to start at every strange face he sees; and that Prince Charles Edward, then relied on to frighten the house of Brunswick, is drunk, morning, noon, and night.

ever was before, for beauty, on a rising ground before the Circus, where my brother's house is, and ten hogsheads of strong beer round it, which drew all the company I desired, and enabled them to sing "God bless great George, our King!" with very good success, with the help of all the music I could get in the Circus. The whole town was illuminated, which, as it is the prettiest in the world, was the gayest thing I ever saw."* Mrs. Anne Pitt would scarcely be the one to sneer at her energetic brother, and say he knew nothing but Spenser. She was one of his most serviceable auxiliaries, at home as well as abroad, and very probably as much so during the Junian period as at any other time. Of this, of course, we have no certainty. We have thought that she might have sometimes been her brother's amanuensis in the business of the letters. Her peculiar character and ability would justify such an idea. But this, also, is a mere matter of loose conjecture, which we dismiss, merely stating our belief that she was in her brother's secret of the letters, or at least some of them. We have not dwelt on this matter, as thinking that the agency of this lady particularly affects the main question, but to impress the idea that the ramifications of the Junian secret go a great way off, and that people who would see them more clearly and minutely than we can show them, must make large *detours* and look liberally about them.

We will close the chapter with a few observations respecting David Garrick. This famous actor was on very friendly terms with Mr. Pitt, who, as we have said, was

* Quoted from the Appendix of Thackeray's "Biography of the Earl of Chatham."

a lover of the drama, and encouraged dramatic amusements among the children of his family. The great orator was always considered a good judge of dramatic literature. We see in Thackeray's life of him, that the Rev. W. Horne, when he published his tragedy of "Agis," had it sent to Mr. Pitt for his opinion, which the latter, who dates from the Pay Office, gives, with his usual judgment and decision. The Great Commoner had the finest and aptest power of common language, as we gather from his speeches, badly described and reported as they are; and the dramatic features of the Junian literature—the dialogue of the Grand Council in 1767 and "Veteran's" conversations of Lord Barrington and Waddlewell in 1772—are full of the peculiar spirit and ability of Mr. Pitt, such as Garrick and his other friends knew him in his accessible days. Garrick would be very apt to recognize the manner of some of those War Office letters, and this, together with other circumstances of a long intimacy, would make Junius very apprehensive of the actor's attempts to come at the secret. But, it is to be remarked, that Garrick's letter to Mr. Ramus did not concern the identity of the Mask—the man himself—but the cessation of his letters: "Junius will write no more." The rapidity with which the knowledge of this private letter to the king's page reached Junius, is a strong proof that he must have communication with some one in the royal household, or very familiar with it. Garrick's interference, though a very slight one, apparently, seems to have disconcerted Junius a good deal; perhaps, as the actor had an interest in Woodfall's paper, he might suspect some collusion between them—some display of the manuscript to a man who was probably acquainted with the handwriting of Lady Chatham, and others of the family. At all events, the angry menace of the note to Garrick shows that Junius was afraid of him, and wished to check his curiosity. The player's voice sinks to a whisper, and he cowers before that awful shadow of a name, as greater men had done before. It is curiously suggestive, that, some months after the date of that fierce little missive to "the vagabond," Lord Chatham, with all his defeats and disappointments rankling in his heart, should have sat down to write those verses to Garrick, which we have already quoted. The talk of a philosophic and contented repose in the country, is mere pretense, as every reader of the earl's history knows, and thus leads us, irresistibly, to the motive. Friendly as the verses seem, Lord Chatham did not go so far as to send them to Garrick. He sent them to Lord Lyttelton, by whom they were transmitted. The actor wrote a copy of verses in return, in which he compared the great earl to Achilles, who could touch the lyre as well as guide the war. We suspect the sentiments of Garrick, on one side, were as forced and affected as those of Lord Chatham on the other. The actor's manner of receiving the abusive and threatening note is noticeable. His reply to Woodfall, published in the Garrick Correspondence, is in a subdued and explanatory tone. He desires it should be intimated to Junius that he would scorn to act the spy or informer—that if he knew who Junius was, he would not reveal his name, seeing that this would be productive of much mischief. No word of disrespect escapes him, and we can plainly see that he regards the masked writer with wonderful deference. He thinks a discovery would cause much mischief. Not, surely, if the man was only Francis, or Lloyd, or Macleane. No doubt Garrick never made any fuss about the name. He says he only reported that the writing would cease. Among the court people, there was not much anxiety about the real name. The king knew it, and others knew it as well. But they shrunk from pronouncing it. The king and court shrank from meddling with Junius, and the highest and best-informed in the land shrunk from naming him. These are the facts which give you a true idea of the masked writer. You see his cotemporaries looking up at him in hatred, or in fear, but, silently, for the most part, and must feel convinced that the being so regarded was the most formidable man in England. Having perused and pondered on evidences like these, so suitable to a mystery of such subtlety and power, and indicating so plainly some shape of magisterial dignity, the reader will probably be disposed to turn, with something like contempt, from the ignorant or insincere theories of those who look for that most terrible of British writers among the clerks, amanuenses, and secretaries, and bewilder us with a barren clatter of quotations, comparisons, and coincidences about Francis, and Macleane, and Barre, and Lloyd, and others of that common herd of able men who, among them all, could not furnish forth one-half the powers of the single real Junius.

CHAPTER XII.

RECAPITULATION — PASSING REMARKS ON THE JUNIAN LETTERS PUBLISHED IN THE GRENVILLE PAPERS AND IN THE CHATHAM CORRESPONDENCE—MR. MACAULAY'S LETTER, AND CONCLUSION.

> Here's a maze trod, indeed,
> Through forthrights and meanders.
>
> TEMPEST.

> I have in this rough work shaped out a man
> Whom this beneath world doth embrace and hug
> With amplest entertainment.
>
> TIMON OF ATHENS.

IN this concluding Chapter, we have only to recapitulate our reasons for regarding Lord Chatham as the Man in the Mask. But we must first take the opportunity of alluding to some late statements concerning the mystery, made in the third volume of the Grenville Papers, lately published. We saw them after having arranged our preceding Chapters, and though they call for no particular notice, they can hardly be passed over in silence. Mr. Smith, late Librarian at Stowe, tries to show that Junius was a Grenvillite—that he was Lord Temple :

> That past, vampt, future, old, revived, new claim.

The *London Athenæum*, the *North British Review*, and other pages have sufficiently set aside that feeble hypothesis—the feebler in this case, that Mr. Smith seems to share the doubts of his readers, and does not argue with the self-conviction necessary to produce conviction in others. *Si vis me credere*, etc. There is nothing new in his arguments. Even those three letters purporting to be from Junius to George Grenville can scarcely be called new, they have been so long talked about. But they are important. No doubt, they prove nothing for any Grenvillite, but they prove the extreme subtlety of Junius, and his profound desire to seem a partisan of George Grenville. The writer intended that in his own day a whisper should go abroad that Grenville had letters of adhesion from Junius, and that posterity should find these letters, read them, and swear by them. The design is evident, and deceives very few. In the letters—dated respectively, Feb. 6, Sept. 3, and Oct. 30, 1768—the writer says he is alone and unconnected. Those fierce and sweeping attacks on ministers and their policy, made by "Lucius," "Atticus," "Valerius," "Correggio," and the rest, proceeded, then, from one totally unconnected—from one looking indifferently on and writing, as it were, mere exercises. He tells Grenville he first began, for his own amusement, discharging his paper bullets of the brain, in fun, against Chatham, Granby, Grafton, Bute, the Princess Dowager, Draper, and so forth. No personal animosity by any means. "No abuse, Hal; none, Ned, none; no, boys, none." No wonder they took him for an Irishman! But, after all, he were a poor strategist, indeed, who could not have such letters as these written to George Grenville or any one else, in order to shield his secret and bother the critics of a future age. And Junius was not mistaken. The critic of the *North British Review*, for August, 1853, shows himself as ready to take the ghost's word as Hamlet. When the Shadow says, "I have no connexion," the critic believes it. He points to it—he puts it in small capitals once and again. He thinks it a capital thing to believe what that arch-deceiver is pleased to say. His notions of the identity are consistent with all this. He says: "We do not believe there is a noble family in the British empire who would claim for an ancestor the literary fame of Junius, when blackened by personalities that would have convicted him of slander, or by deeds that would have brought him to the scaffold. It is among inferior men, like Francis, Barre, Macleane, Wilkes, and Horne Tooke, that the reality of Junius shall be found when the dark shadow of his name shall have received the rites and purifications of baptism. If a nobleman, occupying a high official position, and thus personally connected with the sovereign, Junius can no longer be regarded as a patriot. If a commoner with liberal opinions, a functionary driven from office, a secretary insulted by his chief, or a protegé of statesmen who encouraged or aided him in his denunciation of public corruption or in his attacks upon constitutional government, we may overlook his failings in consideration of the impulses which he obeyed; and in the soundness of his principles and the sacredness of his cause, we may forget the virulence with which it was advocated."*

* *North British Review*, for August, 1853.

The ethics and criticism of this passage are on a par with the logic of it. The assertion, that because a man is a nobleman he cannot be so liable to act unworthily as an untitled man, is made ridiculous by experience, and is untrue to human nature. The reviewer certainly did not trouble his head with the public or private history of that Georgian period. If he did, he might have seen that the meanness, or bad passion, that may have belonged to such men as Wilkes, Tooke, Macleane, and others, seems purity itself compared with some of the wicked doings and sayings of the highest order of people. There is no need to argue such a matter. But let us note the morality of the critic. It would be a shocking thing for a titled man, writing from an intimate sense of wrong and ill treatment—from an ebullition of the blood and a towering of the passions—to be guilty of truculent language against those working against him. But let it be some other man, bowing subserviently before his superior, and, at his command, in cold blood, with an abstract malignity, pursuing, and abusing, and stabbing those who never offended him, in order to earn a dirty bit of daily bread—and that is a pardonable view of the case, and quite allowable.

The reviewer seems to know very little of the world we live in, when he says such an inflamed man as Junius could not be a patriot. Not a band-box patriot, to be sure, such as Fenelon would put in a book and any little politician would profess himself to be; but, nevertheless, one of those patriots turned out or accepted by society to do its terribly rough business of forcing a nation along the broken roads of progress, and making all necessary hubbubs about principles, and so forth. Lord Chatham, in his letters and his life, showed he loved the glory of his country; and he was always ready to tomahawk and trample upon those contemptible and disastrous people who refused to recognize his superiority, and who checked his efforts to raise England to the level of a Roman renown. There have been much worse patriots than his lordship. But this question has nothing to do with patriotism, and we dismiss the matter—merely insisting that the grim earl, striking right and left at his enemies and foaming at the mouth, like many a better man in a passion, is a more natural and wholesome object than a cowering little wretch sitting at another man's writing-desk and assassinating character to order.

The Grenville Letters mean nothing but "miching malheco." In this they resemble the two letters said to have been sent to Lord Chatham by Junius. The first of these Chatham letters is dated January 2d, 1768. In the first place, it has no signature. In the next, it is, on the face of it, a feint. It speaks of respect and veneration for the earl, though, but a few months previously, Junius was abusing his lordship for his villainy, his lunacy, and his gouty legs; and, only a week before, he declared that Lord Chatham had made a national debt which the country could never pay, and that he himself could not bear to see incense offered to an idol who so little deserved it!* The use of the word "idol," in reference to the earl, was greatly affected by Junius. Again, about a month after the above date, he asks why Lord Chatham should hold the Privy Seal, if he cannot do

* Miscellaneous Letter xi. Signed "Downright," Dec. 22, 1767.

the duties of it!* and, in half a year after, he calls him a compound of contradictions, and one who would be as mad in the heart as in the brain if he attempted to deny some former letter, relating to Sir Jeffrey Amherst.† That letter of 2d January, then, is a transparent piece of strategy. The other letter bears date the 14th of January, 1772. At that time the proof-sheets of the letters to Lord Mansfield and Camden were in the hands of Lord Chatham. This letter states that Junius sends them for his lordship's inspection. If the proofs had been traced to Hayes, or seen there by any one not in the secret, a letter from Junius would be necessary, to say he sent them. But this, of course, is mere conjecture, and worthless. It is enough to know that the second letter would mean just as much as the first. Both are parts of a scheme of deception. After what has been set forth in these pages, any further argument on the subject would be superfluous. All these letters, we repeat, Grenvillite and Chathamite, bear the palpable marks of simulation.

As we write, we are captivated by the newspaper heading of a letter from Mr. Macaulay concerning Junius. One more disappointment! Nothing is more attractive than these Junian captions, and, as a general rule, nothing can be more unsatisfactory than the matter which follows. To look for anything in them is like trying to fill your belly with the east wind. When you look for broad views of any of these creeds—some principle and spirit of doctrine—you are treated to a confusion of narrow texts and testimonies,

* Miscellaneous Letter xii., February 16, 1768.

Miscellaneous Letter xxxv. Signed "Lucius," August 29, 1768.

and inevitably bewildered into a feeling of disgust and disrespect. Instead of dwelling—if it were only for novelty—on the great Junian points and features—on the high tone and palpable aim of the letters, say in those onslaughts of 1770, in which Junius, Lord Chatham, and the City of London fought the King, Lords, and Commons of the realm, foot to foot, and hand to hand, Mr. Macaulay, a high critical polemic, takes us into a crypt of the War Office, among all the dry, dusty quillets and quiddities—the Irish half-pay and the English half-pay, and the inevitable Mr. Francis. In the letter before us, he is opposing the Lyttelton theory of the *Quarterly Review*, and the assertion which it makes, that Francis, the War Office clerk, would not have been ignorant of the difference between the Irish half-pay establishment and the English half-pay establishment, and declaring positively that the young man should, on the contrary, have exhibited that very sort of ignorance. That ignorance appears a great argument for the Franciscan theory. And why? Because, when he, Mr. Macaulay, was Secretary at War, he made particular inquiries of two or three of his clerks, and there was not one of them who did not agree with him, viz.: that Francis ought to have made the mistake—ought not to have known the difference between the English half-pay and the Irish half-pay! We cannot see the force of Mr. Macaulay's logic. It seems remarkably feeble and Franciscan. However, having thus satisfied his mind that Junius, who makes the mistake about Draper's half-pay, must have been Francis, who would be ignorant enough to make it, he goes on to say that the case of the young clerk "rests upon coincidences such as would be sufficient to convict a murderer!" Historical criticism surely sinks very low here; and Mr. Macaulay, with his view to the "coincidences" in this Junian question, seems curiously on a par with M. Dupin, the French advocate, who, it is said, sees nothing in the crucifixion of Jesus Christ, so much as a certain point of illegality in the sentence of Pilate. Those "coincidences" would not convict a hen-stealer; and it would be a bad day, indeed, for society, if we could have no more valid kind of evidence against our murderers. In turning away from this lawyer-like mode of criticism, we cannot help saying, what we think, that Mr. Macaulay is really not such a maladroit and helpless critic of this matter as he is pleased to show himself.

The arguments for Francis, we repeat, are not less fatal to his claim than the moral considerations arising out of this mystery. That desire of doing a thing worthy of immortality, and the resolve that the secret of the authorship shall perish with him, show that Junius was a great man, a man of powerful unfaltering will. There is something sublime in the idea of sealing up forever a secret which millions would desire to look into. To such a man as Francis, Boyd, or Macleane, no such idea could ever belong or be attributed. None but a man like Lord Chatham would think of taking that secret into the coffin with him. To any of the small men, what would be the consequence of discovery after a lapse of years, at a late period of life or at the close of it? The fame of an undying literature. Anything like punishment to themselves, or disparagement to their families, would be, if not out of the question, only a trifling consideration when weighed against that *volitare per ora*—that celebrity which should preserve and perpetuate the name of a great writer, and to which few men are indifferent. Francis was not the man to forfeit such celebrity. Sir Edgerton Brydges and George Cholmondeley declared the opinion of all who ever knew Sir Philip, when they said it was not in his nature to conceal his authorship if he were Junius. It was not in the nature, nor in the need of any of these subordinate men. With Chatham the case was different. He could not contemplate a discovery during his lifetime; for this would expose him to a storm of aristocratic indignation, and the general blame attachable to the wilder displays of the passions; nor a discovery after his death, which may be thought to tarnish his glory as a great war-minister and patriot, and be a source of detriment or disagreeable remembrance to his family. He, therefore, pushed aside, with a steady, subtle hand, the renown of Junius, resolved that it never should be reclaimed. The man who had achieved the fame of the greatest orator and the greatest statesman of his time, could dispense with one more less dignified passport to immortality.

Coming now to consider the odium still attached to the memory, so to speak, of Junius—especially in the aristocratic circles of England—we are convinced the Grenvilles of the present day would not permit Mr. Smith to bring forward Lord Temple, if they were not very well aware that he was not Junius, and that the world should never for a moment believe he was. Mr. Smith and his Grenville papers, in fact, have authoritatively extinguished the claims of Lord Temple. But, arguing on special grounds, what should that Junian odium signify to Lord Chatham's fame, or to his de scendants—after such a lapse of time? That nobleman's character could scarcely be more blackened and vituperated than it was in his lifetime. The king, Grafton, Mansfield, and the rest, thought him a man of the wickedest and subtlest passions—"the subtleist-workinest villain that is on the face of the earth," as good Queen Anne used to say of Lord Sunderland—and so did hundreds of others. Lord Waldegrave, a very honest, sincere sort of man, says of him: "He is imperious, violent, and implacable; impatient even of the slightest contradiction, and, under the mask of patriotism, has the despotic spirit of a tyrant."* Again: "I was not ignorant that Pitt could be guilty of the worst actions whenever his ambition, his pride, or his resentment was to be gratified."† What worse could now be said or thought of him as the veritable Junius? The earl's descendants are not, or would not be, justified in any great horror of this imputation, considering the qualities that usually go to make up the world's celebrities. Junius denounced a great many culpable men and discreditable things; he told George III. some glorious truths; and when he thought he saw his country going to the dogs, under the guidance of weak men, he made outcries that rang from one end of the kingdom to the other. No doubt, he often preferred vituperation to calm logic—loved flogging better than preaching. It is also urged against him, that he struck behind a mask (and this seems the *gravamen* of the charge), exhibiting a truculence of passion supposed to belong to no order of human nature above the rank of a justice of the peace, or a baronet at far-

* Lord Waldegrave's Memoirs, p. 18. † Ibid., p. 131.

thest. But not even for such considerations should we think the family of Lord Chatham disparaged by a discovery. If anonymous vituperation were a very heinous offense, half the able editors in the English-speaking lands, generally considered respectable members of society, would be in the Penitentiary. Lord Chatham was a man of genius, and genius has a way of distinguishing men by leveling them to the commonest impulses of the common red earth. As the world goes and has gone, the celebrities have very often most blots to show. Falstaff says that he who has most flesh has most frailties; history seems to show that those who have most mental power have most mental perverseness.

Quitting the philosophy of the question, it may be truly said that there is not a peer's family in the British dominions of which some member, at some time or other, has not done something opprobrious; and yet who thinks of disparaging the family for such a thing? It would be a good thing for the highest families if they had no greater disgrace to remember than that their ancestor, in denouncing the faults or crimes of his fellow-men, gave way to his passions, and grew foul-mouthed—particularly when the gout tormented his great toe, or some rash medicine sent it flying upward, to put toys of desperation into his brain. Lord Chatham's greatness and instinctive sense of rectitude, together with his glory as a minister, are more than a set-off against some of his bitter letters, and leave to his descendants a balance of hereditary credit, larger, perhaps, than that of any other noble family in the United Kingdom. The great statesman and orator belongs to history and literature.

Keats says, that the humblest man shows a grace in his quarrel; and the quarrel of Lord Chatham has a gladiatorial grace which wins admiration, scarcely mixed with any other feeling, now that the passions of his day and generation are all exhaled. He belongs, as we have said, to literature as much as to any family; and literature is not at all ashamed of the author of the Junian letters. A censor is nothing without severity; and we believe very few will doubt that Alexander Pope had more malignity than Lord Chatham, with none of that passionate grandeur of sentiment which could redeem it.

In the foregoing chapters we have shown that the intellectual power, political experience, and political disappointments of William Pitt enabled and prepared him to play the part of Junius; that several years before the Junian period, he was a writer of anonymous attacks; that he was tempted by the persuasions of the king to make that heterogeneous and unfortunate ministry of 1766; that, baited and disgusted, he quitted it, going into the country and shutting himself up on pretense of gout and general debility; that he was not insane during the long time of his retreat, as was reported, and as Lord Mahon still asserts, nor, by any means, overwhelmed with any incapacitating sickness; that it was during one of his most remarkably secluded periods of retirement the letters of the Miscellaneous Series began to come forth; that the very first of these was a simulated attack on Lord Chatham and Lord Camden, whom he came, by degrees, to justify, and, finally, to eulogize; that Junius bitterly avenged every slight and affront offered to Lord Chatham, holding, at the same time, a face of dislike towards him; that he fiercely denounced the personal enemies of that lord, authoritatively rebuked the king for a policy to which Lord Chatham was all his life opposed, and used all his efforts to discredit and beat down those feeble ministries by which the earl was forced from power, and thwarted in his efforts to regain it; that, on the chief questions of national policy, Junius and Chatham thought alike, and used one another's language, and that this is most palpable during the party struggles of 1770 and 1771, when the vehement earl, at the head of the Whig alliance, and aided by all the sedition of the city of London, attempted the complete destruction of the king's friends as a corps; that when Lord Chatham's war upon the ministry resulted in failure, Junius brought his letters to a close, his expressions of despondency and disgust being echoes of those used at the same time in the letters or speeches of the earl; that Francis was the reporter, amanuensis, and ally of Lord Chatham in all this time; that when the letters were about to cease, the young man quitted the War Office, and was, in a few months, removed from a place of £500 a year to an Indian appointment of £10,000 a year—a most extraordinary fact as regards his youth and insignificancy; that the earl exerted himself to procure for him this situation, and thus arranged a coincidence which has attached a suspicion of the authorship to Mr. Francis; that the affectations of the latter during his life prove his complicity and his desire to guard the secret of his patron; that, in fine, the advocates of Francis are now forced to admit that their juvenile Junius had a potent ally, and that this ally was Lord Chatham.

To this conclusion we must all come at last: Lord Chatham and Francis were allies. And if it be conceded that each would play his natural part—that the eloquent and exasperated statesman would act like himself, and the smart little clerk of twenty-seven would stick to his proper vocation, we shall not be very much at a loss, or at variance, about recognizing the truth of the matter; unless, indeed, we should have some other than logical reasons for our particular beliefs. Everything, in fact, leads us to this: JUNIUS WAS LORD CHATHAM. The great orator alone, of all those named from the beginning, of all the public men of his age, covers, easily and powerfully and completely, all the conditions of that anonymous literature. That stumbling-block and dissuasive of so many sincere inquirers—the opening letter of "Poplicola" (echoed in some of those which follow) is the chief condition of the secret. Without those demonstrations of subtlety (a quality, remember, as distinctive of this astonishing writer as his vivid rhetoric), our idea of Junius is not perfect. Nay, the cunning, as we have already said, was beyond the rhetoric; the latter failed in the contest, while the former has, for eighty-five years, succeeded in baffling the curiosity of the world.

We repeat, Lord Chatham covers all the conditions of *Nominis Umbra.* There are no marks of an understrapper's or hireling's pen on these formidable specimens of literature. Even where Junius descends lowest and becomes most truculent, there is certain tone of lordly willfulness in his manner which cannot be mistaken. The high passion of the man saves the worst thing he utters from the charge of vulgarity, and when he scatters his dirt about him, it is with an air of majesty. If any one still speaks of malignity, let us remember how the greatest of men have behaved in the bitter business of controversy; remember the angry paroxysms of John Milton, grinding his teeth and swearing to kill Salmasius after he has been *gouged* in the contest with that enlightened philosopher. Lord Chatham alone had the motives of thwarted ambition and fierce personal resentment which would enable a man to sustain that wonderful epistolary war for five years. The writings of Junius give evidence of a man of mature age—one versed in the experiences of social life, and accustomed to discuss the gravest and most difficult questions of state policy—holding his head as high as any other head in England—not even excepting one, and confronting, on terms of lordly equality, the best of those he vituperated and challenged. His general intrepidity of speech, in fact, shows him to have been as exalted in position as commanding in intellect—an aristocrat of the proudest style; and this may be as easily gathered from the manner of his notes to Woodfall as from his authoritative letter to the king.

Junius must, so to speak, be regarded as the complement of the great minister. Without the literature of Junius, the historic reader must feel that the character of Lord Chatham is strangely incomplete; that the latter part of his biography is out of proportion, and not a little perplexing to those who would comprehend it. On the other hand, without the antecedent statesmanship and polemic experience of a man like the elder William Pitt, such a strange literary tempest, and all the championship and strategy of the Mask would be impossible things. The one is necessary to the other.

Asunder, each has been a puzzle to the world. Brought together, they present a grand character with distinct lineaments. Asunder, they may be imagined as parts of some broken piece of statuary, one portion of which lay buried in the ground and lost in concealment; but we can fancy them yet generally contemplated together in a restored condition, and Lord Chatham still more intelligibly and truly recognized in the attitude so finely sculptured by Henry Grattan—smiting with one hand the house of Bourbon, and wielding in the other the democracy of England.*

* On account of a few similarities of expression—lest they should be thought plagiarisms—it may be observed that a paper from the present writer, sketching, by anticipation, the theory of these pages, appeared, a few seasons ago, in the *Dublin University Magazine*. The reprints of it, and even of *rifaciamentos* of it, in the eclectic periodicals of this country, and the rather out-of-the-way notice a thing so slight met with from some of the great transmarine critics, furnished an interesting reply to the stereotyped assurance that nobody cared to hear any more about Junius. That little straw showed the way the wind blew—but not the trade-wind. And the great literary fact is that, within the last twenty years, the interest in the secret has increased, the inquirers have become more numerous, and their position in society, as well as in the world of letters, has given to the investigation a dignity, so to speak, which did not belong to it in the beginning. Three highly remarkable and important publications (it will be remembered), put forth by the immediate descendants or family relatives of the Earl of Chatham, have, in that time, raised the wind of the discussion to a higher pitch than ever—to say nothing of Campbell, Nicholas, Macaulay, Brewster, and the other *tempestarii* of this literary element; so that, after all, it is no great wonder that, if the poorest sort of paragraph about the identity of Junius shall appear in *John O'Groat's Journal*, the scissors of every newspaper on English-speaking ground must move to it and help to send it round on its grand tour of the world. The theme is certainly still interesting. Everything dark naturally is, and men love so much the discussion of a mystery—the mumbling of the game, so to speak—that, very probably, any too direct attempt to put an end to it would be rather unfavorably received than otherwise.

www.ingramcontent.com/pod-product-compliance
Lightning Source LLC
LaVergne TN
LVHW010237110826
845151LV00004B/1324

* 9 7 8 1 4 2 5 5 2 4 3 6 4 *